Power and Policy
in Communist Systems

Power and Policy in Communist Systems

THIRD EDITION

GARY K. BERTSCH
University of Georgia

MACMILLAN PUBLISHING COMPANY
NEW YORK

COLLIER MACMILLAN PUBLISHERS
LONDON

To J.H., B.M. and M.G.Z.

Copyright © 1985, by Macmillan Publishing Company,
a division of Macmillan, Inc.

Earlier copyright © 1978, 1982, by John Wiley & Sons, Inc.

Macmillan Publishing Company
866 Third Avenue, New York, New York 10022
Collier Macmillan Canada, Inc.

Library of Congress Cataloging in Publication Data:

Bertsch, Gary K.
  Power and policy in Communist systems.

  Includes bibliographies and index.
  1. Communist state. 2. Communist countries—
Politics and government.   I. Title.
JC474.B448 1985   320.9171'7   85-12122
ISBN 0-02-309120-7

Printed in the United States of America

Printing   3 4 5 6 7   Year 6 7 8 9 0

ISBN 0-02-309120-7

PREFACE

Although many outstanding scholars have written about communism, there are still serious deficiencies in terms of what books are available for instruction.[1] I would be the first to admit that this book does not overcome all the deficiencies and to contend that some of them may be irresolvable; yet, I have tried to address what both I and reviewers consider four major shortcomings.

The first is the problem of a unified conceptual scheme. This book takes a straightforward policy approach based on the concepts of policy goals, actions, and outcomes. What do Communist leaders want to accomplish (goals)? What have they done and what are they doing (actions)? What are the consequences of their actions (outcomes)? Second, the policy approach emphasizes the critical forces of politics in Communist states—the historical and environmental settings in which policymaking occurs, the ideological determinants of policy, and the party and government organizations within which planning, decision, and execution take place. Third, the book takes a comparative approach to the study of these topics. Utilizing the distinct Soviet, Chinese, and Yugoslav models for more intensive comparison and other states, such as Poland, Cuba, and Vietnam, for illustration, this approach allows careful study of the similarities and differences among major types of systems. Finally, this book attempts to address what I and others consider a long-standing need in the available textbooks on communism. Assessing books on Soviet communism, Alexander Dallin states the need this way:

> Virtually all texts have, very sensibly and understandably, dealt with the Soviet political system from the top down: this is indeed where the first and major effort had to lie. But I suspect that the time has come to explore what the whole exercise has meant, what it has done—and what it means today—to the Soviet citizen.[2]

Focusing on the domestic front, this book assesses the impact of communism on the lives of the people. To what extent, for example, are Soviet, Chinese, and Yugoslav policies serving the needs and aspirations of the average citizen? How are they enhancing the opportunities for human dignity? Although these are difficult and complex questions, we discuss them in the pages ahead.

Power and Policy in Communist Systems, 3rd Edition, was written to meet what I and (I think) others perceive as the needs of instructors and students who want to study contemporary communism in a single course. I have tried to give proper attention to the questions of facts and values in politics. I have endeavored to explain the significant differences in communist and non-communist perspectives

---

[1] See the reviews of textbooks on the Soviet Union, China, and Eastern Europe in the special issue of *Studies in Comparative Communism*, 8 (3) (1975).

[2] *Ibid.*, p. 247.

on the world and their implications in terms of conflicting conceptions of human dignity. I have also attempted to challenge misleading stereotypes that are often held about communism without making subjective value judgments of my own. Finally, I have written the textbook to challenge the intelligence of students and I have tried to avoid unnecessary concepts, jargon, and theoretical complexity.

In my mind, the twentieth century has provided ample evidence that the establishment and growth of communism is not a temporary historical aberration. Because of its spread around the globe, first in Russia, then, in Europe, Asia, and even Latin America, we must take a critical and careful look at the nature and meaning of social and political life in Communist Party states. Interestingly, the American citizen is both the best and worst observer of such politics. We are sometimes less than astute observers, for example, when it comes to facing an ideology so different from our own. The moment we hear the terms socialism, communism, proletariat, and revolution, we close our eyes and ears and observe what we want to see and hear and ignore what we want to avoid. We are also poor observers because we often compare the best of our society with the worst of theirs. When we see the cheap and poorly constructed apartment complexes of Moscow, we rarely compare them with the ghettos of our large cities, but rather we contrast them to our most impressive suburban communities. Or, when seeing the traditional and backward peasant life of China, we think not of Appalachia but of the mechanized farm life of Iowa or Illinois.

We are capable observers, however, when it comes to information. We may have at our disposal greater quantities of fairly accurate and detailed information about Communist Party states than any other population on earth. To observe, compare, and evaluate, one needs such information and, although we certainly could use more than we possess about Communist states, we now have access to enough to engage in critical study and to make informed observations and judgments. We are also good observers because we have some appreciation of the significance and importance of the monumental issues before us: war and peace, health and disease, starvation and abundance, freedom and oppression. We understand that governments and political systems are intended to help people meet such challenges and we search for clues to the most effective and just ways in which to deal optimally with current and future problems. This will to survive and to do so in a way that preserves human dignity, freedom, and the quality of social life is a valuable characteristic among the American populace. Those of us serious about improving our system of government and the world in which we live will want to take a critical and careful look at communism. What do its adherents stand for? What are they attempting to do? Is there anything to learn from those states called Communist? Have they experienced successes? What are their failures? By carefully studying their political experiences, we may be able to benefit from both their achievements and their mistakes. Let us see if there is anything to learn that can be of value to us.

Power and Policy in Communist Systems, 3rd Edition, is part of a three-volume series. The authors and titles of the other volumes are Professor David M. Wood, *Power and Policy in Western European Democracies*, 3rd Edition, and Professor Robert P. Clark, *Power and Policy in the Third World*, 3rd Edition. Professors Clark, Wood, and I have coauthored a comprehensive textbook, *Comparing Political Systems: Power and Policy in Three Worlds*, 3rd Edition.

GARY K. BERTSCH

CONTENTS

INTRODUCTION
Studying Politics in Communist Systems

COMPARING COMMUNIST POLITICAL SYSTEMS

What do we mean when we refer to a Communist political system?[1] There has been considerable disagreement over the years, for example, about Cuba's advent to communism. Most observers hold that Fidel Castro was not a Communist at the time of his revolutionary victory in 1959. On the other hand, most agree that Castro and Cuba became communist by the middle 1960s. Countries like Poland and East Germany are governed by parties that are not, formally speaking, called Communist, whereas others, such as Italy and France, have large and active Communist parties but are not considered Communist Party states.

In this book, when we refer to Communist systems, we mean the 16 states that are internationally recognized as Marxist–Leninist and are governed by Communist-oriented leaders who purport to be actively engaged in the building of communism. Listed alphabetically, these states are Albania, Bulgaria, Cambodia (Kampuchea), China, Cuba, Czechoslovakia, East Germany, Hungary, Laos, Mongolia, North Korea, Poland, Romania, the Soviet Union, Vietnam, and Yugoslavia. The leaders of these states contend that they are guided by the ideological doctrine of Marxism–Leninism and consider their nations on the road to becoming genuine Communist societies.[2]

Richard C. Gripp has noted that a number of common ideological features are supposed to characterize these Marxist–Leninist states, including: (1) a deterministic and materialistic interpretation of history; (2) a revolutionary transformation of the former system; (3) rule by a dictatorship of the working class, through the Communist Party; (4) egalitarianism of society; (5) anticapitalism and antiimperialism; (6) public

---

[1]Because these states think of themselves as socialist and not yet communist, our reference to them as Communist political systems is somewhat of a misnomer. Because it is widely done, however, we use these designations interchangeably with such other terms as *socialist*, *Marxist-Leninist*, and *Second World* to describe the Communist Party states. Referring to these countries as Second World states corresponds with the growing use of the terms *First World* for the more developed states of North America and Western Europe and *Third World* for the less-developed states of Asia, Africa, and Latin America.

[2]Some possible inclusions, such as Afghanistan, Angola, and Mozambique, are not listed here because of their relative newness, the many uncertainties surrounding their strategies of development, or the fact that they disclaim being communist. For an annual review of the established and aspiring Communist states, see Richard Starr, ed., *Yearbook on International Communist Affairs, 1985* (Stanford, Calif.: Hoover Institution Press, 1985).

ownership and state control of the important economic functions of society; and (7) a commitment to a progressive/humanitarian society conducive to social welfare.[3] Although Marxist–Leninist states share certain ideological principles and ideals, their contemporary policies and practices are often quite different, both from one another and from the original principles and ideals.

Over the years, an area studies rather than a comparative approach has been the primary method for studying Communist Party states. Area studies focus on single countries, such as the Soviet Union, and seldom compare one with another. A result of this approach is that most books on communism concentrate on single countries and explain in considerable detail their historical and contemporary features. One interesting finding revealed by this information is the surprising diversity of the 16 states. Although they adhere to a common ideology and profess rather similar political goals, these states vary markedly in many significant ways. China and the Soviet Union, the two largest and most powerful Communist Party states, differ greatly in how they view and are going about the construction of communism. East Germany and Czechoslovakia are characterized by rather high levels of economic development, but others, such as China and Albania, are considerably less developed. Hungary and China have been experimenting with significant economic reforms while the Soviet Union, at least until recently, has been resisting them. And whereas some, such as Yugoslavia and Albania, carry on foreign policies that are largely independent of the Soviet Union, others, such as East Germany and Bulgaria, are generally attuned to the Soviet Union. Why are these states similar in their founding ideology but different in other equally critical respects, such as foreign or domestic policy? The reasons for these similarities and differences and their causes and consequences can best be determined by the comparative study of communist political systems.

Comparison is an integral part of intellectual activity and one in which we are constantly engaged. To compare means to look for similarities and differences so that we can more fully understand what we are studying. Genuine understanding requires careful, systematic comparison. This book will attempt to compare critical features of the 16 Marxist–Leninist states to better understand the nature of contemporary communism. Why are citizens restive and outspoken in Poland, whereas they are more passive in the USSR? Why do some leaders seem to be less sensitive to human rights or industrial democracy than others? Why do some keep their people isolated from the outside world, whereas others permit a freer flow of ideas and people? Why are some systems more successful in meeting the needs of their people? Comparison will aid in answering such questions.

Comparison of political life in Communist Party states is a particularly difficult and challenging task.[4] One basic reason for this difficulty is that few Americans have ever visited a Communist Party state, and fewer still have lived in one for any length of time. And, indeed, our knowledge and understanding of these countries has not been facilitated by the countries themselves. Most have been closed societies that have not been particularly willing to promote or facilitate exchange and communication. Although improved relations between the United States and these countries during the 1970s considerably eased the general isolation and lack of exchanges, relatively few Westerners will ever have the opportunity to visit the USSR, China, or one of the other Communist nations.

Increased scholarly and educational exchanges over the past decade, however, have added substantially to what we know about the Communist Party states. Many American scholars have spent considerable time conducting research in these countries and have published

---

[3]Richard C. Gripp, *The Political System of Communism* (New York: Dodd, Mead, 1973), pp. 13–14.

[4]For a variety of excellent essays on the systematic, comparative study of communism, see Fredric J. Fleron, Jr., ed., *Communist Studies and the Social Sciences* (Chicago: Rand McNally, 1969). Also, see Michael Waller, ''Problems of Comparative Communism,'' *Studies in Comparative Communism* 12 (2, 3) (1979): 107–132.

numerous books and articles about what they have found. During the last two decades, hundreds of American college professors and graduate students have traveled annually to the Soviet Union and the Communist Party countries of Europe for official, extended periods of research and study. Many more travel informally. In addition, with the normalization of United States–Chinese relations in 1978, these two countries began a period of expanding exchanges. Although there is still a great deal that we do not know, the research compiled puts us in a much better position today to study and compare these states than 10 or 20 years ago.

POLITICS AND VALUES

On returning from a trip to the People's Republic of China, a Western observer was asked to evaluate the impact of communism on this seemingly inscrutable society. The Chinese Communists, the observer noted, have restored human dignity to the Chinese people by making them proud to be Chinese once again. Another visitor made a starkly different appraisal. In his words, communist governments in general and the Chinese Communists in particular have done more to destroy the human dignity of their populations than any governments in modern political history. These two observers, both intelligent and informed scholars who have studied society and politics across the globe, disagreed because they held different value systems and contrasting conceptions of the meaning of *human dignity*.

The more critical scholar approached the Chinese experience from a liberal democratic tradition that considers the promotion and preservation of individualism the primary determinant of human dignity. According to this Western value system, the individual is viewed as an end in himself or herself and is served by, and placed above, the group. Individual liberties and private conscience are considered inviolate rights and conditions necessary for the realization of human dignity. When evaluating the Chinese experience, this scholar saw little evidence of the individual rights and conditions that he considered conducive to the enhancement and protection of his conception of human dignity.

The other scholar, however, attempted to view human dignity in China in somewhat the same manner as the Chinese Communists view it, and, as a result, came away with a starkly different evaluation. Where the first scholar saw repression of individual rights, the second observed a collective spirit that placed the public good before private interests. Where the first perceived a lack of individualism, the second saw greater cooperation and brotherhood and sisterhood. In communist ideology, the term *individual* is typically used in a negative, pejorative sense—the self-centered individual is encouraged to restrain his or her greed and selfishness under communism to serve the common good. Through their identification with, and contribution to, the collectivity, individuals are expected to realize human dignity within a more cooperative social environment.

The Western concept of human dignity tends to be based on individualism, private rights, including freedom of religion, and the principle that both the personal and public good can be best served under a pluralist system of private rights and opportunities. The communist concept is oriented more toward collectivism and individual duties and responsibilities for promoting the public good. In the West, personal liberties are given a higher priority than the regulation of social and economic equalities; in Communist Party states, these priorities are reversed. Such differing concepts resulted in the two appraisals of China noted above, and such concepts are likely to affect our study of Communist systems. For that reason, it is necessary to confront these contrasting value systems and determine how we should utilize them in our study of Communist Party states.

When we study, compare, and evaluate Communist systems, including their policies and performance, should we try to view political life as Communists do or should we utilize our Western values and standards of performance? Unfortunately, an excessive dose of ethnocentrism has characterized many American studies of foreign countries, particularly those with ideologies and value systems different from ours. Even if we consider the American system superior to all other forms of society and politics, we should note that other people, including Communists, often feel equally assured about their value systems and forms of government. Although we neither can, nor should, ignore our own values when we study and appraise political life in Communist Party states, if we want to understand these countries better, we must pay close attention to *their* value systems and how those who hold them view the world. We must ask ourselves, for example, what it is that Communist leaders and their followers are trying to accomplish and how successful they have been.

Communist leaders are constantly exhorting their people to aid in the building of communism. To the true believer, communism is an ideal state of being in which genuine human dignity will be realized.[5] Basing their ideas on the writings of Karl Marx (1818–1883), Communists (or Marxists) assert that communism is the ultimate stage, the final form of socialism, and that it is to be achieved only after the destruction of the remnants of capitalist institutions and ideas. Believing that this change may take a rather long time, present Communist leaders do not claim to have succeeded in attaining genuine communism as yet, but only in making progress toward that end. As they see it, the closer a society comes to being communist, the greater the opportunities for human dignity.

Theoretically speaking, what specifically is the Marxist meaning of human dignity and how is it related to communism? To the Marxist, but not necessarily to the present-day Communist, human dignity might be thought of as a state of being in which: (1) political *power* is shared under a system of participatory democracy; (2) *respect* is given to all individuals on the basis of universalistic norms; (3) *well-being* is provided equally to all people on the basis of need; and (4)

[5]Obviously, communism means different things to different people. For a consideration of its many conceptions, see Alfred G. Meyer, *Communism*, 4th ed. (New York: Random House, 1984).

enlightenment is to be granted to all so that everyone will have the opportunity to become a well-rounded, productive citizen. The ideal society called communism is considered by Marxists as one in which these four values are equally available to all members of the society. The extent to which such a distribution of values is achieved determines the level of human dignity. Because of political exigencies, Communist leaders have often departed from Marxist ideals as they attempted to establish and further Communist rule in their states. As a result, their allocations of the four values outlined above have often shown little resemblance to the Marxist ideal. In the chapters ahead, we will look at the way in which various environmental and political forces affect the distribution of these values and then make some assessments concerning the problems and prospects for enhancing human dignity in the Communist world today and in the future.

But why should a student of politics be concerned with the idea of human dignity? Is human dignity in the contemporary world affected by politics, leaders, and their ideologies? Or, is it totally dependent on such environmental determinants as economics and culture, factors that may seem outside the realm of politics? In other words, do political leaders and ideologies make a difference? Communists certainly believe they do. In no uncertain terms, they contend that the needs of modern men and women will be better served in a socialist system governed by leaders adhering to Marxist ideology. A good example of how they feel is indicated in this recorded interview with the mayor of Moscow:

> Because we are able to plan effectively and to act in the interests of the entire people, our cities are better administered, safer, and more humane. . . . We can avoid the excesses of bourgeois urban development while building the cities of socialist man, and we can provide a model for the rest of the world.[6]

One is also reminded of Nikita S. Khrushchev's "We will bury you" admonition to the

[6]Quoted in B. Michael Frolic, "Noncomparative Communism: Soviet and Chinese Cities," *Journal of Comparative Administration* 5 (3) (1972): 280.

American people. The impulsive Khrushchev made this jolting statement not to threaten us with military superiority but because he sincerely believed his ideology and form of government was better equipped than ours for solving the challenges of the modern age. Although we may be unable to verify authoritatively such assertions in this short book, it should help us to develop a better understanding of the ideological origins of such ideas, how Communist leaders are governing their changing societies, and their records of political performance.

COMMUNIST POLITICS AS THE ALLOCATION OF VALUES

A good deal of research has been conducted through the years trying to determine what people value in life and how political systems go about providing these values to their people. In this book we will examine and compare how four basic values important to people throughout the world are allocated in Communist political systems and then determine how these allocations influence the question of human dignity. Although politics can be viewed in many ways, in this book the term *politics* refers to the process by which the values of *power*, *respect*, *well-being*, and *enlightenment* are authoritatively allocated.[7] Because these four values are so central to the Communists' attempts to construct the new social and political orders associated with communism, they are of central concern throughout this entire book.

The first value, power, means the ability to influence public policy and concerns the distribution of policymaking rights and responsibilities in the socialist state. Struggling to wrest political power from the old elitist governments, the Communist revolutionaries originally fought for a proletarian dictatorship where the workers would rule. This dictatorship was viewed by Vladimir Ilyich Lenin and other early Communist leaders as a temporary stage that would even-

tually evolve into communism, a broader form of democracy, where all individuals would participate in the administration of society. Today, the 16 Communist Party states consider themselves to be at different stages of socialist development. Regardless of the stages, however, we find considerable discrepancies between contemporary realities and the ideal of worker rule envisioned under socialism or the full democracy expected under communism.

Power is the most significant of the four values because it is of great importance in determining how the other values will be allocated. In the words of a leading American political scientist:

> Power can be thought of as the instrument by which all other values are obtained, much as a net is used in the catching of fish. . . . Since power functions both as means and end, as net and fish, it is a key value in politics.[8]

Power in Communist Party states, as in all political systems, is the ability to effect political outcomes and influence the allocation of other basic values. Joseph Stalin held dictatorial power and made many personal choices that determined the distribution of power, respect, well-being, and enlightenment in Soviet society during the quarter century of his rule. Because he had so much power, he was able to monopolize the allocation of values in Soviet society and to dictate who could share this power with him. Some Communist Party officials were advanced under Stalin and allowed to share his power at the top of the Party hierarchy; others, who were not so fortunate, were executed, banished to Siberia, or simply removed from political life. During Stalin's years, the ideal of worker rule was substantially revised and the idea of one-man, or totalitarian, rule became the guiding principle.

Another value all people desire is respect. Respect refers to the desire of most people to enjoy secure and supportive relationships with others, including political authorities. Respect concerns the status, honor, and prestige given to different individuals and groups, and it also in-

[7]These values are derived from the eight-value scheme of Harold Lasswell. See *The Future of Policy Science* (New York: Atherton, 1963) and *A Preview of Policy Sciences* (New York: Elsevier, 1971).

[8]Karl W. Deutsch, *Politics and Government* (Boston: Houghton Mifflin, 1970), pp. 23–24.

volves the feelings of affection and loyalty afforded to such people. To some extent these qualities are represented by the socialist concepts of brotherhood and equality. Marxist-Leninist doctrine posits that the workers' revolution and the establishment of socialism would halt the historical exploitation of class over class. In their now-famous *Communist Manifesto*, Karl Marx and Friedrich Engels argued that the history of all preexisting societies (i.e., slavery, feudalism, and capitalism) was the history of class struggle. One class was pitted against another, which resulted in a condition leading to exploitation, dishonor, hate, and disrespect. In the eyes of Marx and Engels, such previous societal forms as capitalism were incapable of promoting the value of respect, because of their economic structures and resultant class divisions.

Under socialism and communism, economic classes were supposed to be abolished and the basis for socialist equality established. With no classes, there would be no exploitation, and the people would relate to one another as comrades. As truly human social relations developed in this conflict-free atmosphere, the new communist consciousness would facilitate the evolution of the ideal political community called communism, a system supposedly devoid of oppression and exploitation. Theoretically speaking, this is the scenario for socialist development; a careful review of what has really happened in these states provides us the opportunity to compare ideals with realities.

The third value is what we might call social and material well-being. Marx and Engels expected socialism and communism to take root in capitalist countries that had already completed the difficult process of industrialization. Accordingly, they expected fairly developed socioeconomic settings in which there would be plenty of food, clothing, and basic material goods. This material abundance would be accompanied by certain social services such as health, welfare, and comfort. The basic principle guiding social relationships in the new communist society was to be "from each according to his abilities, to each according to his needs"; people were to produce what they could and consume what they needed. To Marxists, socialism and communism were expected to contribute more to the general well-being of their populations than did feudalism and capitalism.

Contrary to Marx and Engels's expectations, however, Communist takeovers came in countries with rather primitive economies and less-developed socioeconomic systems. With a few exceptions, the states were largely peasant and agrarian rather than industrialized societies, and they were marked by economic backwardness and deprivation. In most all Communist Party states, the top priority has been one of rapid industrialization, often at the expense of the welfare sector. Although the value of well-being remains in the developmental priorities of the Communist leaders, the backward socioeconomic settings have made the task of promoting the social and material good of the people much more difficult than anticipated.

The final value, enlightenment, involves the process by which individuals learn about themselves and the world. The value may be allocated in a way that allows some individuals (e.g., the sons and daughters of political elites) to learn more than others. Whereas enlightenment certainly involves formal education and occupational training, it is also related to the ideal of molding a new Communist citizen possessing a new mentality and prepared to contribute to the socialist order. Enlightenment is a multifaceted concept and represents psychological, social, and behavioral components. The enlightened communist citizens are considered individuals who have cast off the bourgeois mentality of the past; they have been educated in the principles of Marxism-Leninism and trained to contribute to the building of communism. They must be ideologically committed, knowledgeable about world affairs, and able to make great sacrifices to serve the construction of socialism and the spread of international communism.

We should remind ourselves that communist preferences concerning the nature and ideal distribution of these four values—that is, who should get what in terms of *power*, *respect*, *well-being*, and *enlightenment*—are likely to be quite different from our own. Although we may disagree with their preferences, we must understand and use them as we set out to study the political process and the leaders' allocation of these values in their states. It is important to emphasize that the nature and distribution of the four values can be understood and appreciated only in their discrete cultural and ideological settings.

THE POLITICAL PROCESS: GOALS, ACTIONS, AND OUTCOMES

As in all political systems, political processes in Communist Party states are marked by a series of *goals*, *actions*, and *outcomes*. The leaders of the Soviet Union, for example, are guided by certain *goals* concerning the way political power ought to be distributed; they carry out policy *actions* to accomplish these goals; and, finally, these actions result in political *outcomes* or consequences that may (or may not) fulfill the desired goals. The political process in the Soviet Union may result in a certain distribution of power or well-being within the populace, but in another state, such as China, a different set of goals, actions, and outcomes may result in a far different distribution of values.

This policy approach, examining the relationship between goals, actions, and outcomes, will provide the framework guiding this book. Many different approaches have been used to examine Communist political systems.[9] We will use the policy approach because it emphasizes and sheds light on the critical human and institutional features of politics that influence the allocation of values.

One important factor affecting the allocation of values is the extent of agreement on their proper distribution. No society is blessed with total agreement as to how such values as power and well-being ought to be allocated. Some observers think that Marxist–Leninist ideology is a widely accepted blueprint for Communist policymakers and that the proper distribution of values is directly deduced from the ideology. Actually,

Marxist–Leninist ideology is a blueprint in only the most general sense, and Communist decision makers disagree violently at times over conflicting interpretations of the values implicit in that ideology. Although most would interpret communist ideology to prohibit private property, for example, a considerable portion of the agricultural land in certain Marxist–Leninist states is still owned by private farmers, a group who have frequently opposed the collectivization of agriculture.[10]

It should be emphasized that it is not only the general, abstract nature of Marxism–Leninism that has led to varying interpretations of its social and political values but also the personal preferences of the policymakers themselves. Considerable evidence suggests that Vladimir Ilyich Lenin, Joseph Stalin, Mao Zedong, and others preferred the flexibility that the abstract ideology provided; it enabled them to adopt and carry out policies to suit their own purposes and the needs they perceived for their countries. Thus, the differing interpretations of Marxist–Leninist ideology have resulted in surprisingly different value priorities and allocations among the different socialist states.

There are also different interpretations among common, everyday citizens in Communist societies about the proper distribution of values—that is, who should get what—just as there are among the political leaders. Some more democratically inclined socialist citizens feel that policymaking is the right of all citizens, but others prefer to leave political power in the hands of a small number of political elites. Indeed, the evidence suggests that the latter preference is that most widely held in the Soviet Union, where security is often valued over democracy and freedom. Although differences of opinion will always exist, political leaders generally attempt to develop a common set of political attitudes among the populace about these value distributions. Communist elites have been particularly active in this respect and have utilized the Communist Party, schools, the mass media, and a va-

[9]For a review of different approaches, see Lenard J. Cohen and Jane P. Shapiro, *Communist Systems in Comparative Perspective* (New York: Doubleday, Anchor Books, 1974), pp. xxi–xxxvii.

[10]In Poland and Yugoslavia over 80 percent of the agricultural land is still privately owned.

riety of different organizations to mold common expectations and values among their peoples. Although they may have had some success in building homogeneous value systems, substantial differences of opinion on the question of value allocation still exist within each Communist Party country as well as among the different countries. Such differences are the basis of political conflict and competition, the very substance of politics.

We will use a plan, or what social scientists call an analytical model, to guide our policy approach to the study of politics in Communist Party states. The basic features of the model are diagrammed in Figure I.1. Briefly, the plan is to examine the impact of aspects of the environment (e.g., history, economics, political culture) on the political system. Probing into the political system, we will determine how the policy process—the relationship between goals, actions, and outcomes—and the environment interact to influence the course of human dignity in communist societies today.

The first three chapters of the book focus on the environment. Chapter One examines the historical background surrounding the establishment of communism in our 16 states. Chapter Two reviews the social and economic features of the different states, and Chapter Three examines political culture—that is, the ideas and values of the people—and the ways political culture is transformed through political socialization. These three chapters provide some basis for understanding the impact of environmental forces on the political process and human dignity.

Chapters Four to Six probe into the political system to examine the ways in which political actors and institutions influence the allocation of values. Chapter Four examines the nature, structure, and roles of Communist parties as well as the leaders within them and how they affect the policy process. Chapter Five concentrates on the nature and structure of the governments and bureaucracies and the various officials within them. In Chapter Six, we examine the way in which policies are made by focusing on the phases of policymaking and the relationships among goals, actions, and outcomes. Examining a number of case studies of policymaking, we get a clear idea of the practical aspects of how decisions are made in Communist political systems.

The final chapter addresses the issue of political performance by examining how the values of power, respect, well-being, and enlightenment have been allocated in Communist Party states and how this affects the human dignity of the people. By focusing on the relationships between environmental and political forces, we intend to develop a fuller and more comprehensive understanding of the determinants of human dignity in the contemporary world.

EVALUATING POLITICAL PERFORMANCE

The contemporary Communist world is marked by a heterogeneous assortment of nation-states. There are relatively wealthy states, such as some of those in Eastern Europe, as well as some extremely poor states in Asia. There are powerful and weak nations; there are large and small. Leaders in all these states, irrespective of their present characteristics, contend that they are attempting to improve their societies and move them closer to the ideals of communism.

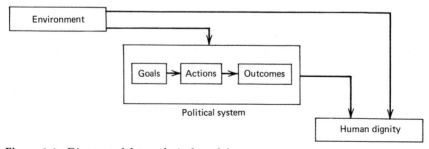

Figure 1.1 Diagram of the analytical model.

In the 1917 Bolshevik Revolution, the Russian Marxists espoused and fought for a new distribution of values. These Communist revolutionaries—Vladimir Ilyich Lenin, Joseph Stalin, Leon Trotsky, and others—felt that too many values to which humans aspire, including power, respect, well-being, and enlightenment, were being monopolized by the exploiting class, which they referred to as the bourgeoisie. They waged a revolution to change the old values of the autocratic tsarist system and to reorder the list of priorities to the benefit of the working class. Although the strategy they have followed since 1917 has met with both success and failure and has incurred many unintended costs, it has drastically changed the nature of Soviet society.

In the mid-1970s, a group of scientists proposed the establishment of a Global Monitoring System (GMS) to appraise the performance of political systems throughout the world.[11] Our study of Communist political systems is also guided by this objective, providing us with an overriding direction (a frame of reference) to facilitate the careful, systematic study of politics. This frame of reference can be supplied by thinking about the following question: *What goals, actions, and outcomes have characterized the different Communist political systems in their efforts to promote the human dignity of their peoples?* Although some may be surprised to learn that Communists are concerned with human dignity, a reading of their ideological writings, policy pronouncements, and speeches indicates that indeed they are—or at least they say they are. Many critics of communism, such as Aleksandr Solzhenitsyn, contend that communism is a disease that destroys all opportunities for human dignity and is inimical to national welfare.[12] Yet countless Communists have proclaimed that human dignity is a fundamental concept and goal of communist relations. But how can we determine if ideological pronouncements of Communists are more than empty rhetoric?

One way we can make this appraisal is by evaluating what they have done in terms of their own standards: power should be distributed broadly among the working population; respect is to be based on the ideal of equality and granted to all individuals regardless of social or ethnic characteristics; well-being is to be provided to all citizens taking into account the socioeconomic capabilities of the state; and enlightenment is to be distributed broadly within the society so that every individual has the opportunity to become a productive socialist citizen. The Marxist state of communism is one in which these values are equally available to all members of the entire political community. Our evaluations can help us determine if the leaders' pronouncements can be taken seriously and the extent to which different societies are approaching, or departing from, the ideals of communism. For example, what has happened in Poland? In the USSR? In China?

By way of brief illustration, we can consider the value of well-being and Leonid I. Brezhnev's repeated pronouncements in the 1970s that raising the citizens' well-being was the highest priority goal of the Communist Party of the Soviet Union (CPSU). According to these promises, the CPSU was going to undertake a series of actions to raise substantially the well-being of the Soviet people. In our study, we can assess the policy outcomes by examining what happened by the 1980s. To what extent did health care, social services, and mass consumption improve during the decade of Brezhnev's pronouncements? Did government expenditures increase in these areas or did the growth in military expenditures place certain limits on social services?

To broaden our understanding we will examine and compare values and policies in other Communist systems. For example, we will consider the value of power and the Yugoslav professed goal to develop a democratic self-managing society based on the concept of participatory democracy. The espoused objective of the self-management system is to make every working citizen a participant in the social and political affairs of contemporary Yugoslav society. To ful-

[11]Richard Snyder *et al.*, "A Global Monitoring System: Appraising the Effects of Governments on Human Dignity," *International Studies Quarterly* 20 (2) (1976).

[12]See, for example, Aleksandr Solzhenitsyn, "Misconceptions about Russia Are a Threat to America," *Foreign Affairs* 58 (4) (1980): 797–834.

fill this goal, the Yugoslav leaders have undertaken a series of actions to set up an elaborate system of participatory structures and institutions—workers' councils, local political organs, and so forth—to enable both direct and indirect participation in the decision-making process. After studying these and other actions, we can consider the policy outcomes concerning distribution of the power value in Yugoslav society: To what extent have the workers' councils and other participatory organs been utilized? What percentage of the population shares power within Yugoslav society and with what effect? To what extent has the average citizen become an active participant in the allocation of the other basic values? And what is being done in the Soviet Union and China today? What will the new Communist Party leader Mikhail Gorbachev do to promote progress in the Soviet Union? And what about Deng Xiaoping, Hu Yaobang, Zhao Ziyang, and the other reformers in China?

In addition to such descriptive appraisals, we are also interested in explanation. We want to know why, for example, democratic goals may lead to democratic outcomes in one political system, whereas they meet with little success in another. Performance of this sort is usually determined by three primary factors: the environment, individuals, and structures. A student's academic performance, for example, can be explained in terms of such environmental factors as his or her family's emphasis on education and the amount of time devoted to study; individual factors, like intelligence and industry; and structural factors, like the organization of particular courses, labs, and so forth.

Political performance in Communist Party states can be explained in similar ways. Although the goals of democratic power diffusion under Yugoslavia's system of self-management have been vigorously pursued, the political outcomes have, in some respects, fallen short of the ideal.

Why? Environmental factors, such as a long history of elitist rule and the nondemocratic political culture and relatively low level of education and democratic training among the Yugoslav populace, have impeded the growth of higher levels of democratic participation and, thus, discouraged a higher correspondence between political goals and policy outcomes. In addition, we can examine the influence of such individual factors as the attitudes of Yugoslav leaders and the orientations of the mass populace and the roles that each play in supporting or obstructing a more democratic distribution of political power. Finally, political structures and institutions also play an important role in determining value outcomes in the society. In the USSR, is the Communist Party's Politburo or the government's legislative body, the Supreme Soviet, a more significant policymaking body? Have the workers' councils in Yugoslavia facilitated mass involvement in political affairs or have they simply been a front for Communist control? In other words, to what extent have the political structures established by the Communist leaders really encouraged democratic policymaking in their societies?

As students of politics involved in the comparative study of Communist political systems, we will be guided by two major questions. The first involves appraisal: *How well are the various Communist systems performing in terms of their goals, actions, and outcomes related to the four values and the cause of human dignity?* The second concerns explanation: *In what ways do environmental, individual, and structural factors affect performance regarding the allocation of these same values?* By addressing these basic questions, we should gain a better understanding of what Communist leaders are (or are not) doing for (or to) their people. We should get a better idea of the sincerity of their claims, how they are trying to achieve them, and what it all means to their people.

Power and Policy in Communist Systems

CHAPTER ONE
Historical Setting

Approximately one-third of the world's population lives under Communist rule. Where do these millions of people thought of as Communists come from? The contemporary Communist Party states they call home represent a heterogeneous collection of different nations, cultures, traditions, and sociopolitical systems.[1] Although there is a tendency to think of Communist Party states and their peoples as being essentially alike, a trip to Moscow, Beijing, and Belgrade will quickly cure that misconception. The present-day diversity found in the Communist world is linked to the past; therefore, to better understand the past, the present and the future, let us briefly examine the historical development of communism. Who originated the ideas of communism and how did different states come to practice them?

KARL MARX AND THE NINETEENTH CENTURY

Contemporary communism cannot be understood without studying the man one American journalist called the least funny of the Marx brothers. The philosophy of Karl Marx has had a greater impact on twentieth-century life than

[1]The adjectives *Communist*, *Marxist-Leninist*, and *Second World* are used interchangeably to refer to the Communist Party states in the chapters that follow. Although none of these adjectives are totally satisfactory, they are the most useful terms available.

any other philosophy or creed. The son of a Jewish lawyer who later became a Christian, Karl Marx was born in Germany in 1818. During his education at the universities of Bonn and Berlin, he became attracted to the philosophies of Georg Hegel and Ludwig Feuerbach. On graduation, Marx became a political writer and joined the staff of the liberal newspaper *Rheinische Zeitung*. After he was named editor, he became involved in various revolutionary causes and, in protest against the Prussian government, moved to Paris in 1843. In France, Marx undertook the serious study of what he called scientific socialism and met many prominent socialist thinkers. One not so prominent at that particular time, but who later became one of the era's great radical philosophers, was another German, Friedrich Engels, with whom Marx formed a lifelong friendship and collaboration.

Engels, the son of a wealthy German manufacturer, had been sent abroad by his father to oversee the family's business interests. While earning his livelihood from the system he so vigorously condemned, Engels came to France where he became involved in socialist thinking and writing. When he met Marx, they formed a deep bond that lasted through Marx's lifetime.

In 1848 Marx and Engels wrote one of the most important political documents of modern history. This document was a short but stirring

Karl Marx (1818–1883), seen here with his eldest daughter, Jenny, was described by some as a warmly affectionate family man. Because of his radical political views, Marx was forced to leave his native Germany. After meeting his collaborator Friedrich Engels (1820–1895), Marx settled in England, where he prepared his major works.

remained for the rest of his life. During his years in Great Britain, Marx worked long hours in the reading room of the British Museum on his chief endeavor, *Das Kapital*. Although the first volume appeared in 1867, the second and third volumes did not appear until after his death in 1883. In contrast to the *Communist Manifesto*, which is a rousing declaration, *Das Kapital* is a mammoth, plodding, scientific study of capitalism that describes its origins and its predicted demise. Because his writings and theories were based on observed facts, Marx wanted to distinguish himself from the utopian socialists. He believed he had developed a scientific theory of socialism. The utopians hoped for socialism; his theory predicted that it was inevitable.[2]

Marx's lifelong endeavor was to discover the laws of human and social development and to provide evidence of their scientific validity. Believing that the world was governed by predictable forces, he spent most of his life trying to understand them. He had a voracious appetite for reading and his typical day in the British Museum began early and ended late. During this exhaustive research he reached several important conclusions.

According to Marx, all traditional societies—for example, feudal or capitalist—were divided into two main classes. Because the interests of these two classes were constantly at odds, they were involved in class struggle. The *Manifesto* notes:

> The history of all hitherto existing society is the history of class struggles. Freeman and slave, patrician and plebeian, lord and serf, guildmaster and journeyman, in a word, oppressor and oppressed, stood in constant competition to one another.[3]

In nineteenth-century Europe, the class struggle between the bourgeoisie (those in control of the means of production) and proletariat (the working class) was generated by the In-

call to arms for the working class and became the creed of the Communist Party. Known as the *Communist Manifesto*, it contains the immortal words: *''Workers of the world unite! The proletarians have nothing to lose but their chains.''* In concise, ringing language, the *Communist Manifesto* sets forth the basic tenets of Marxist philosophy. Telling of the bourgeoisie's (the owners') exploitation of the proletariat (the workers), Marx predicted a proletarian uprising and an end to capitalism and exploitation.

Marx returned to Prussia for a short time following publication of the *Manifesto* but was tried for sedition and expelled from the country in 1849. He then went to England, where he

[2]For a useful collection of the basic writings of Marx and Engels, see Robert C. Tucker, *The Marx-Engels Reader*, 2nd ed. (New York: Norton, 1978).

[3]*Ibid.*, pp. 335–336.

dustrial Revolution. Capitalism had developed in Europe and, although economic development soared, great human costs were incurred. Those in control of the means of production were exploiting the working class in the production process. According to Marx, the proletariat had no means of production and were forced to sell their labor to live. Marx predicted that the exploited working class would develop a political consciousness and throw off the ruling bourgeoisie. This revolution would result in a new form of society—a form called socialist—in which the working class would rule. Because classes would be dissolved, exploitation and class struggle would disappear. This societal form would finally evolve into communism, a perfect state free of classes, exploitation, material scarcity, and government coercion.

Marx was a man of his times. He lived in nineteenth-century Europe and observed some of the worst features of industrialization. Attracted from the countryside to the cities, the new working class was subjected to treatment incomprehensible by today's standards. Because labor unions and collective bargaining had not developed, the proletarian class had no voice against the powerful bourgeoisie, was paid subsistence wages, and lived in deprivation and poverty.

As a humanitarian and social scientist, Marx was forced to rebel against the injustices he saw. Not a man of the sword, although he believed in violence, he utilized the written word to call attention to the degraded state of mankind. Marx wanted the quality of life to be improved for the impoverished masses and he wished to develop a theory that demonstrated improvement was not only possible but inevitable and scientifically predictable.

Before his death in London in 1883, Marx experienced constant hardship and frustration. He and his family lived near the poverty level and suffered from poor housing, lack of nutrition, and inadequate medical care. His two sons and a daughter may have died as a result of these conditions. He was often without any means of subsistence and had to rely on the financial support of his friend and collaborator, Engels.[4]

But to Marx, the physical suffering was minor compared with his broken dream of proletarian revolution. Marx hoped and predicted that workers' uprisings would occur in nineteenth-century Europe. By his death, however, there had been no major proletarian revolution and no founding of a Marxist state. Although we must acknowledge Marx's contribution to the beginning of modern social science analysis, we must also recognize that he was a product of the period in which he lived and was limited by it. It is obvious that he did not predict many of the developmental nuances of the twentieth century.

By the end of the nineteenth century, socialism and revolution were discussed by students, workers, revolutionaries, and other interested observers across the continent. Throughout the coffeehouses of Europe, revolutionaries of different viewpoints and motives plotted to end the injustices they perceived around them. Many were without direction, lacking either political theory or power; others found inspiration and guidance in the writings of Marx and had firm ideas on how power could be obtained. One such individual was the Russian, Vladimir Ilyich Ulyanov, later to become known by the pseudonym Lenin.[5] Born in Simbirsk (renamed Ulyanovsk), Russia, in 1870, Lenin was the son of a school and civil service officer. Although the Ulyanov family was of an apparently conservative and religious background, the children were radical and became involved in a plot to overthrow the tsarist autocracy. Lenin's sister, Anna, and brother, Alexander, were arrested on charges of belonging to a revolutionary organization conspiring to kill the tsar. Alexander was

[4]Isaiah Berlin has written a splendid book about Marx's life: *Karl Marx: His Life and Environment*, 3rd ed. (London: Oxford University Press, 1963); also see David McLellan, *Karl Marx: His Life and Thought* (New York: Harper & Row, 1974).

[5]David Shub, *Lenin, a Biography* (New York: Penguin, 1976); Rolf Theen, *Lenin: Genesis and Development of a Revolutionary* (Princeton, N.J.: Princeton University Press, 1980).

hanged in 1887 along with four fellow conspirators for his complicity in the abortive plot.

One year later, in 1888, Lenin was introduced to Marxism and before long began writing revolutionary materials that plotted the overthrow of the tsarist government. Traveling between St. Petersburg, the capital of tsarist Russia, and the nations of Europe, Lenin established his credentials as a Marxist and a revolutionary. On his return to Russia in 1897, he was arrested and sent to Siberia, where he was incarcerated until 1900.

By the spring of 1900, Lenin was a free man in the city of St. Petersburg (renamed Leningrad in 1924). Dedicated to the overthrow of the autocracy that had imprisoned him and had executed his brother, Lenin plotted with other Russian Marxists. When he returned to exile in Switzerland and Germany, he published the article "What Is to Be Done," in the party journal, *Iskra* (The Spark). In that article, he argued for a small, centralized, revolutionary organization to lead the uprising, as opposed to a broad-based, mass movement. The plan was accepted by a faction of the Russian Marxists, who adopted the name Bolsheviks, and Marxism was soon put to the test.

THE BOLSHEVIK INSURRECTION

At the beginning of the twentieth century, the autocracy of Russia under Tsar Nicholas II was in serious trouble. Europe was industrializing and generally prospering, but Russia, always comparatively backward, was falling further and further behind. Economic difficulties, including a scarcity of food and consumer goods, declining services, and poor wages, were worsened by ill-advised military ventures. The Russo-Japanese War of 1904–1905 proved an embarrassing defeat to Imperialist Russia and a great drain on her available resources. Then, Russia became involved in World War I at enormous cost, and the human and physical resources of the state were further depleted.[6]

During the 1907–1917 period, Russian Marxists were a disorganized, faction-ridden organization, unprepared to assume political power or even to apply pressure to the failing tsarist regime. Many were in exile (Lenin) or imprisoned (Stalin); most of the remainder were involved in ideological disputes and intraparty fighting. One major conflict among the Marxists was between the Bolsheviks (the majority) and the Mensheviks (the minority). While the Mensheviks favored a broad-based movement and a more evolutionary path to power, the Bolsheviks were inclined toward a small, conspiratorial movement that could assume power quickly and decisively. Led by

Vladimir Ilyich Lenin (1870–1924) and his wife, Nadezhda Konstantinovna Krupskaya. In organizing a ''party of a new type'' to engineer the Bolshevik uprising and bring about the Russian Revolution in 1917, Lenin began a tradition of centralized Communist Party rule.

[6]Several books analyze the decline of tsarist Russia. Among the best are Hugh Seton-Watson, *The Decline of Imperial Russia, 1855–1914* (New York: Praeger, 1952); and M. T. Florinsky, *The End of the Russian Empire* (New Haven: Yale University Press, 1931).

Lenin, the Bolsheviks prevailed over all other revolutionary and opposition movements and brought about the Communist takeover.

The stage was set for a Bolshevik victory with the abdication of Tsar Nicholas II in February 1917 and the political vacuum that followed. Power was initially assumed by the non-Communist, but democratic-liberal and socialist Provisional Government of March to November 1917, under Alexander Kerensky's leadership; but it, too, was incapable of quickly resolving Russia's difficulties. Returning from Switzerland to St. Petersburg in April 1917, Lenin organized the insurrection. Under his leadership, the Bolsheviks prepared for their takeover by appealing to the masses with such slogans as ''Bread, Peace, Land'' and by organizing a conspiratorial military organization. Careful planning, utilization of a new organizational weapon (the Communist Party), the use of armed force and propaganda, the revolutionary leadership—all aided in their successful seizure of the Winter Palace, the symbol of Russian authority, on the night of November 7, 1917. The initial Bolshevik victory in St. Petersburg was incredibly easy: the provisional government had few answers and little support; the Russian army had been so consumed by World War I that it had no energy or inclination to try to keep power from the revolutionaries; other opposition and revolutionary groups were largely ineffective. Suddenly in power, Lenin was confronted with almost insurmountable economic and social problems as he began the construction of the first Marxist state.

It may appear surprising that the tsarist regime and the traditional political structure could be toppled by such a small band of untested revolutionaries. But the victory was neither as difficult nor as easy as it may seem. Imperial Russia was a sick and dying state; even if it had been able to cope with the challenges of modernization, its entanglement in World War I proved costly. This situation left the Bolsheviks with a vulnerable opponent, and when the political vacuum developed in 1917, the organized, determined, and politically astute Communists grasped power. The revolution was not easy in the sense that major difficulties for the Bolsheviks came after they had seized power, not from the defeated tsarist autocracy, but rather from other groups (Mensheviks, Socialist Revolutionaries, many anti-Communist groups) that challenged the Marxist leaders. Although the Bolsheviks had grasped power, a struggle for the rule of Russia would continue for many years.

To the Bolsheviks' dismay, the writings of Marx were of little help in the ensuing years. Although Marx went to great lengths to explain the impending fall of capitalism and the victory of socialism, he wrote little *about the nature and construction of socialism*, and, therefore, was of minimal help to the new Russian leaders as they began their difficult task. As a result, Lenin and the Communist leaders had to set out largely on their own. Their problem was worsened because Russia was not ''prepared'' for the socialist victory, in the sense that it had not gone through, although it definitely had begun, the capitalist stage of industrialization and development. According to Marx, socialism would triumph after capitalism had outlived its usefulness. But the Bolsheviks' seizure of power came before Russia had completed that important stage of development. As a result, Lenin and his fellow leaders had to complete Russia's industrialization before they could devote their attention to the construction of communism.

Other pressing problems also confronted the Bolsheviks in the immediate postrevolutionary period. World War I continued to drain Russian resources. In addition, Bolshevik rule was not readily accepted throughout the Russian state, and a bloody civil war broke out (1918–1921) that saw Western intervention (including the United States) on the side of the anti-Communist forces. Subsequently, Western hostility and suspicion of the Bolsheviks and communism precluded the possibility of assistance from abroad. So, although the Bolshevik victory of 1917 placed the Marxists in power, it in no way guaranteed the future success of communism.

Lenin's first objective was to get Russia out of World War I. On March 3, 1918, Russia signed the Treaty of Brest-Litovsk, obtaining peace with the Central Powers in return for yielding valuable land and resources. The Communist leaders then began consolidating the homeland. During the Civil War, opposition movements were eliminated as the Communist Party moved to assert dictatorial control. Then, to facilitate economic recovery, the leaders adopted the New Economic Policy (NEP) (1921–1928) that permitted a partial return to private enterprise and eventually got the economy back on its feet.

During the postrevolutionary construction years, the Communist leaders were concerned with survival, both of the state and of their regime. The Communist Party became a leading organizational tool for consolidating power and organizing political rule. In these building years, the ideals of proletarian rule and democracy were lost among the pressing needs for survival. According to most Western observers, the ideal of a dictatorship of the proletariat in which the workers were supposed to rule became in reality a dictatorship of the Party.[7]

After the death of Lenin in 1924, this dictatorship invested increasing power in the hands of one man, Joseph Stalin. Although a dying Lenin warned the Party against Stalin's ascendancy to the reins of power, a power struggle ensued and Stalin soon achieved dominance. During his rule (1926–1953), Stalin revised Marxism in many ways. Differences in degree grew into differences of kind. The combination of environmental forces (for example, the need to industrialize) and Stalin's pathological character resulted in a highly centralized, totalitarian state. Most observers agree that Stalin's imprint on Marxism during these formative years of development took communism far afield of the more humanitarian theories of Marx, and this Stalinist brand of communism was exported to Eastern Europe and China at the end of World War II.[8]

Joseph Stalin (1879–1953) delivers an order to his foreign minister, Vyacheslav M. Molotov, at Yalta in 1945. Stalin placed the USSR on the road to becoming an industrial and military power, but his oppressive rule cost greatly in terms of social welfare, democracy, and human rights and took Soviet ideology far afield from classical Marxism.

At the time of the Bolshevik victory, the Russian leaders expected victorious revolutions elsewhere in Europe.[9] During the early 1920s, optimism about this possibility began to fade. The recognition that these victories would not occur quickly or easily was made official by Stalin in 1924 when he formulated his famous "socialism in one country" doctrine. According to this doctrine, attempts to promote world revolution would be abandoned.[10]

[7]Solzhenitsyn argues that the roots of the dictatorship of the Party are to be found in the nature of the ideology itself.

[8]Two excellent accounts of Stalin and his rule are Robert C. Tucker, *Stalin as a Revolutionary, 1879–1929* (New York: Norton, 1973); and Adam B. Ulam, *Stalin: The Man and His Era* (New York: Viking, 1973).

[9]At the Third International Party Congress held in 1919, Lenin told the delegates that conflict between the capitalist and socialist worlds was inevitable and that socialism would soon result from proletarian uprisings throughout Europe.

[10]Stalin's policy conflicted with Leon Trotsky's theory of permanent revolution (formulated in 1905). The fiery Trotsky was expelled from the country in 1929 for his views and was assassinated by a Stalinist agent in Mexico in 1940. Trotsky's book, *The Revolution Betrayed* (New York: Pathfinder Press, 1972), provides an interesting personal account of this and related issues.

Because capitalism had temporarily stabilized itself, it was better to turn inward and concentrate efforts on building Russia into a bastion of socialism.

Closely tied to the Bolshevik victory was the establishment in 1921 of the second Communist Party state, Mongolia. Dominated through history by both Imperial Russia and Imperial China because of its unfortunate location between the two more powerful countries, Mongolia finally gained statehood in 1911. Shortly thereafter, the Russian Civil War brought Red Army troops to Mongolian soil. Using Mongolia as a base of operations, renegade White Russian bands were tracked down and destroyed by the Red Army and the partisan Mongols. In 1921, the victors established the Provisional Revolutionary Mongol People's Republic. Since that time, the Soviet and Mongolian states have had close ties and relations.

Although Marxist states were established in Russia and Mongolia early in the century, no other revolutions were successfully carried out until after World War II. But the absence of new Marxist states did not mean the absence of communist revolutionary activity. The most violent, intense, and significant activity occurred behind the Great Wall of China.

REVOLUTION IN CHINA

A powerful determinant of present-day diversity in Communist states is the past. Examining this point, one scholar argues that the remarkable differences in Chinese and Russian revolutionary outcomes can be attributed in large part to the influence of distinct prerevolutionary sociopolitical structures and patterns of economic development. According to Theda Skocpol, old regime structures helped to shape specific variations in the revolutionary outcomes not merely by surviving but also by influencing the Communists' consolidation and use of state power.[11] China's prerevolutionary experience was certainly of great importance.

China's ruling tradition was one of upper-class government; the city ruled over the countryside through a network of local gentry and warlords; and the few ruled over the many. To the peasant, the central government seemed remote and unconcerned with the problems of the masses. A Chinese folk poem expresses what must have been the feelings of the masses.

We work when the sun rises,
We rest when the sun sets.
We dig wells for drink,
We plow the land for food.
What has the Emperor to do with us?

The institutions of family, gentry, and government perpetuated ancient Confucian traditions and provided the mortar that gave China its long, stable history.[12] But the events of the nineteenth century drastically changed the course of Chinese history. Conceived of by its leaders and the masses as the Central Kingdom, China was now battered by Western imperialism, resulting in intense national humiliation. This was intensified in the latter part of the century by unequal treaties imposed on China by the European powers and by her defeat to Japan in the Sino-Japanese War (1894–1895). During this period, parts of China, such as Hong Kong and Shanghai, became Western colonies, where the local populace was subject to foreign law. Evidence of this is the now-famous photograph of a sign in a city park of Shanghai: NO CHINESE OR DOGS ALLOWED!

The twentieth century presented not only the dawn of a new Chinese culture but, more importantly, the birth of Chinese nationalism. The spirit of this movement was Dr. Sun Yat-sen, a radical but compassionate politician, educated in the Chinese classics and Western medicine. In 1911, Sun's political followers

---

[11]Theda Skocpol, ''Old Regime Legacies and Communist Revolutions in Russia and China,'' *Social Forces* 55 (2) (1976): 284–315.

[12]The ancient traditions are deeply embedded in China and represent conservative forces even today. For an excellent analysis of the past, see Mark Elvin, *The Pattern of the Chinese Past* (London: Eyre Methuen, 1973); for a contrast of the past with the present, see Lucian W. Pye, *China* (Boston: Little, Brown, 1972); also see John K. Fairbanks, *The United States and China*, 4th ed. (Cambridge: Harvard University Press, 1979).

toppled the Manchu dynasty and established a Chinese republic based on democracy, socialism, and nationalism. The revolutionary's accomplishment brought about the end of more than 2000 years of dynastic rule in China, but even he was unable to cope with the political, social, and economic problems that contributed to the fall of the Manchus. One major problem was posed by the warlords. From 1916 to 1926, China was torn by strife between provincial dictators, who pitted Chinese against Chinese in their greed for increased power and wealth. Combined with the humiliation at the hands of the imperialist European powers, this internal conflict made it difficult for Sun and his supporters to unite the Chinese and promote social and political development.

By the second decade of the twentieth century, China found a more interested and active sector of the Chinese population committed to speak out against foreign and domestic exploitation. In the spring of 1919, large groups took to the streets to protest foreign domination and imperialism. Known as the May Fourth Movement, a wave of patriotism touched off street demonstrations and political harangues that motivated the Chinese delegation to refuse to sign the Treaty of Versailles at the 1919 Paris Peace Conference, an agreement that would have legitimated and prolonged foreign imperialism in China.

In the early part of the century, several Chinese scholars became acquainted with Marxism and other varieties of socialism, and interest grew when the antiquated Russian autocracy was overthrown in 1917. Many Chinese intellectuals followed the events in Russia closely and began to study the Russian experiment with Marxism; one was Li Dazhao[13] (1888–1927), a history professor and chief librarian at Beijing University. While studying Marxism, Li met with students in his office, which became known as the Red Chamber.

One of the young intellectuals attending these meetings was Mao Zedong, a man soon to take a leading role in the growing Chinese drama.

A major reason for the growing appeal of Marxism–Leninism in China resulted from the Soviet's position on imperialism. To many Chinese intellectuals, Marxism–Leninism represented the key to Chinese development. It told them how to be scientific and "modern" in dealing with the problems of development and how to be uncompromisingly antiimperialist and nationalist in being Chinese. Soon Russian agents from the Communist International (Comintern) arrived in China to aid Chinese Marxist–Leninists in promoting communism. In July 1921, the Chinese Communist Party (CCP) was established and a new actor joined the revolutionary cast.

The Russian Comintern agents advised the Chinese Communists to form a united front with the Nationalists [Kuomintang (KMT)], which was under the leadership of Dr. Sun Yat-sen. Although the native Communists found this a bitter pill to swallow because they preferred to organize for revolution on their own, it was sweetened somewhat by the fact that the Nationalists were also committed antiimperialists. The alliance, although often shaky, lasted through Sun's death in 1925 and the rise of his successor, Chiang Kai-shek. However, in April 1927, Chiang turned on the Communists in Shanghai, slaughtered them by the thousands, and established himself as the head of the new Chinese government. Stalin then ordered the Chinese Communists to seize power, but this only resulted in the killing of more Communists. After Stalin's disastrous plans led to the eviction of all Soviet advisors and a new annihilation of the Chinese Communists, the CCP grew more estranged from the Russian Communists. Stalin turned to his "socialism in one country" doctrine and Mao became more concerned with organizing the peasants.

It was during this period that Mao advanced to power. With a brilliant understanding of the use of organizations, Mao groomed the CCP into a political force that would re-

[13]Chinese names are transliterated in the Pinyin system now standard in China. Familiar names, like Confucius, Kuomintang, Chiang Kai-shek, and Sun Yat-sen are not rendered in Pinyin but follow the Wade-Giles system used in the past.

Mao Zedong (1893–1976) on the reviewing stand at a mass political rally in Beijing. After establishing Communism in China in 1949 by ousting Chiang Kai-shek and the Nationalists, Mao developed a more radical brand of Communism, and split with the Soviets in the early 1960s.

direct the course of Chinese history. In 1934, Nationalist military pressure forced the CCP troops to take an epic trek—the Long March—across 6000 miles of difficult terrain—100,000 Chinese began the march; only 20,000 survived. The conclusion of the Long March, in the northern city of Yanan in the province of Shaanxi, began an important stage of CCP development, commonly called the Yanan period. During these years, Mao consolidated his power within the Party and formulated the ideological and military plans that would carry the Communists to victory. Building on the power of human will, Mao engaged the CCP in a "proletarian revolution" in a peasant society, which lacked any semblance of capitalist infrastructure. Mao and the CCP called on the power of the Chinese peasantry to accomplish the theoretically impossible: the founding of a Marxist state in China.

Chinese involvement in World War II aided the Communists' ascendancy to power.

When China entered World War II against Japan in 1937, Chiang Kai-shek was faced with an important decision—whether to concentrate his forces and efforts against the Japanese, which he referred to as a disease of the skin and body, or against Mao and the Communists, which he considered a disease of the heart and spirit. Considering the latter the more pressing evil, Chiang set out once again to destroy the CCP forces. While the Nationalist and Communist forces were engaged in a civil war, Japan launched a relentless attack on the Chinese mainland that destroyed Chinese industrial capabilities and caused widespread suffering. Under such conditions, the Nationalist government had limited capabilities, few answers, and even less success at resolving the pressing social and economic difficulties facing the Chinese people. The government and KMT Party under Chiang were marked by corruption and were out of touch with the Chinese masses. At the same time, the war gave Mao and the CCP time to consolidate their forces, to appeal to the Chinese masses, and, ultimately, to challenge and defeat the Nationalists. Just as World War I encouraged the downfall of tsarist Russia, World War II did the same to Nationalist China.

With the Japanese surrender in 1945, the Communists and the Nationalists tried to negotiate an agreement to end their conflict. Although the United States attempted to mediate the dispute, it was in a compromising position because of its past and continuing financial and military support of the Nationalists. By 1946, the negotiations had failed and the two factions reverted to a state of civil war. Although the Nationalists had superior equipment and support, the Communists were able to draw on the vast Chinese populace to defeat Chiang's forces. The Nationalists retreated to the island of Taiwan (Formosa) and in 1949 the Communists controlled the entire Chinese mainland. It was at this time that the People's Republic of China (PRC) was formed.

The Russian and Chinese revolutionary experiences were quite different. Whereas the Bolshevik takeover occurred quickly and the real test of the new leaders came after the revolution, the Chinese takeover took several decades.[14] This meant that when Mao and his comrades finally took office in 1949, they had been tested under fire. They were a united, cohesive, militarized group. Because they had won power on their own, they were loath to have someone else dictate to them concerning their postrevolutionary development. As we will see, who wins power is of considerable importance in determining who gives orders after power is won.

Following World War II, China's neighbor, Korea, also became Communist. Similar to the division and occupation of Germany after World War II, Korea was divided at the 38th parallel into northern and southern zones with the USSR and the United States serving as oc-

cupational powers. During the three-year Soviet occupation of the North (1945–1948), the Red Army installed Communist-oriented leaders to manage the affairs of the occupied zone. The head of the Communist government was Kim Il Sung, a military figure who had fought along with the USSR in World War II. The Soviets initially set up a coalition government—the North Korean Provisional People's Committee—before establishing a more monolithic Communist regime. Although the Korean Communists were not initially in a particularly strong position, Soviet assistance and the fusion of the socialists and Communists into the Workers' Party provided the necessary power base to ensure a Communist government in North Korea. In 1950, the Communist regime of North Korea attempted to take over South Korea; this brought about U.S. military involvement on the side of South Korea and Chinese involvement on the side of North Korea. When the Korean armistice was signed on July 27, 1953, the division of Korea into a Communist North and non-Communist South was perpetuated.

COMMUNISTS COME TO POWER IN EASTERN EUROPE

Perhaps more so than in Asia, World War II markedly altered the political setting of Eastern Europe. Before the war, none of the Eastern states were Communist; within a few years after the war's conclusion, all eight countries were governed by Communist regimes.[15] What had happened in this short span to prepare the way for communism? We can identify two distinct patterns: (1) Communist parties winning power during World War II, principally through their own internal efforts (Yugoslavia and Albania); and (2) parties obtaining power through the occupation, pressure, and assistance of the Soviet Union (Czechoslovakia, Poland, Romania, East Germany, Bulgaria, and Hungary).

(margin note:) ? would have been all comm?

[14]For an analysis of the Chinese approach, see Chalmers Johnson, *Peasant Nationalism and Communist Power* (Stanford, Calif.: Stanford University Press, 1962).

[15]For an excellent account, see Hugh Seton-Watson, *The East European Revolution*, 3rd ed. (New York: Praeger, 1956).

COMMUNIST VICTORY
FROM WITHIN

Yugoslavia is a state of recent political origin. Prior to World War I, the South Slavic peoples—who comprise contemporary Yugoslavia—were subjects of larger European empires or lived in independent states. Most of the southern part of the land area was under the administration of the Ottoman Empire, whereas the north was part of the Austro-Hungarian Empire. From the ashes of World War I came a new state, the Kingdom of Serbs, Croats, and Slovenes, later—in 1929—to be called Yugoslavia.

The South Slavic ethnic groups of this new state represented different cultures, languages, religions, and traditions. The northern part of the country used the Latin alphabet, was Catholic, and was mostly Western in culture and tradition; the southern part was inhabited by nationalities who used the Cyrillic alphabet, were Orthodox or Moslem in religious faith, and held more to Eastern cultures and traditions. This complex mix of nationalities and ethnic groups generated intense conflict in Yugoslavia between the two world wars. To quell such conflict, unite the country, and move the state toward its goals, autocratic King Alexander established a dictatorship in 1929. This centralized form of government only exacerbated the existing problems and undermined still further the regime's fading support.

Through the 1920s and 1930s, a small group of Yugoslavs were attracted to Marxist philosophy and what it might do for Yugoslavia. One such individual was Josip Broz, later known as Tito, a young man who had been wounded fighting for the Austrians in World War I and had been taken to Russia as a prisoner of war. On his release in Russia, he became interested in the Bolshevik cause and later returned to Yugoslavia to promote the ideals of socialism and communism. Although King Alexander outlawed the Communist Party, Tito and the Yugoslav Communists were able to organize a secret party that relied on Moscow for guidance and direction.

On March 25, 1941, the government under

Josip Broz Tito (1892–1980) led Yugoslavia during its national liberation struggle in World War II, guided the country through over 30 years of postwar development, and brought about a distinctive Yugoslav brand of communism during his years of leadership. He is shown here at the 10th Congress of the Yugoslav League of Communists in 1974.

Prince Paul, who replaced the King after his assassination in Marseilles, signed the Tripartite Pact guaranteeing collaboration with the Nazis. In the national uproar that followed, the army revolted, deposed the government, and repudiated the pact. Yugoslavia virtually was without a government until the end of the war. In its place, various movements organized, including the Chetnik movement representing the Serbs and the Ustashi, which was pro-Nazi and primarily Croatian. But the most successful was the Communist movement led by Josip Broz Tito.[16]

Tito and the Communist partisans, gaining considerable support from all the South Slavic groups of Yugoslavia, waged a coura-

[16]For an interesting account of the life of Josip Broz Tito, see Milovan Djilas, *Tito: The Story from the Inside*, trans. Vasilije Kojbic and Richard Hayes (London: Weidenfeld: Nicolson, 1981).

geous battle against the Nazis as well as against such other anti-Communist Yugoslav forces as the Chetniks. Because Tito and the Communists were perceived by the West as the most effective force against the Nazis, they ultimately won the backing of the Allied Powers. After years of guerrilla warfare in the mountains of central Yugoslavia, the victorious partisans recaptured the land from the Nazis and quickly established a Communist Party state. This was all accomplished with little aid or advice from the hard-pressed Soviets, a fact significantly affecting the Yugoslav experience as a socialist state.

The Communists' advent to power in Albania was closely tied to the Yugoslav movement. During World War II, Albania was occupied by Italy and later Germany. As in Yugoslavia, various resistance groups arose, one Communist-inspired. This movement received both aid and advice from Yugoslav emissaries and, under the leadership of Enver Hoxha, seized power in 1941 and has held it to the present day. The fraternal ties that originally characterized Albanian and Yugoslavian relations, however, soon deteriorated into fear and suspicion. Today, Albania is an isolated, xenophobic enclave on the southern boundary of Yugoslavia.

COMMUNIST VICTORY FROM WITHOUT

During and following World War II, the Soviet Union was instrumental in uniting antifascist groups and, subsequently, for eliminating non-Communist alternatives and placing Communist Party regimes in power in the remaining six East European states. In view of Soviet military predominance in the area at the end of the war, the USSR was in a strong position to determine the character of the postwar governments in these liberated states. The Teheran Conference of 1943 and the Yalta and Potsdam conferences of 1945 gave the Soviet Union great freedom in determining the political character of postwar Eastern Europe. Some contend that it could have gone so far as

to incorporate the liberated areas into the USSR.[17]

The Soviets chose not to adopt the more radical policy of incorporating these European states into the Soviet Union; instead, they opted for the more gradual policy of national fronts. This meant that the governments in the liberated states were to be reconstituted into coalition governments with the Communists sharing power; at the proper moment, the Communists were to seize complete control. Although there are certain similarities in all cases, there are sufficient differences to warrant brief discussion of each.

The Communists' advent to power in Czechoslovakia occurred under unique circumstances. In the prewar Czechoslovak state, the Communists were an influential and respected political party. Liquidated by Adolph Hitler in 1939, the Czechoslovak government under the noncommunist President, Eduard Beneš, went into exile in London for the duration of the war. But back at home, the Czech and particularly the Slovak Communists formed underground resistance movements to fight against the Nazis. While in London, the Czechoslovak government maintained good relations with both the Soviet and the home Communists and, with the liberation of the country, President Beneš returned to preside over a coalition government with strong Communist representation. Although the coalition appeared to be working well, the Communists staged a coup in 1948—strong Soviet involvement was suspected—and occupied broadcasting stations, government buildings, and other key power organs. Quickly and decisively, the coalition was transformed into a solid Communist Party regime under the leadership of Klement Gottwald.

Like Czechoslovakia, the prewar Polish government went into exile in London during World War II. Resisting the Nazis at home under terrible odds were the Home Army and

[17]In fact, it did so in the case of the Baltic States and the eastern sections of Czechoslovakia, Romania, Poland, and Germany.

underground government. These resistance forces recognized, and were recognized by, the Polish government in exile. Although this non-Communist government initially maintained reasonably good relations with the Soviet Union, a series of disputes ensued, resulting in full Soviet support of the Polish Communists. In 1942, a group of Polish Communists traveled from Moscow to occupied Poland to join the native Communists who had stayed at home. One of these who came from Moscow was Wladyslaw Gomulka, who was to become the head of the postwar Soviet-oriented regime. As the Nazis were driven from the country, a predominantly Communist Committee of National Liberation was formed to administer the liberated areas. Following the full liberation of the country, the committee acted as a provisional government and assumed control of the Polish state. Although the Western powers intervened at the 1945 Yalta Conference and succeeded in having representatives of the London government included, the Communists retained predominant influence. With the help of the Soviet Union, local Communists were eventually successful in eliminating political opposition and in placing Gomulka and his associates in full control.

As in the Polish case, the takeover in Romania was a relatively protracted process occurring at the end of World War II. The takeover began with the Soviet Red Army's "liberation" of the country from Nazi occupation and Soviet diplomatic pressures based on the national front policy. This included disarming the Romanian army, prohibiting non-Communist political parties, and severely restricting political suffrage. Western pressure in 1945 again added non-Communists to the coalition government but dominant power remained in the hands of the Communists under the leadership of Peter Groza. Elections held in an atmosphere of Communist intimidation, the arrest of opposition leaders, and the abdication of King Michael placed Communists in a position of power under the secretary-general of their party, Gheorghe Gheorghiu-Dej.

In East Germany, the Soviet Red Army was the sole occupying power following the war and automatically was placed in a position of exclusive control. Walter Ulbricht, a German who had returned from Moscow to Berlin with the Red Army, assumed the key ruling position in the new government. Although political parties continued to exist and performed certain political and administrative functions, the occupying Soviet officials and German Communists assumed total control. In October 1949, the German Democratic Republic (East Germany) was formed and the dedicated Communist, Ulbricht, and his monolithic Socialist Unity Party were firmly in command.

The Soviet Red Army entered Bulgaria on September 8, 1944 and departed late in 1947. During that three-year period, domestic anti-Communist opposition was crushed and dominant political control of the Bulgarian Communist Party was assured. The day after the Red Army's intervention in 1944, a Soviet-backed coup brought power to a socialist movement called the Fatherland Front. Under the leadership of General Kimon Georgiev, a government was formed that placed Communists in key leadership positions. After a series of political purges and pressure tactics, the Communist-dominated Fatherland Front won 78 percent of the vote in the 1946 elections. This new Bulgarian government was headed by a former general-secretary of the Comintern, a long-time Communist and friend of the Soviets, Georgi Dimitrov.

As in Bulgaria, Soviet intervention in Hungary placed native Communists on the inside track to power. Because Hungary had taken an active part in military operations against the Soviet Union, the Red Army took an aggressive position concerning postwar political developments. The occupying Soviet Army purged non-Communist leaders, accused many of collaboration with the Nazis, and, by 1947, had moved Hungarian Marxists into power, including the leader of the Hungarian Communists, Mátyás Rákosi. Having spent 16 years in Hungarian prisons for being a Communist, Rákosi was now intent on achieving absolute power in the postwar Hungarian state. Although non-Communist parties initially had considerable influence—in the open election of 1945 the Smallholders Party's victory led to the formation of a non-Communist coalition—Rákosi and the Soviets soon achieved a dominant position through the controlled 1947 elections.

Suddenly and somewhat unexpectedly, the political character of Eastern Europe was radically transformed. The proud young states of pre–World War II Europe were now cast behind what became known as the Iron Curtain. The Soviet Union's strategy had succeeded remarkably well in establishing Communist regimes in its neighboring states of Europe. It had established a buffer zone, which helped calm Soviet fears of German invasion and of American aid to a resurgent Europe. Caught up in their own concerns of postwar reconstruction, the Western powers were slow to react. Soviet involvement in and control of Eastern Europe was so complete and so successful that by the time the West fully recognized what had been done, diplomatic action was hopeless. A military response from the Western powers would have undoubtedly brought another violent military conflict. In its place, the Cold War developed—a period of extreme ideological hostility and enmity between the West and the Communist Party states of Europe.

THE SPECIAL CASES OF CUBA AND SOUTHEAST ASIA

Given its proximity to the United States and the continuing acrimony in United States–Cuban relations, the establishment of a Communist government in Cuba takes on special interest and meaning. Closely tied to, and highly dependent on, the United States, pre-Castro Cuba was run by an unpopular and inefficient dictator named Fulgencio Batista. Fidel Castro, a gifted revolutionary who had apparently not yet become a Marxist or Communist in the 1950s, plotted and then fought

against the dictatorship in an effort to promote representative democracy. As a result of growing Cuban sympathy and the support of other groups and sectors in Latin America, and even in the United States, Castro was able to stage a successful revolution against Batista's corrupt and inefficient army.

Castro and his minuscule force of less than 100 persons, subsequently reduced to around a tenth of that, began their takeover with an invasion from Mexico in 1956. Basing their guerrilla warfare in the Cuban mountainous region of the Sierra Maestra, Castro and his forces attacked depots, cities, bases, and other key targets throughout the country. With growing popular suport and revolutionary power, Castro forced the Batista regime to surrender in January 1959 and took over the reins of government. Unlike so many of the other countries discussed, the Cuban countryside was not in a state of total revolution and disorder. Rather, Castro was able to take over a country with a flourishing economy and a relatively healthy populace.

Contrary to considerable opinion, available evidence suggests that the Cuban revolution was not initially directed by a Communist Party or by any political or ideological organization other than Castro's nationalistic, revolutionary band. Apparently, at that time, Castro did not consider himself a Marxist–Leninist.[18] Although there was a Cuban Communist group, known as the Popular Socialist Party, the first contact between it and Castro's forces did not take place until 1958. The Communists were extremely skeptical of Castro's movement and placed their faith in a popular front strategy that would unite all anti-Batista forces.

At what point Castro, or Castro's Cuba, became Communist is still debatable. Castro was and is a radical with a deep desire for the social transformation of Cuba; but he is not a disciplined Communist in the sense of being a

[18]For an account of Castro's ideological philosophy prior to, and during, the Cuban revolution, see Hugh Thomas's monumental work, *Cuba: The Pursuit of Freedom* (New York: Harper & Row, 1971).

strict adherent to Marxism–Leninism or the Soviet Union. Although communist ideology played a minor role in the revolution and initial period of Cuban transformation, that soon changed. It seems clear in retrospect that Castro felt Cuban socialism was threatened by the United States in such challenges as the U.S.-supported invasion in 1961, known as the Bay of Pigs, which prompted him gradually and apparently reluctantly to turn to Soviet patronage and, thus, eventually to Soviet-style communism.

The territory today known as Vietnam had been under French control since the late nineteenth century. During World War II, the rather larger area of Indochina was the scene of warfare between national troops under Ho Chi Minh and the Japanese occupational forces. With the defeat of the Japanese and the withdrawal of the Chinese Nationalist troops from the northern part of the Indochinese peninsula, Ho established the Democratic Republic of Vietnam (North Vietnam). At first, the French accorded it provisional recognition; then, negotiations broke down and the Ho regime initiated military action against French forces and the South Vietnamese (September 2, 1945). Carrying on a people's war, Ho and the Vietnamese Communists were involved in almost constant struggle for the next quarter of a century, first against France (1946–1954) and later against the United States. The United States had come to the aid of the South Vietnamese in the 1960s. On April 30, 1975, the American forces were withdrawn from Vietnam. Under the party leadership of First Secretary Le Duan (Ho Chi Minh had died in 1969), the North Vietnamese entered Saigon, and brought an end to the partition of Vietnam.

Generally refused an enclave on Cambodian soil by the royalist government under Prince Norodom Sihanouk, Ho Chi Minh's Cambodian Communist allies spent most of their time exiled in North Vietnam. With Lon Nol's successful right-wing coup against Sihanouk in 1970, about 1000 Cambodian Communists returned home to wage war against the new republic under Nol. The bloody war that had been raging in Vietnam during the 1960s and had spread to Laos now engulfed Cambodia as well. Old and new revolutionaries, known as the Khmer Rouge resistance movement, waged a relentless guerrilla war against the new and weak Cambodian Republic supported by the United States. The revolutionaries, under Pol Pot, won the conflict and ousted Lon Nol in 1975 and adopted a new constitution the next year that established an independent state called Democratic Kampuchea. In December 1978, the Vietnamese Communists invaded Kampuchea and installed a puppet regime headed by President Heng Samrin.

During the Vietnamese conflict, the Laotian Communist movement, known as the Pathet Lao, controlled the northeastern section of Laos bordering on North Vietnam. Advised and supplied by the North Vietnamese, the Pathet Lao exploited the ineptitude and weakness of the royalist government and spread its control over an expanding portion of the country. Finally, in December 1975, the Lao People's Revolutionary Party emerged from the coalition government to abolish the monarchy and establish the Lao People's Democratic Republic.

It should be apparent by now that the establishment of Communist regimes in Vietnam, Cambodia (Kampuchea), and Laos did not bring immediate peace and prosperity to the area of Southeast Asia. Conflict continues to rage at staggering costs to the people of that troubled region.

A COMPARATIVE OVERVIEW

It is clear that communism came to many different countries, under a variety of circumstances, and for many different reasons. We will now try to identify the most significant similarities and differences by considering the following questions. Generally speaking, *how* did Communist movements come to power? *When* and *where* did they come to power? *Who* led these successful movements? And, perhaps the most interesting and important question, *why* did they come to power? As students of comparative politics, our guiding purpose is to establish some general patterns that explain the advent of communism throughout the world.[19]

HOW DID COMMUNIST MOVEMENTS COME TO POWER?

Most observers of Communist Party states agree that the way in which a party comes to power is important in determining how it uses power and makes policy in subsequent years. Communist parties that come to power through independent revolutionary movements—for example, the USSR, China, Yugoslavia, and Cuba—are likely to assume much more autonomy and latitude in planning and carrying out policy than states—for example, Mongolia, Bulgaria, and East Germany—in which the party came to power through the outside influence of the Soviet Union.

Communist parties have come to power either as a result of independent internal movements, through the imposition of a Communist Party regime by an outside force, or as a result of some combination of the two. The first column in Table 1.1 summarizes the experiences of each country. The two major powers within the Communist world—the Soviet Union and China—came to power primarily as a result of internal movements. In addition, two countries in Eastern Europe—Albania and Yugoslavia—as well as Cuba and Vietnam had independent movements and became Communist largely as a result of their own actions.

In the remaining countries of Eastern Europe, the Soviet Occupation at the end of World War II led to the imposition of Communist-dominated regimes. Although the condi-

tions, timing, and exact strategies varied somewhat from case to case, the idea of a national front served as the guiding policy. Coalition-type governments were initially installed but were soon transformed into Communist-controlled governments. Although it occurred in a different part of the world, the Communist ascendancy to power in North Korea was initially similar to the East European experience, particularly to that of East Germany and Poland. North Korea escaped Soviet domination after 1950, however, when China's influence increased and growing Sino-Soviet competition in North Korea allowed the Koreans to follow a more independent road.

The Vietnamese and Cuban revolutions are quite different from the East European examples where the Soviet Union played a dominant role. Ho Chi Minh and Fidel Castro were both nationalists and revolutionaries intent on ending exploitation and imperialism and bringing democratic socialism to their governments. Unlike the East European cases, they were successful in doing so without major assistance from or the occupation of an outside power. With few exceptions, those regimes that established communism on their own exhibit greater independence and autonomy in the international arena today. On the other hand, with the notable exceptions of Romania and North Korea, those coming to power as the result of an outside occupation show less independence of action, particularly in relation to the USSR. In addition, those leaders coming to power by means of the independent route (e.g., Mao, Tito, Castro) enjoyed relatively cohesive, stable reigns. Although there are exceptions, such as North Korea, those placed in power by outsiders tended to be less popular among their own people and more susceptible to Soviet interference, power struggles, or other developments resulting in abbreviated tenure.

In summary, Communist movements can be, and have been, generated by internal and external forces. Thus, we can conclude that both domestic and international factors deter-

[19]The advent of communism in Communist Party states is analyzed in Thomas T. Hammond, ed., *The Anatomy of Communist Takeovers* (New Haven: Yale University Press, 1975). Also see Hugh Seton-Watson, *From Lenin to Khrushchev: The History of World Communism* (New York: Praeger, 1960).

TABLE 1.1 Chronological Listing of Successful Communist Movements

State	How	When	Where	Who
		Attributes for Comparison		
Soviet Union[a]	Independent movement	1917	Europe	Vladimir Ilyich Lenin
Mongolia	Armed occupation (USSR)	1921	Asia	Sukhe-Bator and Khorloin Choibalsan
Albania	Independent and outside (Yugoslavia)	1944	Europe	Enver Hoxha
Yugoslavia	Independent movement	1945	Europe	Josip Broz Tito
Vietnam	Independent movement (unification)	1945 (1975)	Asia	Ho Chi Minh (Le Duan)
North Korea	Armed occupation (USSR)	1945	Asia	Kim Il Sung
Romania	Armed occupation (USSR)	1945	Europe	Gheorghiu-Dej
Bulgaria	Independent and outside (USSR)	1946	Europe	Georgi Dimitrov
Hungary	Independent and outside (USSR)	1947	Europe	Mátyás Rákosi
Poland	Armed occupation (USSR)	1947	Europe	Wladyslaw Gomulka
Czechoslovakia	Independent and outside (USSR)	1948	Europe	Klement Gottwald
East Germany	Armed occupation (USSR)	1949	Europe	Walter Ulbricht
China	Independent movement	1949	Asia	Mao Zedong
Cuba	Independent movement	1959	Latin America	Fidel Castro
Laos	Independent and outside (Vietnam)	1975	Asia	Kaysone Phomvihan
Cambodia	Independent (Outside—Vietnam)[b]	1975 (1978)	Asia	Pol Pot (Heng Samrin)

[a]The Soviet Union, China, and Yugoslavia are in italics in all figures and tables to emphasize their use as comparative cases.

[b]Vietnam invaded Cambodia in 1978 and installed the puppet regime headed by Heng Samrin.

mine the manner in which communism develops in various nations.[20]

WHEN AND WHERE HAVE SUCCESSFUL COMMUNIST MOVEMENTS OCCURRED?

The chronological listing in Table 1.1 shows that most successful movements occurred at the end of World War II. With the exceptions of the Russian (1917) and Mongolian (1921) takeovers at the end of World War I and the relatively recent Cuban and Southeast Asian experiences, most successful movements followed

[20]It should be noted that Marxist rule was brought to Chile in 1970 through the ballot box. Although elected, the Communist-oriented government of Salvador Allende Gossens was subsequently overthrown by military leaders in 1973.

the serious disorders of World War II. Wars and other major destabilizing forces establish the conditions for revolutionary change. In one way or another, Communist victories tended to come in the wake of international or civil war.

Geographically speaking, Communist movements have been victorious in both East and West. Although most contemporary Communist Party states are concentrated in Eastern Europe, movements in Asia and Latin America illustrate that communism is not bound to any one part of the world. Recent developments in the Third World, particularly in some countries in Africa, and in certain Central American countries like Nicaragua, suggest that communism may have a future in other regions as well.

Communism also shows no particular bounds in terms of culture. When communism first took hold in Russia, some experts attributed its success to the nature of Russian culture. Their Slavic culture, "soul," and general spiritual characteristics (according to these theorists) made them well suited for an ideology emphasizing collectivism and socialism. Because of these spiritual and cultural requisites, scholars noted, communism was unlikely to go to other parts of the world. Subsequent movements and the spread of communism to the different cultures in Asia and Latin America seem to invalidate the idea of cultural requirements.

Communism has also come to power in countries at different levels of economic development. Most have been agricultural societies at the early stages of economic growth. Some, such as Czechoslovakia and East Germany, have had rather advanced economic systems; others have been at intermediate stages of development; still others, in Asia, have had very primitive economic systems. Overall, it is fair to say that Communist movements can occur under many different geographical, cultural, and socioeconomic conditions.

WHO LED THESE VICTORIOUS MOVEMENTS?

Were Lenin, Mao, Tito, Ho Chi Minh, Castro, and others indispensable elements in the revolutionary process or could victory have been achieved without them? Perhaps more important: Which came first—the revolution or the revolutionary? To evaluate an individual's impact on a process as complex as revolution is difficult and risky. What can be said is that most had extremely capable leaders, men who understood their countries well and the military and organizational dynamics of the revolutionary process. Leaders like Mao and Tito were able to seize on international forces (e.g., World War II) and to combine them with domestic needs to build successful resistance and revolutionary forces. Although they were "great" leaders in many respects, we can probably observe that the social and economic

forces were larger than the men. If a Tito, Mao, Lenin, or Castro had not existed, it is likely that some other individual would have come to the fore and directed the revolutionary movement. "Great" men cannot necessarily make history, but they can influence it by recognizing and exploiting emergent social forces. At the very least, the individuals listed in Table 1.1 were the right men in the right place with the foresight and ideas to bring revolutionary visions to fruition.

WHY WERE THE COMMUNIST MOVEMENTS SUCCESSFUL?

Table 1.1 contains no entry with the heading "Why?" Although the why of successful movements is far too complex to summarize in a brief word or two, we can make some broad generalizations about the trends leading to the demise of the old state systems and to the success of communism.

All the regimes that preceded the establishment of communism suffered from a number of severe shortcomings. Most had lost the confidence of the broader society and their leaders were unable to inspire and gain the support of the mass populace. Often there was government corruption and inefficiency that resulted in disillusionment and disappointment with the old autocracy. The difficulties of the times were further exacerbated by forces of international and civil war, conflicts in which the armies were either unable or unwilling to protect incumbent regimes. In every case, either internal or international wars (and often both) contributed to the final collapse of the old regime. What followed was disorder, economic stagnation, and a political vacuum.

But why were the successor states Communist rather than some other political doctrine or creed? One reason for the success of Communist movements concerns the use of a new organizational weapon, the Communist Party. Centralized, conspiratorial, and militant, the party became the organizational agent for affecting revolutionary change. Operating in a period of political disorganization and general social disorder, the organized parties of the revolutionaries capitalized on the unstable setting to grasp the reins of power. It is in this respect that the leaders often showed the attributes of the great-men syndrome. Understanding the use of organizations and the domestic and international contexts in which they were operating, the leaders assumed and consolidated political power.

The revolutionary leaders and the parties they represented also understood the meaning and role of military power. "Power grows out of the barrel of a gun," proclaimed Mao Zedong. Use of the party as a military as well as a political organization was a major factor in most takeovers. In some states, armed force meant the intervention of the Soviet Army and a period of military occupation. This factor represented a key element in the Communists' ability to assume and retain political power, especially in those states often referred to as being in the Soviet bloc.

Although comparison is difficult because of the many differences among the Communist movements, we can identify some general patterns concerning the advent to power. Authoritarianism, misrule, mass discontent, and alienation, when combined with international warfare and foreign imperialism, are the factors that have led to a toppling of old state systems. Then, organized resistance and revolutionary movements, led by astute leaders operating within centralized Communist Party organizations, often with the armed assistance of the USSR, helped establish new Communist systems. Because there are obviously other states that have experienced such conditions and have not gone Communist, we should not consider these patterns universal laws. At the same time, there are enough similar conditions and forces to point up general patterns that involve the establishment of Communist rule.

COMMUNIST PARTY STATE RELATIONS

The national divisions and ethnocentrism that have sometimes caused problems within Communist Party states have been just as pronounced in affecting the relations among them. Although the Soviet leaders anticipated fraternal relations among the new Communist Party states following World War II, the experience has often been marked by considerable conflict and antagonism. The Soviet leaders have attempted to unite the international socialist movement under the leadership of the Soviet banner. History indicates, however, that they have experienced a number of challenges.[21]

The first major crack in the facade of communist internationalism came with the dispute between Stalin and Tito and Yugoslavia's expulsion from the Cominform in 1948. When Stalin sensed that Tito was failing to toe the Soviet line fully, he promptly excommunicated the Yugoslavs from the Communist camp. Yugoslavia's subsequent independent course suggested that the building of socialism was possible (and in the eyes of some, even preferable) outside the Soviet fold. This and other feelings concerning sovereignty resulted in a series of national uprisings in several of the other East European states against the dominant Soviet role and in favor of more autonomous interstate relations within the socialist bloc. The most notable of these uprisings occurred in Hungary in 1956 as the Hungarian leadership and people sought to gain more sovereignty over the building of socialism in their country. After the Yugoslav experience, the Soviet leadership was unwilling to see their hopes of Soviet-directed internationalism suffer another setback; accordingly, they crushed the Hungarian movement in the fall of 1956.

The next great setback to a united movement of socialist states came with the growing disaffection between the Chinese and the Soviets in the late 1950s. Resulting in an open split in 1960, the Sino-Soviet dispute buried all illusions concerning the possibility of socialist harmony.[22] Chinese and Soviet animosities reached the level of open warfare in the late

[21]See, for example, Charles Gati, "Soviet Empire: Alive but Not Well," *Problems of Communism* 34 (2) (1985): 73–86.

[22]See Donald Zagoria, *The Sino-Soviet Conflict, 1956–61* (New York: Atheneum, 1964).

1960s as both sides prepared for war. The Sino-Soviet border became the site of numerous military skirmishes and the encampments of huge armies prepared for war. Although recent years have seen a partial lull in hostilities between the two powers, ideological conflict continues to rage.

With the Chinese split, the position of Soviet leadership in the socialist world was further challenged. Albania also broke away from the Soviet bloc, transferred its allegiance to the Chinese Communists, and became China's beachhead in Europe.[23] Disagreeing with China's new domestic and foreign policies in the post-Mao era, Albania cut its relations with China and now is isolated from both Communist Party and non-Communist states. Romania, too, was affected by the Sino-Soviet dispute and, although it remained in the Warsaw Pact, the Romanians challenged the role of Soviet leadership and began to walk a tightrope between China and the Soviet Union. We will not outline all the points of conflict and contrast among the states, but it should be clear that the view of the Communist world as a monolithic union of like-minded states is a gross misconception.

Suggestions for Further Reading

Brzezinski, Zbigniew K., *The Soviet Bloc: Unity and Conflict*, rev. ed. (New York: Praeger, 1961).

Burks, R. V., *The Dynamics of Communism in Eastern Europe* (Princeton, N.J.: Princeton University Press, 1961).

Drachkovitch, Milorad M., ed., *Marxism in the Modern World* (Stanford, Calif.: Stanford University Press, 1965).

Fejto, Francois, *A History of the People's Democracies* (New York: Praeger, 1971).

Gasster, Michael, *China's Struggle to Modernize* (New York: Knopf, 1972).

Goodrich, L. Carrington, *A Short History of the Chinese People*, 3rd ed. (New York: Harper & Row, 1959).

Hammond, Thomas T., ed., *The Anatomy of Communist Takeovers* (New Haven, Conn.: Yale University Press, 1975).

Hunt, R. N. Carew, *The Theory and Practice of Communism*, 5th ed. (Baltimore: Penguin, 1963).

Johnson, Chalmers, *Peasant Nationalism and Communist Power* (Stanford, Calif.: Stanford University Press, 1962).

Lichtheim, George, *Marxism: An Historical and Critical Study*, 2nd ed. (New York: Praeger, 1965).

McCrea, Barbara P., et al., *The Soviet and East European Political Dictionary* (Santa Barbara, Calif.: ABC-Clio, 1984).

Meisner, Maurice, *Mao's China: A History of the People's Republic* (New York: Free Press, 1977).

Pares, Bernard, *A History of Russia*, 5th ed. (New York: Knopf, 1949).

Schapiro, Leonard, *The Origins of Communist Autocracy* (Cambridge: Harvard University Press, 1955).

Seton-Watson, Hugh, *From Lenin to Khrushchev: The History of World Communism* (New York: Praeger, 1960).

———. *The East European Revolution*, 3rd ed. (New York: Praeger, 1956).

[23]Harry Hamm, *Albania—China's Beachhead in Europe* (New York: Praeger, 1963).

Selden, Mark, ed., *The People's Republic of China: A Documentary History of Revolutionary Change* (New York: Monthly Review Press, 1979).

Singleton, Fred, *Twentieth Century Yugoslavia* (New York: Columbia University Press, 1976).

Snow, Edgar, *Red Star over China* (New York: Random House, 1938).

Trotsky, Leon, *A History of the Russian Revolution,* trans. Max Eastman (3 vols.) (New York: Simon & Schuster, 1932).

CHAPTER TWO
The Contemporary Setting

People often think of the Communist world as a monolithic bloc of gray, nondescript, undifferentiated states. This stereotype is a gross misconception and has led to an unfortunate amount of naiveté and misunderstanding about the countries we call Communist. If we examine them closely, we will find extreme diversity in their social, economic, and political features. In 1980, the USSR had a gross national product (GNP) of $1.2 trillion, making it the second largest economy in the world. Albania in Europe and some of the Asian Communist states, on the other hand, have economies that are among the smallest in the world. Other countries have rather high per capita GNPs, while some are extremely low. East Germany had a per capita GNP of $7226 in 1980 while that of Laos was under $100. When considering ethnic and cultural characteristics, we learn that North Korea is ethnically homogeneous—almost totally Korean—whereas the USSR is made up of over 100 diverse ethnic and national groupings. Understanding the nature of politics in Communist Party states requires careful study of this rich variety of national characteristics.

In the following chapters, we will concentrate on three rather different types of Communist political systems. Using the comparative approach, we will consider many of the 16 Communist Party states discussed in the previous chapter, but concentrate our attention on the USSR, China, and Yugoslavia. As our study will illustrate, these three states represent contrasting and, in many respects, competing models of communism. In this chapter we will examine the different economic, social, and demographic characteristics and the role they play in determining the setting in which politics takes place.

THE ECONOMIC SETTING

Economics is at the heart of Marxist ideology. Marx predicted that the socialist revolution would occur in capitalist countries that had undergone the Industrial Revolution. In point of fact, communism arose in agriculture-based societies where the proletarian sector was a very small percentage (generally 5 to 25 percent) of the working population (see Table 2.1). The countries of Asia—China, Cambodia (Kampuchea), Laos, and Vietnam—were even more agriculturally oriented than their European counterparts. The United Nations estimates that nearly 80 percent of China's present-day labor force still works in agriculture. Therefore, although Marx predicted that economic abundance and equality would come with the victory of socialism, the social and economic conditions of most aspiring Marxist states were not conducive to the realization of Communist ideals.

TABLE 2.1 Working Population before Socialism, by Sector of Economy

	Czechoslovakia (1934)	Hungary (1930)	Poland (1931)	Romania (1930)	Bulgaria (1935)	Yugoslavia (1936)
Industry	38.3	24.1	19.4	7.7	8.0	9.9
Agriculture	25.6	53.0	60.6	76.9	80.0	76.3
Trade	9.2	5.9	6.1	3.3	2.4	4.2
Other	26.9	17.0	13.9	12.1	9.6	9.3
Total	100.0	100.0	100.0	100.0	100.0	99.7

SOURCE: Walter D. Connor, *Socialism, Politics, and Equality: Hierarchy and Change in Eastern Europe and the USSR* (New York: Columbia University Press, 1979), p. 31.

THE SOVIET UNION

The initial challenge facing Lenin and the Communist leaders after the Bolshevik victory was Russia's reconstruction. After extricating the country from World War I, the Bolsheviks went about the task of consolidating power and building socialism within their country. In 1918, Lenin's decree nationalized heavy industries, land, and the means of production; private ownership of land and industry was strictly forbidden. During the ensuing period of civil war and foreign intervention (1918–1921), however, little could be done to set up a rational system of economic administration. It was during this period of ''war communism'' that economic output fell to 20 percent of what it had been before the outbreak of World War I.

To get the economy going again, the Russian leaders adopted the New Economic Policy (NEP) in 1921. Although large industries remained nationalized, this new policy called for a mixed economic strategy that denationalized small industries and agriculture. Representing a temporary return to capitalism, the NEP saved the Bolshevik government from bankruptcy and got the Russian economy back on its feet again. By 1926, economic output had reached its prewar levels.

With Lenin's death in 1924 and Stalin's assumption of power, Russia's leadership embraced the monumental task of rapid industrialization. With the first Five-Year Plan of 1928–1933 (a centralized plan coordinating economic goals and policies for the entire country), the Stalinist strategy of economic development began to materialize. Because there was no real possibility of bringing foreign capital into the country—the socialist leaders did not want to become dependent on the capitalist West and the West was suspicious of, and unwilling to support, Russian development—Soviet economic policy had to devise a method of generating capital internally. By adopting a policy that exacted high costs from the peasantry and that funneled nearly all economic surpluses back into the industrial sector, the Soviets attempted to accumulate funds on their own. To achieve the Party's economic goals, Stalin established a centralized administrative structure and re-adopted the policies of nationalization and collectivization. Designed to mobilize the population to attain what many people felt to be unreasonably high economic goals, this developmental policy incurred great human costs. Individuals or groups who disagreed with nationalization or the collectivization of agriculture were sent off to Siberia or annihilated.[1] The human costs surrounding Stalin's programs were high, but the economic benefits were substantial. Even in view of the devastation and economic setbacks caused by World War II, the Soviet economic strategy propelled the USSR to the stature of a world

[1]Stalin's collectivization drive of 1920–1936 was a radical program to transfer the private ownership of land to collective farms under state administration. The drive ended with the abolition of 90 percent of private farming and the deportation of over 1 million peasant households.

TABLE 2.2 Socioeconomic Indicators, 1980

Country	GNP (million US $)	GNP per capita (US $)	Global Economic-Social Standing[a]
Albania	2400	898	56
Bulgaria	37,390	4219	31
Cambodia	na[b]	na[b]	134
China	300,000	298	91
Cuba	18,000	1864	35
Czechoslovakia	89,260	5821	27
East Germany	120,940	7226	19
Hungary	44,990	4200	28
Laos	300	87	122
Mongolia	1420	854	54
North Korea	20,500	1151	76
Poland	139,780	3929	34
Romania	85,500	3851	35
Soviet Union	1,212,030	4564	25
Vietnam	8600	161	103
Yugoslavia	59,132	2651	46
USA[c]	2,583,700	11,347	9

[a]Represents average rankings based on 140 countries for GNP per capita and education and health indicators.

[b]Not available.

[c]The USA is included for comparative purposes.

SOURCE: Adapted from Ruth Leger Sivard, *World Military and Social Expenditures*, 1983 (Leesburg, Va.: World Priorities, 1983), pp. 21–29.

power by the end of the Stalinist era in 1953. Utilizing a command-type economic system based on government control of the means of production, central planning, and a high rate of capital investment, production in the Soviet Union drew close to, and even surpassed, that of some of the Western powers.

Between 1950 and 1980, the Soviet Union's economy grew even further. In 1950, the Soviet GNP was estimated at less than one-third that of the United States. By 1965, Soviet GNP had grown to approximately half that of the United States and three times that of Great Britain; by 1980, the Soviet economy continued to grow (see Table 2.2). The general economic goal through the first 60 years of Soviet development had been that of basic capital investment.

Stated simply, the Soviets opted for the development of heavy industry—hydroelectric plants, steel mills, and so forth—at the expense of the consumer sector.[2]

CHINA

Assuming power in 1949, Mao Zedong and the Chinese Communists faced an even less developed economy, more devastated country, and a more chaotic economic system than the Bolsheviks confronted. The economy was in such a deteriorated state that it did not even have the

[2]For an excellent economic history of the Soviet Union, see Alec Nove, *An Economic History of the USSR* (London: Allen Lane, 1969).

capability to manufacture the primary vehicle for Chinese transportation, the bicycle. Unlike the Bolsheviks, Mao and his compatriots did not rush to nationalize industry and collectivize agriculture. To stimulate economic recovery, they attempted to use capitalist industry and redistribute agricultural land among the peasants; nationalization and collectivization would occur gradually over the span of several years. This policy of gradual transformation was carefully followed during the 1949–1952 period and resulted in political consolidation, economic recovery and growth, and improved internal and international prestige. Slowly, the leadership began to transform privately owned enterprises into a cooperative form of state/private management. At the outset of the first Five-Year Plan in 1953, these joint enterprises accounted for approximately half of China's economic output; by 1956, practically all private enterprises had been changed to the cooperative private/state operation. The first Five-Year Plan (1953–1957)—based on a general conception of Stalin's model although benefiting from the hindsight of Soviet mistakes—resulted in substantial material growth and economic progress. Utilizing aid and advice from the USSR and East European states, China appeared well on the way to economic recovery.

Soon after the second Five-Year Plan was proclaimed (1958–1962), however, the recovery encountered a number of serious setbacks, the first of which was the Great Leap Forward campaign beginning in 1958. Based on the general line of "going all out and aiming high to achieve greater, quicker, better, and more economical results in building socialism," this radical program was intended to make China a world economic power in a matter of decades. With expectations of surpassing Great Britain in industrial output in 15 years, the strategy called on both modern and traditional (what the Chinese refer to as "walking on two legs") methods of development. Sacrificing quality for quantity and suffering from poor planning and execution, the Great Leap Forward resulted in a "small step backward." Planning

became difficult, product quality declined, economic imbalances were experienced, and the idealistic but misguided campaign ended in disgrace.

The period of 1959–1961 also brought a series of natural calamities, such as droughts and floods, that further reduced Chinese economic capabilities, diminished agricultural production, and hindered development. In their midst came the Soviet Union's withdrawal of material aid and technical assistance in the summer of 1960. Precipitated by a growing ideological dispute, the Soviet Union's withdrawal interrupted many developmental programs that relied on foreign assistance.[3] At this point in Chinese reconstruction, the future looked bleak indeed.

In the early 1960s, the Chinese brought an end to the Great Leap Forward program and began to reevaluate their economic policies. This period ushered in an emphasis on greater self-reliance and a search for policies uniquely suited to Chinese needs and capabilities. The reappraisal changed the general strategy from one emphasizing heavy industry (the Soviet Union's approach) to one emphasizing agriculture. The new order of priorities became agriculture first, light industry second, and heavy industry third. As recovery proceeded and the third Five-Year Plan entered its second year in 1967, however, the economic system encountered another destabilizing campaign. Intended to "take firm hold of the revolution and stimulate production," the Great Proletarian Cultural Revolution (GPCR) of 1966–1969 once again set the economic system into a state of disarray. Young revolutionaries, the Red Guards, were dispatched to the factories and all other social and economic organizations to stimulate production through revolutionary and ideological means; their intrusion had certain political benefits but also great economic costs. Although intending to rejuvenate the

---

[3]These and other events resulted in the so-called Sino-Soviet conflict, a dispute characterized by hostile interstate relations through the 1960s and 1970s and continuing into the present.

revolutionary spirit of the populace, the GPCR exacted a considerable price before it ended in 1969.

YUGOSLAVIA, EASTERN EUROPE, AND CUBA

Always less developed than Western Europe, the East European countries were further devastated by two world wars. During their evacuation of Yugoslavia at the end of World War II, the Nazis destroyed much of the country's transportation system and industrial facilities. The Yugoslavs began the task of reconstruction by nationalizing and collectivizing private holdings according to the Stalinist mode of development. However, growing friction between Joseph Stalin and the Yugoslav leaders culminated in a decision that shocked the world. Unexpectedly, in 1948, Stalin expelled Josip Broz Tito and the Yugoslavs from the international Communist organization, Cominform, and initiated a sudden freeze in Soviet-Yugoslav relations.[4]

A few years after the expulsion, Tito and his associates began considering alternatives to the Soviet command-type economic system. Slowly experimenting with and implementing a number of reforms, the Yugoslavs moved to a decentralized form of market socialism that based production more on the laws of supply and demand, less on the expectations of a central economic plan. Movement to a market-based economy was in part motivated and certainly hastened by the Soviet's economic blockade of Yugoslavia that followed their expulsion from the Cominform and the socialist camp. Weathering this blockade and severe natural catastrophes with economic assistance from the United States, the Yugoslavs began a steady period of economic growth. Through the 1950s and 1960s, the Yugoslav economic growth rates were among the highest in the world.

Although some countries fared worse than others, World War II also unleashed destructive forces on the economies of the other East European states. The extent of these damages and the amount of reparation required by the region's victor, the Soviet Union, largely determined the initial pace and extent of postwar recovery.[5] In many cases, the Soviets stripped factories of machinery or dismantled entire plants for shipment to the USSR to help pay for war damages. By the early 1950s, however, all the states were back to their prewar levels of production. East Germany was the last to reach this level because of the unusually high extent of war damage and equally high reparations to the USSR.

Following similar policies of Soviet-oriented socialist construction, the economies of the East European states were virtually all nationalized by 1950. Emulating the Soviet economic model and working within the supranational Council for Mutual Economic Assistance (CMEA or COMECON) established in 1949, the different states adopted rather similar economic policies and procedures.[6] Attempting to expand the industrial base (particularly mining, machine building, ironworks, and steelworks) while simultaneously retarding personal consumption, the states hoped to increase the margin for capital investment. The resultant economic systems were generally in-

[4]The Communist Information Bureau (Cominform) was established in 1947 to bind the East European socialist states more closely to the USSR. In a letter of March 27, 1948, addressed to Tito and the Yugoslav Communists, Stalin and the Soviet Central Committee castigated the Yugoslav leaders and excommunicated them from the socialist camp. Because they considered themselves loyal to the Soviet Union, this was initially a bitter blow to the Yugoslav Communists. For a firsthand account of their reactions and subsequent search for alternative economic and social policies, see Vladimir Dedijer, *The Battle Stalin Lost* (New York: Universal Library, 1972).

[5]For a discussion of Soviet demands for reparation payments from the new Communist Party regimes to cover war damages inflicted by the Axis Powers, as well as other forms of Soviet involvement in the postwar economic setting of Eastern Europe, see Nicholas Spulber, *The Economies of Communist Eastern Europe* (Cambridge: MIT Press, 1957).

[6]COMECON was established as a response to the Western Marshall Plan and was intended to coordinate reconstruction, planning, production, and foreign trade within Eastern Europe. It originally included Bulgaria, Czechoslovakia, Hungary, Poland, Romania, and the USSR. Subsequently, it was broadened to include Albania (since withdrawn), Cuba, East Germany, and Mongolia.

efficient. Economic recovery from the ravages of war was achieved at unnecessarily high costs in terms of poor working conditions, low salaries, and a scarcity of basic consumer goods.

Unlike the war-torn countries of Europe and Asia, Cuba had a relatively stable and productive economy to greet Fidel Castro on his assumption of power. In a series of moves to punish the followers of the ousted dictator Fulgencio Batista, Castro expropriated properties, including factories, shops, hotels, and so forth; reduced rents; lowered property values; raised wages; and prohibited the export of capital. Soon after, he nationalized the oil industry and expropriated all foreign companies. All these policies helped to undercut the former capitalist system and, by 1960, Cuba was well on the road to socialism.

SOCIALIST ECONOMIC FORMS

The ideal of communism described by Karl Marx envisioned an economic system based on the principle "from each according to his abilities, to each according to his needs." This principle presupposes an economic system in which there are no shortages and where the members of society do not have to pay for food, goods, or services. Individuals work and produce according to their abilities and consume only what they need. A cursory review of economic relations in contemporary Communist Party states indicates that this level of development is still an ideal and rather far removed from reality.

To move toward the ideals of communism, all Communist Party states have established some sort of socialist economic system. Under socialism, workers produce according to their ability and are paid according to their contribution. In this economic system, theoretically speaking, the factors of production are owned collectively and controlled by the public. Marx believed that this system was a lower stage than Communism but, although it was an unjust system because more important work

would be more highly rewarded than less important work, it would accomplish certain necessary benefits. Basically, socialism would produce a system of material abundance in which the state would "wither away," and the "oppressive government of men" would be replaced by the "administration of things." For Marx, socialism provided these necessary socioeconomic prerequisites for the emergence of true or pure communism.

The Communist Party states of today display a variety of socialist institutional arrangements and policy preferences, each officially designed to facilitate the evolution from socialism to communism. The Soviet Union's economic system has often been referred to, especially by its Marxist detractors, as one of state socialism.[7] In this system, state ministries and government bodies at different levels manage the factors of production. Because industries and enterprises receive their directives from central planning agencies, the term *command-type system* is also used to describe the Soviet economic system. Although the market and the idea of supply and demand have some effect on production, the planning agencies assume primary power and responsibility for determining the type and level of economic output. Profits and losses accrue to the state, not to the enterprise or to the workers.[8]

The centralized economy under the model of state socialism allows the central government to control key policy decisions, but there are still some economic interests and enterprises that remain outside direct government control. Some agricultural and industrial cooperatives, usually quite small, administer their own economic affairs. There are also private artisans (jewelers, tailors) and professionals (doctors and dentists) in some Communist Party countries who, although required to be

[7]Because the state rather than the public owns the factors of production, the term *state socialism* is widely used to describe the Soviet economic system.

[8]For a review of the organization and functioning of the Soviet economy, see Robert W. Campbell, *Soviet Economic Power: Its Organization, Growth and Challenge* (London: Macmillan, 1967).

registered, function very much on a private basis. At the same time, ownership of the majority of the means of production resides in the hands of the state and is under the control of government authorities. In theory, at least, this system is to serve the collective interest and avoid the type of "man over man" exploitation that Marxists contend characterizes private ownership in the capitalist system.

Although a basic purpose and desired benefit of the centralized, administered system of state socialism is that of economic efficiency, many economists have called attention to considerable waste and inefficiency in the Soviet and East European systems. The administered system is useful in tackling high-priority tasks, like the development of heavy industry or the decision to promote intensive capital investment. However, vesting ownership in the state and control in the government ministries has ruled out certain economic dynamics that promote efficiency and development. A key example involves the attitude and commitment of the average worker. Marx contended that under capitalism workers had become estranged from their work, but that under socialism they were to regain control of their work because the work enterprise was to be publicly owned. But under a centralized system of state socialism, as in the Soviet Union, workers have once again been separated from their work. In the eyes of many observers, the state has merely replaced the bourgeoisie and, thus, the role and attitude of the worker has not changed significantly.

There have been a number of reactions to this development in the form of experimentation with alternative forms of socialism. Perhaps the most far-reaching and interesting is the Yugoslav experiment with their self-managing form of socialism. Referred to by a variety of terms, including decentralized socialism, *laissez faire* socialism, or a mixed free enterprise/public ownership system, the Yugoslav experiment represents an attempt to resolve some of the problems of state socialism. Hoping to eliminate excessive bureaucracy, low

productivity and efficiency, and a relative absence of motivation and initiative, they have developed a hybrid economic system that combines elements of both socialism and capitalism.

Beginning in the early 1950s, Yugoslavia began to abandon many features of the Soviet command-type system. In a series of reforms, Yugoslav leaders deemphasized centralized planning, provided economic enterprises with more decision-making autonomy, and made competition and profit a central motivating feature of the economy. All these and additional policies came under the movement toward self-managing, market-oriented socialism.

Although accounts of the motivating forces behind self-management vary, most include Yugoslavia's desire to put power in the hands of the worker, where, according to Marx, it rightly belongs. The first major move in the early 1950s involved the establishment of workers' councils in economic enterprises. These councils of elected workers were to assume major responsibility for running the affairs of the firm. Under this system, central government planning was deemphasized while the autonomy of the enterprise was increased. That is, considerable authority was transferred from central planning ministries to the enterprises themselves, and the enterprises began to base their decisions on the market. This change had a drastic effect on the economic system and the broader society. Rather than produce what the central plan required, enterprises began to produce what would sell on the market. This action upgraded the quality of Yugoslav goods and made them more competitive both domestically and internationally. It also moved the economy in a more consumer-oriented direction because the enterprises were motivated to produce goods that the consumer would be willing to buy. This has made the Yugoslav system one of the most consumer-oriented economies of the Communist Party states we are studying.

As one might expect, the Yugoslav form of socialism came under hostile attack from both the Chinese and Soviet leaders. A pamphlet published in Beijing in 1964 noted:

> Although the Tito clique still displays the banner of "socialism," a bureaucrat bourgeoisie opposed to the Yugoslav people has gradually come into being since the Tito clique took the road of revisionism, transforming the Yugoslav state from a dictatorship of the proletariat into a dictatorship of the bureaucrat bourgeoisie and its socialist public economy into state capitalism.[9]

The Soviet leaders also looked with disdain on the economic revisionism being followed in Yugoslavia and warned their fellow leaders in the other European socialist states to stay clear of this heresy.

Taking the advice of the Soviet leaders, the East European states have adopted a much more orthodox (Soviet-oriented) path to economic development. In these states, an initial mixed-economy period after World War II was followed by the adoption of a command system emulating the Soviet model. Launching Five-Year Plans that emphasized industrial development, nationalizing trade and industry, and subordinating labor unions to the Communist Party, the economic models of the other East European states looked initially like miniature copies of the Soviet system.

From the late 1950s to 1980, however, many of the East European states began to experiment with reforms. Some observed with keen interest the successes of economic experimentation in Yugoslavia. Many felt that the planned economies established in their countries with Soviet assistance after World War II were impeding optimal development. Having experienced prewar histories of rather successful economic growth and possessing definite economic potential, economic planners in some of these states blamed their present difficulties on the Soviet-style administered system. Although the responses differed from country to country, many were eager to experi-

ment with new economic forms. Significant policy changes based on economic liberalization were initiated at different times in a number of the countries, particularly Czechoslovakia, Hungary, and Poland. However, because the USSR perceived these policies as endangering the preservation of the command system, the Soviets often intervened and forced these countries back into more orthodox positions. Witness, for example, the Czechoslovak experience in the late 1960s when they attempted to undertake far-reaching social and economic reforms. One dimension of this experiment was economic liberalization designed to take some of the planning and policymaking functions away from the party and central ministries. Although significant economic progress was being made and other social and political reforms were gathering momentum during the spring of 1968, Soviet reservations about the advisability of these reforms resulted in military intervention that brought an end to Czechoslovak economic and political liberalization.[10] Organizing a joint intervention by the Warsaw Treaty Organization (WTO) states, troops and tanks from Bulgaria, East Germany, Poland, and the Soviet Union marched on to Czechoslovakian soil on August 20, 1968, and brought an end to what had become known as "the Prague spring."[11] Many Czechoslovak leaders, including the Communist Party leader, Alexander Dubcek, were ousted as the country returned to the more orthodox position that

---

[9]*On Khrushchev's Phoney Communism and Its Historical Lessons to the World* (Beijing: Foreign Languages Press, 1964), p. 47.

[10]The Soviet leaders were worried by factors other than economic liberalization. There were fears, for example, concerning Western influence and involvement in Czechoslovakia and the possibility that the reforms would result in withdrawal from the Warsaw Treaty Organization (WTO) and COMECON pacts.

[11]The Warsaw Treaty was signed in 1955 by Albania, Bulgaria, the German Democratic Republic [GDR (East Germany)], Hungary, Poland, Romania, and the USSR as a response to the establishment of the North Atlantic Treaty Organization (NATO). Like NATO, the treaty pledged mutual military assistance in the event of an attack on one of the signatories. The so-called Brezhnev Doctrine that grew out of the 1968 intervention in Czechoslovakia appeared to broaden the assistance to include perceived domestic threats to socialism.

characterizes the economic systems of the other WTO and COMECON states.

The Chinese and Cuban economic systems have both significant similarities to, and differences from, the Soviet and East European forms. Involved in a cyclical, or zigzag, course over the years, the Chinese system has moved back and forth, emphasizing more radical and more moderate economic forms. At some periods, particularly during the Great Leap Forward (1958–1960) and at the height of the GPCR (1966–1969), the Chinese approach to economic development was based primarily on mass ideological mobilization of the populace. The hope was to attain higher output and greater growth through the human efforts and ideological commitment of the Chinese people. During these periods, revolutionary values and attitudinal changes were emphasized at the expense of technological expertise. The motto of the workplace, ''Higher profits through greater study,'' meant study of the *Quotations from Chairman Mao*, China's ideological primer. Since Mao's death in 1976, more moderate and less ideological methods have prevailed.

In 1984 the Chinese announced sweeping economic reforms, what the top leader Deng Xiaoping referred to as a ''revolution.'' The reforms call for greater decentralization of industrial management and more competition among factories. At the core of the reforms is an attempt to invigorate the state enterprises by granting them more autonomy. The reforms are intended to introduce more market forces in industry and make businesses compete so that, in the Chinese Communists' words, ''only the best survive.'' Another key component of the reforms is the drastic modification of centralized planning. The reforms reduce the scope of mandatory planning to include only items that are vital to the national interest and people's livelihood, such as the production of energy and raw materials. Service industries and the production of small commodities, on the other hand, are to be left to market forces.

There was further evidence of dramatic change in China in 1984. In the autumn, the Chinese Communist Party newspaper, *People's Daily*, said that although the works of Marx and Lenin should be studied, they are not necessarily applicable to problems and challenges confronting China today. In a front-page commentary, *People's Daily* noted that ''Marx died one hundred and one years ago. . . . We can not depend on the works of Marx and Lenin to solve our modern day questions.'' This dramatic statement was qualified somewhat the next day when the newspaper ran an inconspicuous three-line ''supplementary correction'' which said the last part of the commentary should have read: ''We can not depend on Marx and Lenin to solve *all* our modern day questions.'' (Italics added.) A few days later, a senior Communist Party ideologist, Yu Guangyuan, told foreign journalists that although Marx was a great revolutionary whose ideas still underpinned Chinese theory, he did not provide practical answers and advice on how to build a socialist economy. Yu noted that some of Marx's theories were far from enough to resolve the contemporary problems of socialist economic construction. Although these fascinating explanations qualified the original *People's Daily* statement somewhat, this discussion and other reports from China call attention to a country that is reconsidering fundamentally the conventional way of doing things and that is currently engaged in sweeping experimentation and reform.

The selection of the young and purportedly reform-minded Mikhail Gorbachev as Soviet party leader in 1985 raises questions of political reform and change in the USSR as well. Although it is rather early to assess the Gorbachev approach to Soviet economic problems, it is an issue that students of Communist affairs will want to follow closely in the years ahead.

However, it should be noted now that after nearly two-thirds of a century of socialism in the Soviet Union and over one-third of a century in other Communist Party states, the utopian socioeconomic state of communism still remains an ideal. During the current stages of socialism, the leaders continue to experiment with different economic strategies and formulas. Let us now see where they stand.

CONTEMPORARY ECONOMIC CAPABILITIES

The Marxist–Leninist states of the Second World vary markedly in their levels of production, total wealth, and resources. The most frequently employed index to measure these economic capabilities, GNP, shows that one of these states (the Soviet Union) has the second highest capabilities in the world, whereas others do rather poorly. The East European countries tend to rank behind the highly developed Western countries of the First World but ahead of the less-developed nations of the Third World. Laos and Cambodia (Kampuchea) rank among the lowest in the world.

Table 2.2 shows some of the diversity in economic capabilities among the states. The Soviet Union has a GNP about four times that of its nearest competitor, China. This is particularly noteworthy when we realize that the USSR has a population about one-fourth that of the Chinese. The East European countries reflect two definite subgroups, one representing the northern states (Czechoslovakia, East Germany, and Poland) and the other representing the southern states (Bulgaria, Hungary, Romania, and Yugoslavia). Albania is far less developed than the rest of the states of southeastern Europe and assumes a position even below some Asian states.

When we compare the growth rates of the East European states with those from the West during the critical years of postwar development, we find generally higher growth rates in the East. In fact, some of the postwar growth rates (those of Romania and Yugoslavia) have been among the highest in the world. We should note, however, that the impressive growth rates can be attributed in large part to the decision to emphasize industrial instead of consumer-oriented development. This policy means the building of hydroelectric plants, steel mills, and heavy industries while de-emphasizing the light industry and manufacturing related to expansion of the consumer sector. Such an investment policy can lead to advancements in the overall output of goods and services, which are clearly reflected in the GNP figures of the socialist states, but which also contribute to dire shortcomings in mass consumption. Travel to Eastern Europe and the Soviet Union will quickly reveal the people to be widely deprived of the wide range of consumer items taken for granted in the West; this includes foodstuffs and clothing, autos, and appliances. Shopping is a depressing ordeal throughout most of the Communist Party states of the Second World.

There has been considerable debate in the East and West about Soviet economic reform. The new Communist Party leader Gorbachev has emphasized the need to achieve a decisive breakthrough in the intensification of the economy. To achieve this, he has stressed the need to accelerate scientific and technical progress and to improve training and skills at all levels. In addition, the post-Brezhnev leaders have experimented with a variety of ''economic reforms.'' Although this term is rarely used in the Soviet Union, there has been considerable discussion and a series of experiments to ''improve the economic mechanism.'' For example, in accordance with a decree adopted under then First Secretary Andropov in July 1983, 700 enterprises of five industrial ministries began to pursue a ''large-scale economic experiment in industry.'' The principle of the experiment was often stated as ''greater independence, greater responsibility.'' The issue of economic experiment and reform will be of considerable importance in the Gorbachev period.

While the economies are unlikely to collapse, a number of them are in considerable trouble. The Soviet economy is still growing, but it is growing at a much slower rate than in the past. Labor shortages in the industrial areas, low productivity, waste, and inefficiency are among the problems placing considerable restraints on Soviet economic development. Poland's problems are much more serious, and include:

1. Wages growing faster than production. Factories have been increasing wages in an attempt to stimulate output. The result is considerable money in the hands of workers but far too little to buy. This leads to further frustration and a thriving black market.

2. **Low product quality.** The low quality of goods produced in Poland causes problems in the domestic economy and damages the prospects of an export-led economic recovery.

3. **Chronic shortages of imported materials and components.** Since the imposition of Western economic sanctions and the credit squeeze of the early 1980s, Polish imports have plummeted, leading to further problems in the domestic economy. Poland's economy remains a very sick patient in the mid-1980s.

Although many of the other East European economies—for example, Hungary and Bulgaria—are doing better, Communist economic systems cannot be called unqualified successes.

However, most economic indicators point to significant changes in the realm of industrial development. Historical experience reveals, for example, that industrialization and general socioeconomic development are typically accompanied by decreases in the agricultural work force. The rural-urban figures changed rapidly in socialist countries as peasants moved from the countryside to assume jobs in the cities where they are likely to find employment in the growing number of factories. Overall, the changes since World War II have been most significant in Eastern Europe—whereas approximately 75 percent of the work force was involved in agriculture before the war (see Table 2.1), less than 50 percent now holds such occupations.

The growth in industrial capacities is also marked by an increase in energy consumption. On a per capita basis, the Second World Communist Party states are among the top energy consumers in the world. As Western experience has shown, energy sources will be increasingly valuable resources in the future. Some Communist countries are (comparatively speaking) quite wealthy in energy resources. Untapped oil and gas reserves in the USSR, Mongolia, and China represent vast storehouses for the future, although they may re-

quire Western technology to exploit them. Other countries, especially those of Eastern Europe, rely heavily on foreign sources of energy and have begun to feel the serious consequences of energy dependence.

Another key to future economic development involves scientific and technological capabilities. Most socialist states have emphasized the role of education and scientific progress in the development process, yet they still lag behind the First World in these areas. Considerable investments have been made over the postwar years in scientific research institutes, institutions of higher education, and advanced technical schools. This emphasis has been particularly strong in the Soviet Union and the Eastern European states, where great investments have been made in scientific education as well as in the importation of science and technology from abroad.

China's emphasis on scientific and technological development, on the other hand, has been less clear and somewhat cyclical. During Mao's rule and the GPCR, for example, many universities and schools were closed and study became synonymous with a careful reading of the ideological exhortations of Chairman Mao. While visiting a Chinese medical hospital during the GPCR, a Western observer asked some advanced medical students what books they used in preparing for the medical profession. All held out Chairman Mao's *Little Red Book* of ideological quotations. As the students' professor began to name some more conventional sources, he was quickly silenced by the students and told to refrain from questioning the advisability of mixing medicine and Maoism.

The Maoist emphasis on ideology did great damage to Chinese modernization and economic development. Members of the intelligentsia were sent to rural communes for physical labor and ideological study. The importance of science and technology to development was denied. Interestingly, Mao's successors appear to recognize the costs of the previous ideological campaigns and upheavals. During the current post-Mao period (which began in 1976), Chinese leaders have been giving considerably more emphasis to the important role that science and technology can play in promoting national development. Stressing the four modernizations—agriculture, industry, national defense, and science and technology—the leaders are encouraging the indigenous development and importation of scientific and technological expertise.

In the 1970s, most all countries of the Second World turned to the West for increased technological and scientific expertise. Permitted under the policy of detente, which relaxed tensions between the Communist and non-Communist worlds, the flow of technology into the socialist states grew significantly during the 1970s. The motives of the socialist states were clear. Party leaders hoped that the infusion of Western technology would obviate the need to undertake massive economic reforms required to salvage their sagging economic fortunes, and they hoped to avoid the decentralization of economic control that would challenge their monopoly of power. They also hoped that the importation of Western technology would promote industrial development and result in a saving of time and resources that the indigenous development of these capabilities would require.

Although the importation of Western technology may have provided some assistance, it did not solve the economic problems of the Communist Party states of the Second World. The socialist economies continue to confront a variety of pressing challenges. There are problems concerning the output and efficiency of collective farms, which remain less productive than private farms. The quality of industrial output is often substandard and consumer demands still go unmet. There are also problems of poor planning, waste, and inefficiency in all sectors of the economies. These and other problems, including the worldwide recession, have resulted in significant slowdowns in the economic growth of the socialist countries. Finally, there are the growing concerns with energy resources and how shrinking reserves and future shortages will affect economic growth. As we will see, these economic issues are important environmental forces that help determine the availability of certain values and their distribution in socialist societies.

THE SOCIAL SETTING

Gross National Product per capita is sometimes used as one indicator of the social well-being of a population. In 1980, the GNP per capita (GNP divided by population) in the United States was $11,347, whereas in China, it was only $298. Obviously, at least by this measure, the well-being of the average American citizen is considerably higher than that of the average Chinese.

One must be careful in interpreting GNP per capita figures, however, for a number of reasons. First, the proportion of the GNP invested in the social and consumer realms may vary markedly from one country to another; second, the distribution of wealth from one individual to another or from one social group to another may differ considerably. In comparing Communist Party states, however, these two factors are not of great importance because the amount of GNP expended in the social and consumer realms is relatively constant from one country to another, as is the level of income inequalities between individuals and groups within each country. For these reasons, the GNP per capita figures presented in Table 2.2 provide fairly useful comparative measures of at least one indicator of social welfare in the 16 states.

In addition to per capita income contrasts, differences in consumer-oriented investment can result in considerable and obvious contrasts in the levels of consumption among the various socialist states. Although it has a GNP per capita below that of Bulgaria and Romania, for example, Yugoslavia has traditionally exhibited higher consumption levels among its population. That is, although living in a relatively less developed socialist state, Yugoslavs have enjoyed an unusually high level of consumerism. Cars, boats, vacation homes, and other items considered bourgeois luxuries in most socialist states have become commonplace within this particular country.[12] The Yugoslavs' relatively high level of consumption is a result of their market-oriented economy and illustrates the impact that economic policies can have on the populace.

Televisions, refrigerators, and automobiles are by now common features of many households in the European Communist Party states, but they are still seldom-seen luxuries in their Asian counterparts. One observes television antennas throughout the East European countryside, including even in the most remote villages, but they are seldom found in China. In economic terms, the Asian socialist states and, perhaps, Cuba and Albania might more appropriately be classified with the Third World states. As one might suspect, the leaders of these states have been the most outspoken critics of the individualism and excessive materialism associated with Western and particularly American conceptions of well-being. Although we tend to emphasize private accumulation of goods and services, communist ideology considers well-being a public good entitled by all. As we note later, there are considerable differences among the Communist Party states—say, between China and Yugoslavia—differences clearly reflected in the social milieus of the countries.

Although consumerism is much higher in many other parts of the world and particularly in Western Europe and North America, social services such as health care and education are impressive features of the social setting in Marxist–Leninist states. When examining overall socioeconomic standing based on GNP per capita, education, and health indicators, most Communist Party states rank behind most of the Western states of the First World and ahead of most of those in the Third. The Soviets, Yugoslavs, and Chinese rank 34th, 46th, and 120th, respectively, out of 140 countries. The

abysmal rankings of the Cambodians (Kampucheans), Laotians, and Vietnamese call attention to the perilous socioeconomic conditions in Southeast Asia. Now, let us examine how certain ideological principles influence the distribution of wealth in Marxist–Leninist systems.

SOCIALISM AND EQUALITY

In the *Communist Manifesto*, Karl Marx and Friedrich Engels wrote: "The history of all hitherto existing society is the history of class struggles." According to their theory, modern industrial society had given birth to the proletariat and bourgeoisie, the two antagonistic classes of the capitalist stage of development. With the establishment of communism, a new historical epoch was to occur. This socioeconomic system was to be free of classes and exploitation and based on the principles of social equality.

The avenue leading to communism, said Marx and Engels, leads through the socioeconomic stage of socialism in which property is made public and private ownership abolished. According to Marxist theory, private property is the force that divides people during the capitalist stage of development. If you forbid private property, you dissolve the basis for class antagonism.

In the Marxist–Leninist states, the ruling Communist parties moved, sometimes quickly and at other times more gradually, to nationalize private property and place power, at least theoretically, in the hands of a proletarian dictatorship. Although the dissolution of private property was more gradual in some states, such as in China where Mao wanted to use the capitalists and avoid class warfare, or incomplete, as in some East European societies where small private farms and businesses still exist, large holdings of private property were outlawed and transferred to collective social or state ownership. Under socialism the proletarian dictatorship was to be a temporary arrangement preceding communism, the idealized classless society. The basic question concerning

---

[12]In the early 1970s, however, Tito declared war on Yugoslav "millionaires" who had acquired seaside villas, large savings accounts abroad, and other material excesses accumulated under the liberal Yugoslav economic system. More recently, Yugoslav economic problems have lowered the standard of living there significantly.

For the Soviet Union, despite advances in the consumer realm, long lines to purchase the basic staples of daily life are not uncommon. Here, women in Moscow wait to buy bread in the GUM department store on Red Square across from the Kremlin.

this theory and the hypothesized developments involves their validity. Would socialism necessarily lead to equality? Would class boundaries and distinctions dissolve under Communist Party rule? Would this lead to the development of the classless community of peoples envisioned under communism?

The experience of the Communist Party states suggests that, although inequalities have been radically reduced, development of a classless society under socialism is not, at least in the short run, a certainty. There are a number of forces making the transition difficult, if not impossible, and these involve some central features of an industrializing society. Most social theorists maintain that a division of labor is a necessary prerequisite to or at least a component of industrialization. Division of labor refers to the structure of jobs and the specialization of occupational skills most likely to achieve optimal industrial development. For example, an industrializing society requires engineers, planners, and workers; these occu-

pations vary in terms of training and skills. Because some occupations are more necessary than others, additional rewards may have to be attached to them to attract people into training for them. As we have noted, the guiding principle of socialism is "from each according to his abilities, to each according to his contribution"; therefore, those occupations that contribute more important skills receive greater rewards. All the countries we are studying have adopted this philosophy of a differentiated reward system during their present socialist phases of development. The communist ideal of "from each according to his abilities, to each according to his needs" still remains remote.

Although Vladimir Ilyich Lenin and the Bolsheviks initially instituted a policy of wage leveling, they soon opted for a system providing incentives in the form of rather sizable wage differentials. Through the 1930s and 1940s, Stalin was quite willing to rationalize inequality in wages as a necessary incentive to attract workers into desired occupations. Soviet industrialization during this phase of development required skilled workers, planners, and engineers as well as clerical and administrative personnel. These and other occupations provided crucial functions required of an industrializing society; they represented the division of labor that characterizes all modernizing societies. Although Nikita S. Khrushchev launched a campaign in the 1950s to reduce these wage differentials, they were never eliminated and remain in the USSR today.[13] Table 2.3 indicates the differentials between some selected occupations in the USSR and four East European countries. Using worker salaries as a base unit (100), the data indicate that although pay generally became more egalitarian between 1960 and 1973, particularly in the USSR, significant differences according to occupation still remained.

It is easy to see why a growing specialization and division of labor has made the establishment of a classless society difficult. When you have a relationship between skills and occupations as well as considerable differences between the highest- and lowest-paid workers, you encounter strong forces encouraging the formation of classes. Communist leaders would refute this argument by noting that although their societies do exhibit occupational and wage differences between individuals and groups, they do not represent the traditional classes of earlier forms of society. In a capitalist society, they would argue, the *bourgeoisie* control and exploit the working class. In earlier societies, the nature of class differences led to an inevitable class struggle—"the history of all hitherto existing society." Therefore, Marxists contend that although wage and status differences may exist in their societies and may lead to a system of social stratification, they will not result in the social classes and resultant conflict of old. Although the question is debatable, we can at least conclude that social divisions are

TABLE 2.3 Average Pay by Occupational Category[a]

	1960	1973
Bulgaria		
Intelligentsia	142.1	132.1
Routine nonmanual	93.8	95.5
Worker	100.0	100.0
Peasant	92.1	91.5
Czechoslovakia		
Intelligentsia	116.8	120.4
Routine nonmanual	77.0	81.3
Worker	100.0	100.0
Peasant	79.2	98.1
Hungary		
Intelligentsia	157.2	142.4
Routine nonmanual	94.8	92.4
Worker	100.0	100.0
Peasant	na[b]	94.1
Poland		
Intelligentsia	156.7	144.3
Routine nonmanual	105.1	100.1
Worker	100.0	100.0
Peasant	na[b]	77.5
USSR		
Intelligentsia	150.9	134.1
Routine nonmanual	82.1	84.5
Worker	100.0	100.0
Peasant	57.7	76.5

[a]Intelligentsia, routine nonmanuals, and workers (all in state industry) and peasants (workers in state/socialist agriculture).

[b]Not available.

SOURCE: Adapted from Walter D. Connor, *Socialism, Politics, and Equality: Hierarchy and Change in Eastern Europe and the USSR* (New York: Columbia University Press, 1979), p. 231.

present in Communist societies and that they do have some of the characteristics of social classes under capitalism.[14]

[13]Wage differentials remain a characteristic of all socialist societies, even within the most allegedly egalitarian, the Chinese. See William L. Parish, "Egalitarianism in Chinese Society," *Problems of Communism* 30 (1) (1981): 37–53.

[14]For a revealing review of the issue of classes in post-Mao China, see "On Class and Class Struggle," *Beijing Review* 23 (20, 22, 25) (1980): 24–26, 24–26, 13–16, respectively. (With the change to the Pinyin system in 1979, *Peking Review* became *Beijing Review*. Most libraries catalog the periodical under the former title for issues before 1979 and under the latter for issues after that year.)

Another factor that works to deter the development of a classless society is the old value structures that are holdovers from the presocialist societies in each country. Throughout history, attitudes and values associated with certain occupations and pursuits tended to divide people. Income, education, and occupation, among other factors, placed some individuals in more privileged groups than others. The landed gentry in China and the old aristocracy and landholding classes in Europe represented privileged groups that became part of the new Communist Party societies. The societal values that supported and rationalized these traditional divisions were deeply imbedded in the value structure of the people. The mere event of a proletarian revolution did little to wipe away the status and class consciousness of the past. Values concerning privileges and perquisites are displayed constantly in contemporary Soviet society. Marriages among different groups—for example, the daughter of an intellectual with the son of an industrial worker—are uncommon. It is often beneath the dignity of one of a more privileged tradition to associate with those of a working-class background. Although the egalitarianism of the current ideology is intended to combat such presocialist values, particularistic value systems still pervade the societies of the Communist Party states.

Before we can develop a better understanding of the ways in which these social distinctions affect the political process, we should get a fuller picture of their presence and meaning in the Communist Party states of the contemporary world.

SOCIAL STRATIFICATION

The division of society into a hierarchy of strata partly results from the political process: Who gets what, when, and how? In most societies, different strata, or classes, are distinguished by unequal shares of the values received by individuals and groups. The landed gentry of traditional China, for example, enjoyed greater respect, well-being, enlightenment, and power than did the peasantry; the bourgeoisie in tsarist Russia had a disproportionate share of these values when compared with the proletariat. Although the ideology of communism is based on the principle of equality, contemporary socialist societies also have strata possessing a disproportionate share of the values their citizens deem important. Most of the states have undergone campaigns where concerted efforts were made to abolish differences of this sort. In the immediate postrevolutionary years in Russia, for example, the Bolsheviks abolished all official ranks and titles as well as such preferential treatment as different class accommodations in rail coaches and public facilities. Although now changed, before Mao's death all ranks in the People's Liberation Army (PLA) were abolished, thus precluding any outward distinction between the lowest-ranking foot soldier and the highest-ranking officer. Castro has gone into the sugarcane fields to labor among the workers. But, whereas serious efforts have been made to promote equality, various forces continue to create inequality and stratification in these societies.

Occupational and income differences are among the primary attributes associated with social stratification in contemporary socialist societies. A top-ranking engineer or a dean in a university is much more likely to have a disproportionate share of respect, well-being, enlightenment, and power than a blue-collar worker. The official ideology maintains that all occupational roles contribute equally to the building of socialism, but some are considerably more valued than others. A nuclear physicist at Moscow State University, an engineer in Poland, and the director of a thriving economic enterprise in Yugoslavia command a higher income and more respect than rank-and-file workers. In addition, their opportunities for attaining the values associated with enlightenment are greater, as are their opportunities for achieving a preferred state of well-being and political power.

Although it is rather dated now, a classic

and still accurate study based on written questionnaires from 2146 former Soviet citizens shows how occupations are related to such values in Soviet society.[15] The study ranks 13 occupational groups on the basis of the respondents' evaluations of the occupations in terms of five characteristics (general desirability, material position, personal satisfaction, safety, and popular support). Surprisingly, the study shows an occupational hierarchy in the Soviet Union that corresponds very closely with that of Western societies, including the United States. Doctors rank first in terms of general desirability and popular respect, for example, and workers rank last. In fact, all professional occupations, such as engineers and accountants, rank considerably higher than agricultural or rank-and-file workers. This interesting finding, taken along with similar research conducted in other countries as well, points to a general pattern of stratification in industrializing Communist societies.[16] Although the proletarian revolution was intended to establish a workers' state, blue-collar occupations under socialism still command considerably less respect than professional and white-collar positions.

As a result of such value systems, families encourage their children to go to the universities and prepare for careers that will bring greater respect, material wealth, and personal satisfaction. Although the official ideology and propaganda attempt to emphasize the importance of working-class occupations in building socialism, a certain stigma is still attached to them. As in the West, an upwardly mobile, achievement-oriented citizen does not aspire to a career on the collective farm or in the factory. Like his or her Western counterpart, the citizen tends to dream of a career in law, medicine, science, or some other professional line of work. Students in the Soviet Union and Eastern Europe seem every bit as achievement-oriented as students in the United States. They value university study and strive to excel because a diploma is often a necessary condition for a desirable occupation.

Joining the Communist Party is also a key to advancement in these societies. Nonconformists sitting in university coffee houses can be heard ridiculing classmates who are particularly achievement-oriented and who joined the Party in order to climb the ladder of social and economic success. Being a Party member and becoming part of the establishment usually means opening doors for future employment and advancement that are often closed to the equally qualified but less conforming citizens.

Although those of us in the West sometimes equate socialism with welfarism, Communist Party states have tended to abide by the principle "He who does not work, neither shall he eat." In most states, health and social services are provided through the work place. For one to eat and enjoy medical care and other social services, one must be gainfully employed. This means that all employed persons are guaranteed a minimal level of health and social welfare. This system is not followed for reasons of control or coercion but rather for administrative convenience. For those who are retired or unable to work, the state provides at least a subsistence standard of living. At the same time, if one has the financial resources, irrespective of whether or not one is employed, he or she can privately buy higher quality care. Paying an extra fee for a choice of medical doctors or simply buying private medical care from a moonlighting physician are common practices in most all socialist states.

The type of employment is of considerable importance in determining the size of one's personal income. The Soviet Communist Party leader is rumored to make approximately 900 rubles a month, whereas an average agricultural worker makes nearer 100 rubles. A director of a research institute will average between 500 to 700 rubles, whereas an industrial worker will take home around 150 rubles a month (1

[15]Peter H. Rossi and Alex Inkeles, "Multidimensional Ratings of Occupations," Sociometry, 20 (3) (1957): 247.

[16]Walter D. Connor, Socialism, Politics, and Equality: Hierarchy and Change in Eastern Europe and the USSR (New York: Columbia University Press, 1979).

ruble equals approximately $1.50).[17] Of course, we must remember that party leaders and other officials enjoy important perquisites in addition to their incomes. Shopping in exclusive stores set aside for party leaders only, superior medical care and attention, personal attendants and chauffeurs, and so forth, are examples of the special privileges they enjoy. Yet, evidence suggests that retiring leaders have seldom accumulated vast private holdings and resources while in power. Most leaders retire to a comfortable apartment or *dacha* ("country villa") on a healthy pension, but only a few enjoy luxury or opulent income.[18]

The gap between the highest- and lowest-paid occupations tends to be smaller in Communist Party than in non-Communist states, and it is unusual for anyone to accumulate great wealth, yet the hierarchy is still there. In the Soviet Union and East European states, the difference in salary between a factory director and a skilled worker may average around 5 to 1. In China, Cuba, and the Asian states the range tends to be somewhat less.

The distinguished American sociologist Gerhard Lenski notes that the range of salaries and incomes seems generally to have been reduced in Marxist societies to levels well below those in most comparable non-Marxist societies.[19] His research indicates a ratio of 50 to 1 between top salaries and the minimum wage in the USSR in the 1970s, 40 to 1 in China prior to Mao's death, and 7.3 to 1 in Cuba. By contrast, the corresponding ratio in the United States in recent years has been approximately 300 to 1.

As Lenski cautions, these figures should not be taken at face value because they do not provide a direct measure of differentials in living standards. However, Lenski concludes that the Marxist experiments have, in fact, resulted in the reduction of inequalities in income and living standards in Communist societies. At the same time, he calls attention to a number of Marxist failures, including: (1) the persistence of very high levels of political inequality, (2) the persistence of worker alienation, (3) the persistence of sex inequalities, (4) the persistence of rural-urban inequalities, and (5) the failure of these Marxist societies to give birth to the new socialist man.[20]

Urban and rural distinctions contribute to a stratified society. The differences between the modern pulsating life in Moscow, Warsaw, or Belgrade and the backward peasant life of the villages is extreme. Urbanization has been a major agent of social change and, in some respects, has had a leveling effect on a whole host of social differences. The common experiences of city life have softened some occupational and cultural differences, whereas life in the agricultural areas remains parochial and provincial. The social differences between the typical college student in New York City and in Moscow are considerable but tend to be no greater than those between the Russian student in that city and his same-age counterpart in a remote Siberian village.

Communists stood and fought for the emancipation of sexes as well as workers. In some respects, however, sex also tends to stratify societies within the Communist world because women predominate in many of the unskilled "physical" professions (e.g., construction workers, machine operators, bus drivers). Unlike the situation in many First and Third World societies, in socialist states women represent an extremely large and important sector of the total work force. And while women predominate in many of the unskilled, "physical" occupations, they also rep-

---

[17]Mervyn Matthews, "Top Incomes in the USSR," in *Economic Aspects of Life in the USSR* (Brussels: NATO Information Service, 1975), p. 133.

[18]There are some exceptions to this general rule. President Tito of Yugoslavia, for example, was known to possess and enjoy the excessive luxuries of many villas, a private island retreat in the Adriatic Sea, numerous cars, boats, and so forth. Former President Richard M. Nixon's reminiscences of General Secretary Brezhnev also draw attention to Brezhnev's appreciation for material goods, notably expensive automobiles.

[19]Gerhard Lenski, "Marxist Experiments in Destratification: An Appraisal," *Social Forces* 57(2) (1978): 370–371.

[20]*Ibid.*, pp. 371–376.

resent an important sector of the work force in many professional occupations. Soviet women predominate in such "mental" occupations as those of economic planner, doctor, and dentist.

The greatest sex discrimination in the Soviet Union, and in most other socialist states as well, is in the area of politics. One expert notes that although there is a relatively high proportion of women in ceremonial political roles, there is a very small percentage in significant positions of real power in either the party or government.[21] Underrepresentation of women is also evident for some nonpolitical directing posts, such as in hospitals, factories, and in the field of higher education. Another interesting and more subtle form of discrimination seems to take place in the home. After putting in a full day as a machine builder, bus driver, or economic planner, a woman typically returns home to assume all the household responsibilities. Perhaps to a greater extent than in the West, Soviet and East European men do little to share in the burdens of housework. Social discrimination against women, deeply imbedded in the traditional value structures of the cultures, will have to be further eradicated before a genuine equality of sexes can be achieved.[22]

One of the features that strikes Westerners most as they travel to socialist states concerns the contrasts in the material standards of the people. Some are dressed in the finest tailored suits and are motored around the cities in sleek Mercedes; others wear drab work clothes as they walk or pedal by bicycle to their work place. Some eat regularly at posh cosmopolitan restaurants, whereas still others are unable to purchase the basic cuts of meat at the neighborhood market. The leaders of these states are certainly aware of such inequalities, but they tend to view them as necessary evils at their country's particular stages of socioeconomic

development. They hope that development will blur the distinctions between job types and reduce differences in financial rewards, leading to greater equality in lifestyles. Some states are indeed marked by more extreme inequalities than others. At the same time, substantial income differentials persist in all of them.

We should now be aware that standards of living and the systems of social stratification with which they are associated vary considerably among the socialist states comprising the Second World. Although some of these differences can be attributed to political choices, environmental factors such as socioeconomic development help determine who gets what in the socialist states. Nobody gets very much in China simply because there is not very much to pass around. The average citizen gets a little more in the Soviet Union, primarily because the state is at a somewhat more advanced economic level. Then, the average citizen in Leningrad or Moscow enjoys a higher standard of living than his or her counterpart in the less developed republic of Kazakhstan, largely owing to the fact that the socioeconomic capabilities of the Russian Soviet Federated Socialist Republic (RSFSR) are higher than those in Kazakhstan.

Yet there are political choices that account for some of the differences in the values people enjoy. Since Mao's death in 1976, the Chinese leaders have moved to abandon the egalitarian goals that were so prominent in the Maoist period. In an attempt to restore a link between individual effort and individual reward and to promote more rapid economic development, the Chinese leaders are allowing a more unequal distribution of wages and the value of well-being.

Similar choices confront the leaders of the Soviet Union. They could give all of the Soviet people more if they decided to lower their investments in the industrial sector or lower their exorbitantly high levels of defense spending and increase them in the consumer sector. Also, the Soviet Government could see that the citizens of Kazakhstan got the same as their counterparts in the Russian Republic if it de-

---

[21]Norton Dodge, "The Role of Women in the Soviet Economy," in *Economic Aspects of Life in the USSR*, pp. 186–188.

[22]See Barbara Wolfe Jancar, *Women under Communism* (Baltimore: Johns Hopkins University Press, 1978); and Gail Warshofsky Lapidus, *Women in Soviet Society* (Berkeley: University of California Press, 1978).

cided to subsidize more heavily the former republic with income from the more highly developed republics. In addition, Soviet decision makers could see that a street sweeper would earn the same income as a nuclear physicist if they decided to level all income inequalities in the Soviet state. These are the perplexing questions and choices of politics. Although the socioeconomic environment in which the citizen resides helps determine the level of welfare and human dignity, the political choices of the decision maker also have an effect in determining the total picture. Some of the differences outlined above are the products of these choices, a topic to which we return in much greater detail in Chapters Six and Seven.

SOCIAL MOBILITY

It is common knowledge that inequalities in social characteristics such as status and income do exist in the Communist Party states, yet equality (or inequality) of opportunity is another question. That is, although some theorists say that perfect social equality is both impossible and undesirable in modern society, equality of opportunity is usually considered a desired feature of the just political system. Little is generally said about this notion in socialist states because general equality of reward is still considered theoretically synonymous with socialism.

As in other parts of the world, this intention is easier said than done. General social laws deeply ingrained in society place those on top—that is, those with higher levels of status, income, and education—in privileged positions vis-à-vis those at the bottom of the social hierarchy. The son or daughter of a Soviet engineer or high Communist Party official may have certain opportunities that result from their social circumstances and that are not available to the children of workers and peasants. The individual in a more privileged position may have connections that promise easier entrance into the university, the opportunity to travel and study abroad, a highly desired job, or other privileges that are not open to the

rank-and-file citizen. These facts result from social conditions or laws that tend to transcend ideology and government action and that seem to be at work in all states throughout the world. To counteract the special opportunities that are open to more privileged sectors of socialist society, special government actions are necessary.

All Communist Party states have acted to establish equality of opportunity in their societies. These actions have taken a number of different forms and are discussed in considerable detail in subsequent sections of this book. We will see that most of them involve the provision of equal educational and employment opportunities. Table 2.4 shows, relatively, the high level of educational advancement in the European Communist states. Enrollment in education is generally high, as are levels of literacy. The relatively low levels of educational development in the Asian states result from their less-developed socioeconomic positions and, in the case of Vietnam, Cambodia (Kampuchea), and Laos, the political conflict and warfare that have plagued Southeast Asia for decades. If these countries stabilize, they are likely to improve their performance in the educational sector as well.

Soviet leaders are particularly proud of and call attention to their general success in opening up what, during the tsarist years, was a relatively closed social hierarchy. Observers traveling with Khrushchev during one of his trips to the United States tell how he and a Hollywood movie millionaire traded rags-to-riches stories. As the Hollywood magnate boasted of his Horatio Alger story and extolled the virtues of the "land of opportunity" in America, Khrushchev was not to be outdone. Where else but in the USSR, he countered, could a miner of peasant origins become the leader of one of the strongest nations on the face of the earth?[23]

[23]For an interesting comparison of John F. Kennedy and Khrushchev's backgrounds and ascents to power, see Zbigniew K. Brzezinski and Samuel P. Huntington, *Political Power: USA/USSR* (New York: Viking Press, 1963), pp. 129–190, 235–268.

TABLE 2.4 Demographic Indicators in Contemporary Communist Party States

Country	Population			Area		Education	
	In 1000s	Percent Urban	Life Expectancy	1000²km	Density per 1000²km	Literacy	Percent of School-age Children in School
Albania	2671	37	70	29	92	72	61
Bulgaria	8862	64	71	111	80	94	57
Cambodia	5692	15	40	181	31	48	23
China	1,006,712	21	64	9597	105	66	59
Cuba	9658	65	73	115	84	95	68
Czechoslovakia	15,255	63	71	128	119	99	59
East Germany	16,737	77	72	108	155	99	62
Hungary	10,711	54	71	93	115	99	59
Laos	3458	14	43	237	15	44	42
Mongolia	1662	51	63	1565	1	95	61
North Korea	17,815	60	64	121	147	85	64
Poland	35,578	57	72	313	114	99	55
Romania	22,201	50	71	238	93	98	62
Soviet Union	265,542	62	70	22,402	12	99	59
Vietnam	53,511	19	63	330	162	87	62
Yugoslavia	22,304	42	70	256	87	87	60
USAa	227,704	77	74	9363	24	99	85

aThe USA is included for comparative purposes.

SOURCE: Adapted from Ruth Leger Sivard, *World Military and Social Expenditures*, 1983 (Leesburg, Va.: World Priorities, 1983), pp. 32–41.

Although varying somewhat by country, a careful review of the backgrounds of Communist Party officials, dentists, doctors, lawyers, and other professionals would show many to be of humble social and economic backgrounds. This phenomenon is particularly true regarding party officials, because those of humble socioeconomic origin are naturally more attracted to the ideology of communism. Communist doctrine attracts such individuals because it explains the perceived injustices in their backgrounds and how they can be improved under socialism.

The two forces that have done the most to enhance the opportunities for social mobility in the Second World Communist-run states are ideology and rapid socioeconomic change. The ideology of socialism has a strong egalitarian base and, although perfect equality is impossible, socialist elites have felt some responsibility in protecting equal opportunity. Gaps have often existed between the ideal and the reality, yet the principle of equality has motivated all governments to promote the ideal of equality and the opportunities for upward mobility.

The rapid pace of socioeconomic change that has characterized the Second World states is the second force that has promoted social mobility and the value of equal opportunity. During phases of rapid industrialization and growth and the increasing need for the new training and skills they bring, great opportunities are open to the populace. The Soviet need for construction engineers in the 1930s and 1940s and their need for nuclear physicists in the 1970s provided great opportunities for personal advancement, regardless of one's social background. Educational opportunities combined with new occupational opportunities open many doors to an upwardly mobile society.

In summary, the social consequences of modernization and industrialization, including social stratification, inequalities, and mobility, are of great importance to the building of communism. If stratification and inequalities are unavoidable outcomes of socialist modernization and industrialization, then it may be impossible to attain the communist ideal of genuine equality. Like the economic forces described earlier, these social forces are part of the environment impacting on what Second World leaders refer to as "the building of communism."

DEMOGRAPHIC CHARACTERISTICS

Close to one-third of the world's population lives in the 16 Communist-ruled states. Roughly a quarter of the world's population (close to 1 billion) lives in China, making it by a large margin the world's most populous state. Ranking behind China and India, the Soviet Union is the world's third most populous state. The remainder of the Communist Party states are of average population size, with three—Albania, Laos, and Mongolia—ranking among the world's smallest populations (see Table 2.4).

Despite certain benefits, a large population also presents definite hardships. The problems of food and living space present particular difficulties for China, where over 90 percent of the population is concentrated on one-sixth of the land. Less than 20 percent of the land is agriculturally productive. Its cultivated land is only 70 percent that of the United States, which has about one-fourth of China's population. Feeding the immense population in China has been a difficult task through the centuries and still represents a problem not fully resolved. The Soviet Union also has difficulty in feeding its large population and has

had to rely on foreign countries to survive. The sale of American grain has helped the Soviet people avoid severe shortages in basic foodstuffs. Despite government efforts and exhortations, Soviet and Chinese agriculture has not been productive when compared to the West and has suffered from a shortage of arable land and inefficient production methods.

The area of a country and the resources on which its economic might is based have important effects on political behavior. The Soviet Union is the world's largest state with a land area of approximately 22.4 million square kilometers. The USSR has approximately the same area as the United States and the 14 states of the NATO Alliance put together. Slightly larger than the United States is China, the world's third largest state (Canada is second). The next largest Communist state, Mongolia, has the smallest population of all socialist states and the lowest population density of any state in the entire world. With 1 person per square kilometer in Mongolia, compared to 155 in East Germany, the Mongolian steppes provide plenty of space for future expansion.[24]

Land area and population size are important attributes in the world of international politics. If a country has a labor shortage (such as East Germany) or a surplus (such as Yugoslavia) or food shortages (such as China and the Soviet Union) or energy shortages (such as much of Eastern Europe), it is forced to enter into dependency relationships with other countries. Although small states are sometimes able to defy larger states, as Albania and Yugoslavia have defied the Soviet Union, political power and international relations are closely associated with the population and physical size of states. Smaller, weaker states without abundant resources are naturally de-

[24]With its small land area, sizable population, and high level of industrialization, East Germany is quickly depleting its natural resources. The contrasting conditions in Mongolia provide many opportunities for future growth and development. The Mongolian birth rate, among the highest in the world, will provide an expanding work force for this process of socioeconomic expansion.

pendent on states that can ensure their security and meet their resource needs. In this respect, the Communist states of Eastern Europe are highly vulnerable, and therefore dependent on the Soviet Union.

The contemporary settings in Communist Party societies are also very much affected by the sociocultural features of nationality and ethnicity. In the *Communist Manifesto*, Marx and Engels predicted that nationality was a dying force in the contemporary world. They believed that with the increasing freedom of commerce in the international market and with the growing uniformity of production and conditions of life, national differences would dissolve; furthermore, as exploitation and antagonism between classes under socialism began to cease, so, too, would hostility among nations. As national differences began to disappear (according to Marx and Engels), we would witness the development of internationalism within the socialist world. In this phase of historical development, workers of the world would be united by the bonds of socialist or proletarian internationalism and the forces of nationalism and ethnocentrism would cease to exist.

As we witness international politics in the contemporary world, we can see that Marx and Engels underestimated the power of nationalism. Nationality, or nationhood, is a strong and enduring sociocultural force that grows out of the history, geography, language, and culture of groups of people. As we enter the last few decades of the twentieth century, we seem to be witnessing a growth rather than a decline in nationalism, which has a definite effect on world politics. The continuing Sino-Soviet conflict, the tension among states in the Soviet bloc,[25] and the animosity that at times surfaces among national and ethnic groups within socialist states point to the importance of the idea of ethnicity and nationhood in the international arena today.

Although we usually refer to the "nations" of the Communist world, strictly speaking, this is misleading. Some of the socialist states are composed of many distinct nationalities, each with its own language, customs, and sense of the past. Yugoslavia, for example, is a multinational state comprised of five South Slavic nationalities—Croats, Macedonians, Montenegrins, Serbs, and Slovenes—as well as other national and ethnic groups. Tending to be concentrated in rather homogeneous regions and constitutionally guaranteed a high level of autonomy within the federated Yugoslav system, these groups maintain a strong sense of individual identity.[26]

The Soviet Union is also a multinational state and includes such nationalities as Russians, Ukrainians, Armenians, Georgians, Latvians, Tatars, a variety of Asian nationalities, and many, many others. There are over 100 different national and ethnic groups in the Soviet Union. Although Russian, the official language of the state, tends to be spoken by most members of all groups, the Soviet Union still displays a rich mix of languages which represent many distant points in Europe and Asia.

The largest Soviet nationality by far is Russian, which comprises just over half of the total population. The bulk of these Russians reside in the Russian Republic (RSFSR), which stretches from Moscow and Leningrad eastward to the Pacific (see the map of the USSR). This one republic in the Soviet Union has almost twice the area of the United States. The Russian Republic contains 16 autonomous republics, 5 autonomous regions, and 10 national areas, representing a heterogeneous multinational mosaic of groups. The next largest Soviet nationalities are the Ukrainians,

[25]The term *Soviet bloc* is often used to refer to the member nations of the WTO. Over the years, there have been a number of national conflicts among these nations, the major ones being Hungary in 1956, Czechoslovakia in 1968, and Poland in the early 1980s.

[26]For a superb analysis of the role of nationality in Yugoslav politics, see Paul Shoup, *Communism and the Yugoslav National Question* (New York: Columbia University Press, 1968).

who reside primarily in the Ukrainian Soviet Socialist Republic, and the Uzbeks, who inhabit the Uzbek Soviet Socialist Republic. The fourth largest are the Byelorussians, or White Russians, and they, too, have a republic within which members of their nationality predominate.

Administratively, the Soviet leaders designed a federal political arrangement to reflect the extreme diversity in the society. This federal structure divides the Soviet state into 15 union republics, which in some cases contain autonomous republics, autonomous regions, and autonomous areas. The 15 union republics and the autonomous republics are indicated on the map. The units coincide with the complex array of national and ethnic groups in the state and vary in status according to the size and strength of the groups. The powers of the various units are described in detail in the Soviet Constitution.[27]

Demographic changes in the USSR are of considerable political importance. The Muslim Turkic nationalities of Central Asia, Kazakhstan, and the Azerbaidzhan Republic are growing at a much faster rate than such western nationalities as the Russians and Ukrainians. The Soviet Union already has the fifth largest Muslim population in the world, exceeded only by those of Indonesia, Pakistan, Bangladesh, and India. Important political choices confront the Soviet leaders. How should they respond to the possibility of Islamic movements that may spill over from other southwest Asian countries? Because there is a severe labor shortage in the industrial, western part of the USSR, what should be done to encourage the Central Asians (who have been reluctant to migrate) to move and fulfill this labor shortage? What can be done to raise the level of development of the Central Asian areas? Zbigniew K. Brzezinski has observed that the nationality problem in

the USSR could become a political issue of greater importance than race has been in the United States.[28] It is clear that interethnic differences and tensions persist and that the Soviet Union has not yet developed a fundamentally new social and international community as its leaders contend.

China also is a heterogeneous multiethnic state. Although 94 percent of the population is of basic Chinese stock (the Han people), it is divided into groups characterized by many social, cultural, and linguistic differences. The spoken word of one Chinese group, such as the Cantonese, may be completely unintelligible to another group. In addition to the Han people, China has over 50 million members of minority groups, more than double the total population of Yugoslavia. Of these, over 50 groups have been designated as minorities and have been given 98 autonomous areas at the provincial, intermediate, and county levels. These autonomous areas, usually named after the group (or groups) who predominates, provide the minorities greater freedom and government rights—although all these rights are subordinate to national programs, laws, regulations, and organizations. The map of China outlines the 21 provinces and 5 autonomous regions. Autonomous regions are areas heavily populated by non-Chinese minorities.

The environmental factors surveyed in this chapter provide the setting for our political analysis that follows. The economic setting tells us something about what contemporary leaders have to allocate. The social setting provides us with some idea of the status and stratification of various groups. The demographic setting gives us a clearer picture of the individuals and groups with which the leaders have to deal. Politics is the art of the possible and these environmental forces set the boundaries for political action and performance.

[27]For a description of the ethnonational setting in the USSR and Soviet nationality policy, see Edward Allworth, ed., *Soviet Nationality Problems* (New York: Columbia University Press, 1971).

[28]Zbigniew K. Brzezinski, ed., *Dilemmas of Change in Soviet Politics* (New York: Columbia University Press, 1969), p. 161.

OCEAN

BERING
SEA

Wrangel I.

SEVERNAYA
ZEMLYA

NEW SIBERIAN
ISLANDS

LAPTEV
SEA

S O C I A L I S T   R E P U B L I C S

SEA
OF
OKHOTSK

YAKUT A.S.S.R.

R E P U B L I C

S O C I A L I S T

Sakhalin I.

Kuril Islands

BURYAT-MONGOL
A.S.S.R.

TUVA
A.S.S.R.

MONGOLIAN

REPUBLIC

CHINA

SEA
OF
JAPAN

JAPAN

NORTH
KOREA

SOUTH
KOREA

EASTERN EUROPE

The Eight Communist States

CHINA AND
SOUTHEAST ASIA

Suggestions for Further Reading

Barnett, A. Doak, *China Economy in Global Perspective* (Washington, D.C.: Brookings Institution, 1981).

Bergson, Abram, *Soviet Post-War Economic Development* (Stockholm: Almqvist & Wiksell, 1975).

Bonavia, David, *The Chinese,* rev. ed. (New York: Pelican, 1982).

Carrère d'Encausse, Hélène, *Decline of an Empire: The Soviet Socialist Republics in Revolt* (New York: Newsweek Books, 1979).

Connor, Walter D., *Socialism, Politics, and Equality: Hierarchy and Change in Eastern Europe and the USSR* (New York: Columbia University Press, 1979).

_____, *Deviance in Soviet Society* (New York: Columbia University Press, 1972).

Dubey, Vinod, *Yugoslavia: Development with Decentralization* (Baltimore: Johns Hopkins University Press, 1975).

Eckstein, Alexander, *China's Economic Revolution* (Cambridge: Cambridge University Press, 1977).

Gati, Charles, ed., *The Politics of Modernization in Eastern Europe* (New York: Praeger, 1974).

Hinton, Harold C., ed., *The People's Republic of China: A Handbook* (Boulder, Colo.: Westview, 1978).

Hoffman, George W., *Regional Development Strategy in Southeast Europe* (New York: Praeger, 1972).

Hohmann, H. H., M. Kaser, and **K. C. Thalheim,** eds., *New Economic Systems of Eastern Europe* (London: Hurst, 1975).

Jancar, Barbara Wolfe, *Women under Communism* (Baltimore: Johns Hopkins University Press, 1978).

Lane, David, *Politics and Society in the USSR* (New York: Random House, 1971).

Lewis, Robert A., et al., *Nationality and Population Change in Russia and the USSR* (New York: Praeger, 1976).

Matejko, Alexander, *Social Change and Stratification in Eastern Europe* (New York: Praeger, 1974).

Matthews, Mervyn, *Privilege in the Soviet Union* (London: Allen & Unwin, 1978).

Mickiewicz, Ellen P., ed., *Handbook of Soviet Social Science Data* (New York: Free Press, 1972).

Mihailovic, Kosta, *Regional Development Experiences and Prospects in Eastern Europe* (The Hague: Mouton, 1972).

Perkins, Dwight H., ed., *China's Modern Economy in Historical Perspective* (Stanford, Calif.: Stanford University Press, 1975).

Sirc, Ljubo, *The Yugoslav Economy under Self-Management* (New York: St. Martin's Press, 1979).

Tyson, Laura D'andrea, *The Yugoslav Economic System and Its Performance in the 1970s* (Berkeley: University of California, Institute of International Studies, 1980).

U.S. Congress, Joint Economic Committee. *China under the Four Modernizations* (Washington, D.C.: U.S. Government Printing Office, 1982).

CHAPTER THREE
Political Culture and Political Socialization

What do we know about the political attitudes and ideas of the millions upon millions of ordinary citizens who live in Communist-run societies? Do they support their leaders? Would they revolt if they had the chance? Are there signs of psychological and attitudinal change in these societies? These important questions take us to the topics of political culture and political socialization.

Because of Communist leaders' strong public commitment to build communism, and because of the important human dimension of the building process, the concepts of political culture and political socialization are of special significance in our study. Gabriel Almond, the distinguished American political scientist, has noted: "Every political system is embedded in a particular pattern of orientations of political action."[1] This pattern of attitudes and beliefs that people hold toward their system is referred to as political culture; it represents the orientations that define the setting in which politics takes place. The political culture of the Soviet Union is the total composite of that society's ideas about political life. Orientations

about justice and democracy, welfare and equality, and other political issues all represent dimensions of the larger Soviet political culture. As in all other states, these orientations have an influence on power and policy in Communist political systems.

Although we refer to a Chinese political culture, a Soviet political culture, and so forth, we should realize that it is a simplification to speak of the total set of attitudes and values of the populace and to consider it a homogeneous whole. Obviously, like other societies, the Communist societies of the Second World are heterogeneous in their beliefs and values, just as they are in social and economic characteristics. But, when we discuss and compare societies, it is useful to have a general concept to refer to the general attitudinal and psychological setting within political systems. *Political culture* is the term for such a concept.

How can one study something as abstract as political culture? What does one try to observe? Some researchers have conducted massive opinion surveys of large samples of national populations. For example, in their book *The Civic Culture*, Almond and Verba surveyed attitudes and values of over 5000 citizens from the United States, Great Britain, West Ger-

[1]Gabriel A. Almond, "Comparative Political Systems," *The Journal of Politics, 18* (3) (1956): 395.

May Day ceremony in Moscow's Red Square, with the Kremlin in the background, draws the country's leaders, who adorn the reviewing stand atop Lenin's mausoleum, as rank-and-file Soviet citizens crowd the adjoining streets. State celebrations illustrate the patriotism and nationalism that is deeply embedded in Soviet political culture.

many, Italy, and Mexico to better understand the political cultures of these states.[2] There is also a large study of political culture in Yugoslavia that analyzes the political orientations of over 1000 Yugoslav citizens.[3] Bertsch and Zaninovich in that study were able to determine more accurately the political cultures of the various Yugoslav nationalities—Croats, Macedonians, Montenegrins, Serbs, and Slovenes. In these and other studies, researchers went into the countries and gathered massive amounts of opinion data that allowed detailed, systematic studies of the people's political orientations. With the partial exception of Yugoslavia and a few other cases, this quantitative approach to the study of political culture is generally not possible in Communist Party states because their governments are usually unwilling to allow Western scholars to study such sensitive issues. In this book, we take an inductive approach and base our study on a large body of research conducted by native and foreign scholars. Although this research is not always based on scientific surveys, it draws on the personal contacts and research of scholars who know these countries well.

Political culture has certain things in common with—but is quite distinct from—a state's ideology. Although the term has been concep-

[2]Gabriel A. Almond and Sidney Verba, *The Civic Culture: Political Attitudes and Democracy in Five Nations* (Princeton, N. J.: Princeton University Press, 1963).

[3]Gary K. Bertsch and M. George Zaninovich, "A Factor Analytic Method of Identifying Different Political Cultures: The Multi-National Yugoslav Case," *Comparative Politics* 6 (2) (1974): 219–244.

tualized in many ways, ideology commonly refers to the set of arguments and beliefs used to justify an existing or desired social order. Although there is bound to be considerable overlap, the ideologies of the Second World states deviate in certain important respects from their political cultures. Though Marxist–Leninist ideology represents the official arguments and beliefs set forth by the Communist parties to explain and justify their social order, the political cultures of these countries represent the personal values of the broader society. In some respects, these two sets of beliefs differ. Although a Communist Party official would be able to enumerate (and sincerely believe) the basic ideological tenets of the state, his son or daughter might hold political attitudes that conflict with the prevailing ideology. Currently, there is considerable concern in many Communist Party states that the political culture of the youth is not sufficiently supportive of official ideology and that efforts must be made to bring young people more in line with the official doctrines.

This issue and attempts to mold political culture introduce us to the concept of political socialization. Most political scientists conceive of political socialization as the process by which official or prevailing attitudes and beliefs are transmitted to a society and particularly to newcomers, such as children or immigrants. Because Communist Party states adopted the revolutionary ideology of Marxism–Leninism rather recently in their political histories, in a sense all of their citizens are newcomers and great efforts have been made to inculcate political orientations conducive to the building of socialism. Because the prerevolutionary societies in these countries have had distinctive traditions and political cultures of their own, the transmission of new political orientations to the populace has not been easy. The leaders of the new states have realized that if their political and economic pol-

At a sports event, 10,000 students with placards form the backdrop for the marching People's Liberation Army (PLA) and People's Militia during a parade in Beijing's Workers' Stadium. Such events were typically combined with political and military presentations during the highly politicized Maoist period.

icies are to be carried out successfully, traditional political beliefs must be replaced. In their place, the leaders hope to develop a new set of attitudes and values, orientations that correspond with and support their interpretations of Marxist–Leninist doctrine and their drives for modernization and rapid industrialization. It is this task that makes the topics of political culture and political socialization so interesting and important in the study of contemporary communism.

CHANGING THE TRADITIONAL POLITICAL CULTURES

When Vladimir Ilyich Lenin, Mao Zedong, Josip Broz Tito, and others assumed power in their states, the traditional political cultures were not conducive to, and (in many respects) were even hostile toward, changes the leaders felt were necessary for building socialism. The political orientations of the people in these countries had been molded over hundreds, even thousands, of years. Centuries of tsarist rule in Russia, imperial rule in China, and foreign domination and dictatorial rule in Yugoslavia taken together with peasant societies and backward socioeconomic traditions resulted in undemocratic, elitist political cultures. We must remember that all three societies and most others that went Communist were composed primarily of peasants, with the bulk of the population working the land. These tillers of the soil generally accepted the prevailing social hierarchy: the strong ruled, the weak were ruled. In all three countries, the traditional belief was that the select few who governed the masses had been chosen by divine mandate. The coronations and the ritualistic ceremonies such as those accorded the Russian tsars, Chinese emperors, and East European kings and ruling families made the rulers and masses acutely aware of the divine significance of the rulers' power. The masses were expected to remain passively in the background sowing the crops, working in factories, or laboring in

whatever jobs they could find. The thought of popular politics and the ideas of democracy were as remote as distant North America. When the peasants heard news of democratic rule in the West, they neither understood its meaning nor comprehended its significance to their backward lot. As the age of democracy grew in other parts of the globe, the masses of these three countries remained largely isolated and, for the time being, unaffected by the winds of change.

When the Yugoslav Communist Party seized power in 1945, for example, the existing political culture was based on authoritarian, elitist, and nonparticipant norms. Centuries of foreign domination by the Ottoman and Austro-Hungarian empires as well as the more recent periods of nineteenth- and twentieth-century rule under indigenous authoritarian regimes served to mold a resigned, apathetic, and conformist society. The authoritarian Stalinist approach to political life, initially followed by Tito and the Yugoslav Communists at the end of World War II, corresponded with the nonparticipant political culture of the populace. The masses had never been widely consulted and involved in the affairs of politics before and did not really expect to be included after the war.

In China, the traditional political culture was steeped in the ideal of harmony with nature and a strict, hierarchical set of social and political relations. Power was entrusted to the emperor or empress, his or her supporting officials, and those who had worked their way up the hierarchy through intellectual attainment. To the masses, political power was the right of the emperor; the hierarchy was viewed as natural and the government tended to be remote. On those few occasions when the common peasant or laborer had contact with the government, the authorities appeared unjust and harsh. Because of this experience, the large bulk of the society was resigned to a life of political passivity and acquiescence. In a large peasant society, the common man and woman had little interest in, and few orientations about, politics. An early Chinese Communist leader commented on this fact in 1922:

> The peasants take no interest in politics. This is common throughout the whole world, but is particularly true in China. . . . All they care about is having a true Son of Heaven [emperor] to rule them, and a peaceful bumper year.[4]

Mass values about democracy and power in China, Russia, and Yugoslavia were shaped by centuries of authoritarian rule. Although the leaders of these countries—the rulers, ministers, counselors, representatives, magistrates, and others who served the empires—possessed a set of political orientations that represented an authoritarian political culture, the masses were characterized by a general absence of political sentiment.[5] They held few political feelings and were uninvolved in politics because of their isolation from political affairs. To transform this massive parochial, nonparticipant sector of society into one that would support and advance the ideas of Communist rule was a major task facing the new leaders in the postrevolutionary periods.

The leaders of the Communist political systems recognized that the building of communism would be difficult, if not impossible, because of the political cultures (and subcultures) inherited from the pre-socialist states. Accordingly, they adopted heavy-handed strategies of political socialization to mold the orientations required for their ideal societies.

Perhaps it should be pointed out that all countries, including the United States, attempt to foster attitudes and beliefs in their people that are supportive of their systems of government. For example, in our country children at an early age are taught the Pledge of Allegiance, "The Star Spangled Banner," and the stories of our founding fathers; we may call it civics or citizenship training, but it is political socialization aimed at instructing the newest generation about the functioning of our political system. The key question in regard to this topic is not whether it exists, for it exists in all societies; we must instead examine who determines what ought to be taught, how it is accomplished, and how far governments go in changing the belief structures of their people. Do they stamp out all differences or are they tolerant of diverse beliefs and opinions? Our exploration of this issue in Communist Party states will point to the fact that a higher premium is placed on ideological purity in these states than in our own country.

A variety of different tactics have been used in Communist Party countries to reform the minds of the citizenry and to develop a new "enlightened" community of Communist citizens. After the revolution in China, emphasis was placed on thought reform, self-criticism, and rectification programs. Those with bourgeois mentalities were given the opportunity to reform themselves and become productive members of Chinese society.[6] In some countries, more coercive methods, such as deportation, imprisonment, terror, and even death and genocide, were used to force transformations in political culture. Stalin was notorious for brutal tactics as he ruthlessly sought to transform Soviet society to suit his purposes. Still others used less violent and more effective methods. One of Castro's strategies for dealing with Cubans of hostile or nonconforming political orientations has been to deport them. Thousands of Cubans came to the United States during the 1960s and again in 1980 because, among other reasons, they were unable or unwilling to change their beliefs and opinions concerning socialism in Cuba.[7] Perhaps the most significant element in changing political culture is simply time itself. After over

---

[4]Chang Kuo-tao, cited in Jerome Chen, *Mao and the Chinese Revolution* (London: Oxford University Press, 1965), p. 193.

[5]An authoritarian political culture represents a set of beliefs and attitudes supporting or, at least, tolerating nondemocratic (autocratic) political rule.

[6]Robert J. Lifton, *Thought Reform and the Psychology of Totalism: A Study of "Brainwashing" in China* (New York: Norton, 1961).

[7]See Richard R. Fagen, *The Transformation of Political Culture in Cuba* (Stanford, Calif.: Stanford University Press, 1969).

a half century in the USSR and a quarter century in most other Communist Party states, attitudes appear to conform more and more with the leader's expectations. This observation must be qualified to some extent, however, in view of the events in Poland in the 1980s. Once again, Polish citizens spoke out and voiced their dissatisfaction with government policy and leadership. What was particularly noteworthy about the most recent demonstration was the coalescence of worker, intellectual, and other sources of opinion in opposition to Communist Party rule. The Polish events of the early 1980s may go down as one of the most significant chapters in Communist history. At the very least, Polish demonstrations of popular opinion on a number of occasions in the 1970s and 1980s should suggest to all that citizens in Communist Party states will not, necessarily, remain docile and apathetic.

The leaders in Communist Party states have used a number of important agents of political socialization, that is, institutions or instruments by which orientations are transformed. If we examine the processes of political socialization in these countries over

In Chinese classrooms during the Maoist period, revolutionary posters and slogans accompanied daily lessons. Although political consciousness still is considered a necessary ingredient of the new socialist person and Chinese political culture, more emphasis now is placed on scientific training and expertise.

the years, we will find that the family has played an important role. After reviewing the results of Soviet research on the topic, one scholar concludes that "most children seem to learn their values from the social environment of their families."[8] Soviet leaders and scholars alike recognize this fact, and, although there is little they can do to force families to promote desired attitudes and values, they do make it clear on occasion that the regime has high expectations about the personal examples set by mothers and fathers in the home.[9]

One agent of socialization that has continued to plague the socialization intentions of the leaders is the church. Particularly in the East European states where the Catholic and Orthodox religions are deeply imbedded in the cultures of the people, the church is a troublesome institution with which the party must contend. At some points in Communist history, the parties undertook aggressive and oppressive campaigns to eradicate religion from their countries. At other points, when they needed to mobilize support for the government and promote unity within the country, they eased their politics of persecution.[10] At all times, however, the leaders have correctly assessed the incompatibility between communism and religion and viewed the latter as an obstruction that impedes the optimal development of communism. Some regimes, like the one in Poland where Catholicism is very strong, have perceived religion as a necessary evil with which they have to live. Others, like Albania, consider religion an evil they can ill afford and have undertaken coercive policies to

[8]William K. Medlin, "Education," in Allen Kassof, ed., *Prospects for Soviet Society* (New York: Praeger, 1968), p. 257.

[9]Editorials in *Pravda* and elsewhere exhort parents to set examples that are in the best interests of building communism.

[10]Stalin's persecution of religion was abandoned in 1941 in an effort to foster greater support and national unity to address the Nazi threat. Nikita S. Khrushchev resumed the more oppressive policies and initiated a campaign (1960–1964) to eliminate religious life completely from the Soviet Union.

eradicate fully its presence and influence from their societies.

The agent of political socialization that Communists take the most interest in and (unlike family life and religion) over which they find it easiest to exert considerable influence is the school. The educational system in all Communist Party states is closely controlled by the Party. Through the coordinating arm of a central ministry for education, the Communist parties have great influence in designing curricula, selecting texts, and setting instructional policies within the schools. Although the Party leaders do not usually become directly involved in these activities, they recommend certain policies, which are implemented through the ministries and by the local organs. The content of courses, textbooks, and the general educational philosophy, however, vary markedly among the different states.

Perhaps the most politicized and ideologically infused education system in Communist history was that of the Chinese during the Maoist period. Throughout the Great Proletarian Cultural Revolution (GPCR) (1966–1969), Maoist doctrine accompanied almost every lesson. In elementary school mathematics, for example, the exploiting capitalist and the downtrodden peasants were typically found in the daily exercises:

> PROBLEM: If a peasant works 4 plots of land and the capitalist takes the products of 3, what does that leave the peasant?

The writings of Chairman Mao played a major role in the educational process during the Cultural Revolution. Pictures from China showed the ever-present *Little Red Book* held proudly by the Chinese grade-schooler. Bulletin boards and texts were adorned with pictures of the Communist leaders and the slogans they extolled to mobilize the masses. Even at the more advanced levels of Chinese education, including the universities, ideology represented a significant element in the course content. One did not even approach the topics of medicine or physics without recognizing the relevance of Maoist ideology to them. Western observers

Science and ideology coexist in Soviet education, as shown by the artifacts in this classroom in Moscow. Major Soviet advances in science attest to the success of its educational system. The effects in the area of ideology are less clear.

witnessed college seminars dedicated solely to the reading of Chairman Mao's sacred thought.

To what extent these Maoist methods brought about enduring changes in Chinese political culture is open to question. What is clear is the changing emphasis in Chinese education in the post-Mao period. Less stress is now placed on ideology and much more is placed on the scientific understanding needed to promote modernization and development. In 1980, the new premier of China, Zhao Ziyang, noted:

> There is an urgent need for training talented people for the modernization program. For this reason, we are attaching importance to teaching work and to the study of cultural and scientific

knowledge. It is our duty to arm the minds of youngsters with the cultural legacy of mankind and with scientific and technological knowledge; we must train our generation into people with genuine talent.[11]

Although Soviet and East European schools are also important, highly regimented agents of socialization, they, too, take a much less politicized and ideological approach than Maoist China. Politics and ideology are, of course, important parts of their lessons, and textbooks are infused with the themes of patriotism, socialist morality, and internationalism. However, the Maoist parroting of ideological slogans and the long and intensive periods of political training are generally not found. Specific courses on ideology, such as the typical high school course "The Bases of Our Ideology," are common. These courses are infused with Marxism–Leninism and take a value-laden approach to the interpretation of national and world events.

The Yugoslav approach is even less ideologically inclined than the typical Soviet or East European, although there is considerable emphasis on the study of "self-managing socialism," Yugoslavia's unique interpretation of Marxism–Leninism. Teachers are expected to provide the proper ideological interpretation of events and issues when the occasion arises, but the emphasis is much more on general education and considerably less on political indoctrination.

Another influential agent of socialization carried out through the schools is the youth organizations. These youth groups range from the elementary-grade Young Pioneers through the high school and college-age youth leagues. Although all Communist Party states have similar groups, they vary widely in functions and behavior. The Chinese Communist Youth League in the 1970s, for example, constituted the primary training ground for what the leaders called revolutionary successors. It had a

militant philosophy and was infused with the Chinese revolutionary spirit. During this period, Young Pioneers in China were even instructed in the arts of making revolution. Whether marching in parades, chanting Maoist slogans, or operating rifles with live ammunition on the firing range, these elementary schoolers were taught the finer points of Maoist strategy for revolutionary warfare. Youth organizations in the post-Mao period have assumed a less revolutionary, more pro-modernization orientation. Premier Zhao comments:

By organizing various levels and absorbing activities involving astronomy, geology, zoology, botany, chemistry, biology, culture and art, the Young Pioneers play a special irreplaceable role in discovering and training young personnel.[12]

New members of the Young Pioneers in the USSR pledge to "warmly love my Soviet motherland" and to "live, to study, and to struggle as Lenin willed and as the Communist Party teaches." The new member also promises to observe the following rules:

The Pioneer loves his motherland and the Communist Party of the Soviet Union. He prepares himself for membership in the Komsomol.

The Pioneer reveres the memory of those who have given their lives in the struggle for the freedom and the well-being of the Soviet motherland.

The Pioneer is friendly with the children of all the countries of the world.

The Pioneer studies diligently and is disciplined and courteous.

The Pioneer loves to work and to conserve the national wealth.

The Pioneer is a good comrade, who is solicitous of younger children and who helps older people.

The Pioneer grows up to be bold and does not fear difficulties.

The Pioneer tells the truth and guards the honor of his detachment.

The Pioneer strengthens himself and does physical exercises every day.

[11]Zhao Ziyang, "Educating the Younger Generation Is a Great Task," *Beijing Review* 23 (24) (1980): 14–16.

[12]*Ibid.*, p. 16.

During Mao's reign, art and culture in China were expected to communicate the goals and values of the revolution. "The Red Detachment of Women," a folktale made into a revolutionary ballet, exemplifies the adoration of Mao and his *Little Red Book*. Today, the Chinese leaders take a more relaxed attitude concerning political socialization.

The Pioneer loves nature; he is a defender of planted areas, of useful birds and animals.

The Pioneer is an example for all children.[13]

Like members of Western organizations, Young Pioneers do not always take these promises seriously.

To some extent, it is instructive to compare Young Pioneers in the USSR and Eastern Europe with Boy and Girl Scouts in the West. Although the Communist Party administers centralized control and guidance, and, therefore, more emphasis is placed on ideological and political themes, children in Communist Party countries enjoy the Young Pioneers just as children in the United States enjoy Scouting. The children in Communist Party states view the Young Pioneers as a fun group where they can meet playmates, go on field trips, and spend a week or two at summer camp. Social service projects are a main activity of the organization, but children participate primarily because they enjoy the recreational activities.

Social service and political education are more important functions of the organization for teenage youth, the Communist Youth League (Komsomol).[14] These groups represent the primary training ground for future generations of socialist society. Leonid I. Brezhnev referred to their mission as that of "bringing up youth in the spirit of communist commitment" and to carry on the "cause of their fathers, the cause of the great Lenin." However, many teenagers in Eastern Europe and the Soviet Union seem bored by the group activities; they often complain that they are ineffective organi-

[13]Allen Kassof, *The Soviet Youth Program* (Cambridge: Harvard University Press, 1965), p. 79.

[14]In the Soviet Union, the Komsomol accepts people of ages 14–28, the Pioneers 9–14, and the Octobrists 7–9.

zations for social work and that the activities do not interest them.

The mass media—television, radio, newspapers, books, and the like—are also controlled by the Communist parties and represent important agents of political socialization. All television networks schedule a heavy dosage of ideological and political programming. These propaganda programs assume a variety of formats but always present the Party, government, and the country's leaders in a complimentary light. Propaganda does not have the pejorative meaning in Communist Party states that it holds in the West. Lenin felt that all Party members should act as theoreticians, propagandists, agitators, and organizers. Propaganda means advertising the Party's work in an attempt to win new adherents to the cause. Even those programs that are expressly intended for entertainment will typically have a political message; the vast majority of novels, short stories, and magazine articles will include the same. This concern with ideology has had a sobering effect on the written word in all socialist countries. The loading of ideology into almost everything from newspaper reports to romance novels has severely reduced the quality of writing. Writers unwilling to yield to ideological themes—often some of the very best writers—are forced to pick other professions to survive.

Some of the East European countries—most notably Hungary, Yugoslavia, and Poland before the imposition of martial law in 1981—have experimented with less censorship and more freedom of expression in the mass media and particularly in film, theater, and the demonstrative arts. These less ideological (and sometimes nonideological) expressions have met with wide approval among the masses and illustrate the great interest in apolitical or nonideological culture and arts among East Europeans.

Yugoslavia is again a deviant case when it comes to ideology in the mass media and arts. The vast majority of movies shown in Yugoslavia come from the West, most from the United States. Many television programs on the Yugoslav networks are American reruns; Western literature dots bookshelves and newsstands. Yugoslavia is the only country in the Second World where you can walk up to a newsstand and buy a copy of the Paris edition of the *Herald Tribune*, or *Newsweek*, or *Playboy*. The apparent philosophy in Yugoslavia is to let communism compete with other ideologies and values in a freer market place of ideas. This is only to a relative degree, however, because the Yugoslav Communists have made it clear that they will not allow the present system of socialism to be overturned.

Although the emphasis is definitely on youth in the socialization process, adults are certainly not ignored. The Communist parties and trade unions have vast networks concerned with ideological training and propaganda. Often the training is tied to one's job—classes and programs are offered to heighten workers' political consciousness and to call attention to the continuing class struggle. Although many adults ignore such activities, the social pressures are great enough to generate a significant level of participation.

The primary agent of political socialization in Communist Party states is of course the Party itself. As will be noted in more detail in Chapter Four, the Communist Party controls public information in the Second World states and, in so doing, plays a powerful role in determining what people see, hear, and learn. Because of their organization and socializing strategy, the Communist parties are able to oppose the agents of socialization that may run counter to the desired political culture (e.g., church, family) and use those agents (mass media, schools, youth organizations) that are under their direction. For example, Communist Party organizations are present in factories, collective farms, and other places of work. Members of these organizations are expected to be exemplary citizens and to set good examples for their peers. In addition, the mere presence of Party members and Party organizations in the work place and throughout the society has a powerful socializing impact of its own. Party propaganda is the responsibility of spe-

Even in Yugoslavia, which is considerably more open to a diversity of ideas than most Communist Party states, much of the art deals with heroic themes and symbols. Here, a Yugoslav monument pays tribute to soldiers lost in World War II.

cial departments of the Central Committee in most Communist Party states. ''Agitprop'' activities (short for agitation and propaganda) are controlled by the Communist parties and often furthered by such organizational vehicles as the ZNANIYA Society (Society for the Dissemination of Political and Scientific Knowledge) in the Soviet Union and their equivalent organization in other states.

Finally, when these less coercive agents of socialization fail, the Communist parties have been quite willing to utilize a number of more coercive agencies to deal with citizens who may threaten regime goals and political culture. Included are local militias, intelligence agencies, and the armed forces. In the Soviet Union, for example, the KGB (Committee for

State Security) is charged with the security of the Soviet state this responsibility, the KGB (a part in other Communist Pa wide-ranging authority to cc revolutionary activities'' and the state.'' The frequent presence of unidenti fied KGB operatives in Party, governmental, military, and other organizations has a powerful impact on attitudes and behavior in Communist societies.

Now that we have reviewed the traditional political cultures and the various agents used to change them, we will take a look at the type of new political cultures the Communist leaders desire.

DESIRED POLITICAL CULTURES

One way of viewing the political cultures Communists desire and consider most conducive to their political goals and the building of communism is to examine what they expect of the ideal citizen. The Soviet leaders would like their citizens to live by what they have identified as the ''Moral Code of the Builder of Communism'':

> Devotion to the pursuit of Communism, love for the socialist homeland, for the countries of socialism;
>
> Conscientious labor for the good of society; whoever does not work does not eat;
>
> The concern of everyone for the conservation and increase of social property;
>
> A high consciousness of social obligation, an intolerance toward infringements of social interests;
>
> Collectivism and comradely mutual aid; one for all and all for one;
>
> A humane relationship and mutual respect among people; one person to another person—friend, comrade, and brother;
>
> Integrity and truthfulness, moral purity, simplicity, and humility in social and personal life;
>
> Mutual respect in family life, concern for the upbringing of children;
>
> Implacable opposition to injustice, parasitism, dishonesty, careerism, greed;

e friendship and brotherhood of all the peoples of the USSR; intolerance toward nationalist and racist hostility;

Implacable opposition toward the enemies of Communism, the pursuit of peace, and the freedom of nations.[15]

Soviet leaders would like their people to be devoted and patriotic, conscientious and industrious, comradely, respectful, truthful, pure, and humble. In other words, they want good socialist citizens who will listen to, and support, the leaders and do a full day's work without expecting unreasonable rewards in return. One gets the distinct impression that the Soviets view their citizens as authoritarian parents view their children; that is, they are to be seen but not heard. The leaders want their people to participate in politics but not challenge the party line, to be industrious and generate resources but not question where these resources will be spent. These are the decisions to be reserved for the Party elite. If all Soviet citizens were to hold these traits, it would of course make the leaders' tasks in governing much easier. A political system characterized by an environment of committed, yet like-minded citizens, is much easier to govern than a citizenry that is actively outspoken and divided by deep political cleavages.

Mao also recognized the importance of political socialization and the desirability of a new political culture. Over 40 years ago, he noted:

It is necessary to train a great many people as vanguards of the revolution. People who are politically far-sighted. People imbued with the spirit of struggle and self-sacrifice. People with largeness of mind who are loyal, active, and upright. People who never pursue selfish interests, but are wholeheartedly for liberation of the nation and society. People who fear no difficulties, but remain steadfast and advance courageously in the face of difficulties. People who are neither high or mighty nor seekers after the limelight, but are conscientious

and full of practical sense. If China has a host of such vanguard elements, the tasks of the Chinese revolution will be successfully fulfilled.[16]

Like the Soviet leaders, Mao also wanted an ideologically committed and active political culture. In fact, Mao placed more emphasis on political participation and, during certain periods of his rule, mobilized what may have been the highest level of mass political activity in modern history. Yet, Mao and the Chinese leaders also placed severe limits on the nature of participation. The people were expected to work within the system, and this meant parroting Maoist slogans and supporting the official party doctrine. There was to be no dissent, but rather a united, mobilized populace led by the Great Helmsman, Mao Zedong.

Mao's successors also recognized the importance of political culture to Chinese development and have attempted to outline its ideal features. In 1980, one high party official emphasized the following points:

1. loving the socialist motherland;
2. utilizing Western things useful to the four modernizations and rejecting things unhealthy and against the national spirit;
3. making the ideal of communism a guide to action; and
4. cultivating and strengthening communist ethics.[17]

The political culture desired by the post-Mao leaders is both "Red" and "expert." Red means that the culture is thoroughly communist; it should recognize the importance and validity of communism and abide by a code of communist morality. Expert means that the culture should also be based on knowledge, skills, and scientific know-how. The political culture desired in contemporary China is, therefore, based on many of the ideological principles of the Maoist period (although em-

---

[15]Donald D. Barry and Carol Barner-Barry, *Contemporary Soviet Politics* (Englewood Cliffs, N.J.: Prentice-Hall, 1978), p. 360.

[16]Cited in "Transform Schools into Instruments of Proletarian Dictatorship," *Peking Review* 19 (11) (1976): 7.

[17]Wang Renzhong, "Striving for the Future of Socialist China," *Beijing Review* 23 (24) (1980): 16–19.

Pope John Paul II, the former Archbishop Karol Wojtyla of Krakow, Poland, walks among a crowd of fellow Poles after celebrating a mass in Warsaw's Victory Square on June 2, 1979. To the right is the late Cardinal Stefan Wyszynski, the former primate of Poland. The Catholic Church represents a powerful agent of political socialization with which the Communist leaders have to contend.

phasizing that they should not be carried to extremes), but it adds a new dimension—knowledge—which is required by the new emphasis on modernization. In addition, there has been a greater opportunity for discussion, different points of view, and even some dissent in post-Mao China. Although the new leaders have experimented with the development of a more modern political culture (*i.e.*, less ideology, more skills and knowledge), they have been explicit in setting certain boundaries and reminding the people that the Chinese Communist Party (CCP) is still in charge.

The Yugoslav leaders place even less emphasis on ideology and more on knowledge in the political culture they desire. Giving special attention to the needs of self-management, Yugoslav political culture is one in which individuals, at least theoretically:

> Become familiar with the essence of socioeconomic relations, political structure, and the rights and duties of citizens in the self-managed socialist society; in addition, they should be prepared for direct decision-making on the conditions and results of their work, and for progressive changes in social relations; finally, they must master democratic methods in the realization of personal rights and freedoms and develop a sense of solidarity in work and in communal life.[18]

The ideal political culture to the post-Tito leaders is one that reflects the attitudes and

[18]*Resolution on the Development of Education on the Basis of Self-Management* (Belgrade: Contemporary Administration, 1971), p. 9.

skills required by the developing, self-managing Yugoslav system. In addition, it should be tolerant of the national differences within the country and support the idea of a united Yugoslav state. Finally, it should support the Yugoslav foreign policy on nonalignment and the independent Yugoslav road to socialism.

There are common elements in the political cultures desired by the leaders of all three countries. They all prefer patriotic, devoted, and industrious citizens, and they want them skilled and knowledgeable and willing to live according to certain communist ethics. That is, of course, the ideal. The important and interesting differences among these countries concern two basic features: first, the balance between ideology and knowledge; and second, what the leaders are willing to do to see the culture they desire implanted in the minds and behavior of the people.

Mao's regime went the furthest in emphasizing ideological themes in the Chinese political culture. More recently, however, the post-Mao leaders have attempted to balance ideology and knowledge. Yet, they still appear to emphasize ideology more than do the leaders of the USSR. The Yugoslavs have gone the longest way in deemphasizing ideology and encouraging the knowledge and skills required in a modern industrial state.

The Communist parties of the Soviet Union and China have gone to greater lengths and utilized more extreme tactics to implant the desired political cultures in their people than have most of the East European states, Yugoslavia included. In the latter states, the people and the social and religious organizations to which they often belong have often resisted the parties' forcing certain value patterns on them. For example, the predominantly Catholic population of Poland has made it difficult for the Polish leaders to take an antichurch stand in their socialization strategies. As a consequence, there is a tacit, but precarious, truce between the Catholic Church and the Communist leaders on the nature of Polish political culture. The desired political culture, then, has to be based on certain social, political, and cultural realities, even in Communist states.

THE DOMINANT POLITICAL CULTURE

Dominant political culture is a term we use to describe the prevailing beliefs and opinions that define political life in the Communist Party states today. This does not mean that every citizen subscribes to an all-encompassing set of beliefs and opinions, but rather that we can identify an average or modal set of values that fairly accurately describes the political cultures of these countries. Later we note that the dominant political culture is not accepted by all and that a full understanding of the topic requires an examination of certain subcultures within the various countries.

Because we want to examine those orientations that most significantly affect politics, we will address those related to the four values outlined in the introduction of this book: power, respect, well-being, and enlightenment. For a political system to allocate these values in an authoritative and peaceful manner, the citizens of a particular state ideally should have uniform expectations concerning their proper distribution. If 50 percent of the population feels that political power ought to be confined totally to a small number of leaders within the Communist Party, whereas the other 50 percent strongly feel it should be shared broadly among the entire society, it will be difficult for policymakers effectively to satisfy both sectors in their decisions. On the other hand, if the society widely shares one distribution or the other or if its members are largely apathetic, the policymakers may have an easier time accomplishing their objectives. A useful way of viewing the dominant cultures, then, will be to examine mass orientations and behavior relating to the four values defined earlier.

POWER

The first value and dimension of political culture concerns the role of the individual citizen in the policymaking process. Should the average Soviet, Chinese, Yugoslav, or East European citizen be involved or should he or she leave political affairs in the hands of a small number of Communist Party officials? Based on the goal of worker control and mass participation, one of the basic reasons for the socialist revolutions was to destroy what was perceived to be a dictatorial state that prohibited mass involvement in political affairs and replace it with a more democratic set of social and political relationships. Accordingly, such institutions as legislatures, public courts, and mass organizations have been established in all socialist states to facilitate the goals of worker and mass participation. But, although Marxist ideology emphasizes democratic participation and mass involvement in political life, political practice and the political cultures of the different states deviate considerably from the ideal.

One leading scholar of Soviet political culture uses the term *subject-participatory* to describe this aspect of the dominant political culture in the USSR.[19] Barghoorn notes: "Subject-participatory denotes the relationship among Soviet citizens of subordination to superiors in one or more bureaucratic chains of command and the obligation of all citizens to do their best to assure the performance of the collective."[20] Barghoorn contends that although mass participation definitely occurs in the Soviet Union, it does so "within a framework of values, directives, and controls emanating from a ramified national bureaucracy subject to the commands of the Moscow Polit-buro."[21] Some observers of the Soviet Union feel that participation is much less controlled than Barghoorn describes it, but the prevailing opinion seems to correspond with his position.[22]

Over the 70 years of Soviet development, political orientations reflecting the subject-participatory culture have been ingrained rather effectively throughout all sectors of the society. The average Soviet citizen, whether inhabiting the far eastern reaches of the Russian Republic or the political center in Moscow, possesses a set of beliefs and attitudes defining his or her subject role in the political system. Even those persons whose attitudes and beliefs deviate from official Communist Party doctrine tend overwhelmingly to accept their roles as passive participants without protest. Most citizens in and out of the Communist Party endorse the norms of partisanship (*partiinost*), the collective (*kollektiv*), and a sense of responsibility (*otvetstvennost*) corresponding with the official ideology.

The idea of partisanship or party-mindedness represents a belief in the validity of the Marxist–Leninist way. Tolerance of other points of view is seldom demonstrated, nor is a willingness to change one's own viewpoint. The average Soviet citizen is quick to provide an ideological response to almost any sociopolitical event in the world. Accordingly, if you ask a Soviet worker about the situation of American laborers or if you ask a Soviet official about race relations in the United States or foreign affairs in Africa, be prepared for a response grounded in Marxist–Leninist doctrine.

The ideal of the collective is also supposed to hold an important place in the Soviet citizen's orientation concerning political power.

[19]The term *subject-participatory* comes from Almond and Powell's three basic varieties of political culture: a "parochial" political culture where individuals manifest little or no awareness of the national political system; a "subject" culture where individuals are oriented to the political system and the impact it has on their lives but are not oriented to participation; and a "participant" political culture of individuals oriented to engage actively in the political process. (Gabriel A. Almond and G. Bingham Powell, Jr., *Comparative Politics: A Developmental Approach* [Boston: Little, Brown, 1966].)

[20]Frederick C. Barghoorn, *Politics in the USSR*, 2nd ed. (Boston: Little, Brown, 1972), p. 23.

[21]*Ibid.*, p. 25. The Politburo is the highest decision-making authority within the Communist Party.

[22]Professor Jerry F. Hough has written a number of pieces arguing that Western evaluations of participation and power in the USSR have not been altogether unbiased. For a statement of his argument, with supporting data, see Jerry F. Hough, "Political Participation in the USSR," *Soviet Studies 28* (1) (1976): 3–20; and "The Soviet Experience and the Measurement of Power," *Journal of Politics 37* (3) (1975): 685–710.

All citizens are expected to be politically involved, yet they should not do so to serve their personal self-interests or those of a particular group or organization; rather, it is the interests of the collective that must be promoted. Whether the collective is a factory, the community, or the entire Soviet population, the common citizen is expected to develop a public spirit and to participate to serve the common or collective good. Yet, after over 60 years of socialism, the typical Soviet citizen still puts self-interests ahead of those of the collective.

A majority of the Soviet people tend to feel some responsibility for participating in public life, but far fewer participate with any real commitment and enthusiasm. Although the ideology justifies the special role of the Party leaders in making policy, the citizens are told of their personal responsibility in participating in the affairs of the state. From kindergarten age through their adult years, the Soviet citizens are reminded that building socialism and achieving communism is not a task to be assumed by leaders alone. All citizens, young and old, white- and blue-collar, must share a common responsibility by participating in the social and political order. Soviet citizens are confronted with a contradiction. The party tells them to participate, yet places firm constraints and limits on the nature of their participation.

When we explore the policymaking structures and processes of the USSR in later chapters, we will notice that there is a clear distinction between leaders and followers in Soviet society. Most leaders apparently hold elitist values protecting and justifying their dominant roles in the policymaking process. Many workers, peasants, and white-collar personnel, on the other hand, could not care less about participation. They prefer the role of followers and remain apathetic regardless of the ideological exhortations of the party leaders. Others, however, hold orientations contending that communism can best be achieved through the active participation of all. They feel that political power is both a right and a responsibility. And, although it is carefully coordinated within an oppressive Party bureaucracy, those who desire the role of political activists have the opportunity to involve themselves in political affairs. The opportunity to participate means working within the system, however, and unorthodox forms of political involvement (e.g., demonstrations) are seldom tolerated.

Obviously, Communist Party leaders and officials hold the preponderance of power in the USSR. How the people view these leaders and whether they consider them legitimate are important issues. Soviet people do, for the most part, seem to respect their leaders and believe that their government is basically a just and honorable one. As we saw when we explored the topic of political socialization, the government has gone to considerable lengths to ensure that the masses gain a complimentary picture in this regard. To do so, the leaders take great care to see that government misdeeds go unreported. When misdeeds are reported, they are presented in a way complimentary of the reigning authorities—for example, showing the vigilance of the party in wiping out corruption and serving the people. There would never have been a Watergate exposé in the Soviet Union. Soviet leaders would have covered their tracks more effectively than did the Richard M. Nixon administration; and, if they had not, they would simply have prohibited by fiat any reporting or investigation of the misdeeds.[23]

Occasionally, Soviet leaders do report certain indiscretions that call into question the honor and goodness of their comrades. In 1972, the First Secretary of Georgia's (a republic along the Turkish border) Communist Party was dropped from his position. It was discovered that his wife was in partnership with an individual who was sentenced to 15 years in prison for embezzling about 1 million rubles in state funds, for establishing a vast network of underground retail outlets, and for committing

[23]In fact, because of the close and friendly relations between Nixon and Brezhnev during the period, Soviet newspapers generally refrained from reporting on Watergate. When they finally did, they described it as a plot by those Democrats opposing détente who wanted to evict Nixon from office.

a variety of other crimes. Although the First Secretary was not personally indicted, his successor had numerous officials and party functionaries arrested in an effort to restore respect in the Georgian government.

A campaign against bribery and corruption, begun under Andropov and continued under Chernenko and Gorbachev, has called public attention to a host of examples of official misbehavior. In December 1982, Interior Minister N. S. Shchelokov was dismissed from his position; in June 1983, he and a regional party secretary, S. F. Medunov, were dismissed from the CPSU Central Committee for "mistakes in their work." Finally, in November 1984, Shchelokov was expelled from the party altogether and lost his military rank for "abuse of position for personal gain and conduct discrediting the military title of General of the Soviet Union." In early 1985 Shchelokov was reported to have committed suicide. Another example reached close to a former Soviet leader. Brezhnev's daughter, Galina, and her husband, Y. M. Churbanov, were banished to Murmansk, and Churbanov was dismissed as First Deputy Interior Minister in early 1985 for conduct unbecoming of the Party elite.

A far more significant reporting of government misdeeds was First Secretary Khrushchev's so-called secret speech at the 20th Party Congress in 1956. Apparently against the advice of his closest associates and other Soviet leaders, Khrushchev denounced the deceased Stalin and his excesses at this important forum of the Communist Party of the Soviet Union (CPSU).[24] By calling into question the infallibility of Soviet leadership (or at least of Stalin), Khrushchev set the USSR on the course of de-Stalinization. Although this episode might have temporarily lowered the Soviet peoples' respect of and trust in the CPSU and the government, they developed increased respect for Khrushchev's openness and the proposed new course.[25]

Because of the close connection between the political systems of the USSR and the six Warsaw Treaty Organization (WTO) states (Poland, East Germany, Czechoslovakia, Hungary, Romania, and Bulgaria), the political cultures of these states have certain similarities. However, there are important differences, such as stronger democratic and participatory values within certain nations (e.g., Czechoslovakia), which grew out of a more democratic political heritage. The adoption of the Soviet political model, on the other hand, has tended to dilute the national differences and the idea of a subject-participatory culture tends to hold for these states as well. In some of these nations, there appears to be considerable tension resulting from the contradictions between democratic rhetoric and the authoritarian realities involving contemporary political life.[26] The dramatic events in Poland in the early 1980s called attention to this fundamental problem. Many people began to speak out. They wanted to be more than subject-participants.

But to what extent can people really speak out about politics in these countries? All are keenly aware of the limits of dissent and the accepted rules for working within the system. At the same time, the Western stereotype of mute citizens' councils and oppressive party demagogues serving out orders in commissar fashion is overdrawn. People participating on local committees and in community councils do speak out and frequently argue in support of their personal and collective interests. At the same time, however, they realize that there are certain institutions (e.g., the CPSU) that are not challenged and certain individuals who are not criticized (e.g., the party leaders). Individual dissenters, such as Andrei Sakharov,

[24]In his memoirs, Khrushchev notes: "We exposed Stalin for his excesses, for his arbitrary punishment of millions of honest people, and for his one-man rule, which violated the principle of collective leadership." (*Khrushchev Remembers*, trans. and ed. Strobe Talbot [Boston, Mass.: Little, Brown, 1974], p. 250.)

[25]Khrushchev's speech was not universally acclaimed. Many party leaders and sections of the country were openly critical—Stalin's homeland, the republic of Georgia, for example, was rocked with widespread anti-Khrushchev demonstrations a few weeks after the speech.

[26]Ernst Kux, "Growing Tensions in Eastern Europe," *Problems of Communism* 29 (2) (1980): 21–37.

Aleksandr Solzhenitsyn, and Andrei Amalrik, overstepped these bounds and were either imprisoned, exiled, or harassed.[27] The well-known Soviet writer Georgy Vladimov and one of the founders of the Group for the Establishment of Trust between the USSR and the USA, Sergei Batovrin, were forced to emigrate in 1983. The well-known historian and political commentator Roy Medvedev was warned, also in 1983, by Soviet authorities that he must cease his ''anti-Soviet activities'' or face criminal proceedings. Many others like them in the USSR and other Communist Party states have been brutally suppressed. It is clear that citizens in these countries are not at liberty to challenge or criticize the basic tenets of the system.

We should also ask to what extent individuals feel they should become involved in committees and councils and participate in local and national policymaking. Although it is difficult to get a full and objective picture without greater opportunities for field research and opinion studies, most observers agree that there are large cadres (groups of elected or appointed officials performing professional, political functions) and nonprofessional participants who are willing to involve themselves in politics. And most of those who are not active participants tend to view the government as legitimate and are quite willing to accept political outcomes as the authoritative allocation of values.[28]

In contrast to the USSR, Mao's China (1949–1976) was intended to be a system of mass involvement, what some scholars refer to as a mobilization system, in which all individuals—leaders and peasants alike—were expected to become involved actively in the struggle for socialist construction.[29] During the early years of Chinese communism right through to his death in 1976, Chairman Mao was the primary mobilizer and undertook a variety of campaigns and programs to encourage active and voluntary political participation. Following the ideal of populism, the leaders expected all citizens to participate in communal affairs and to serve the people. Although there was a distinction between national and local political cadres and the masses, subordination and privilege were to be removed from all other social relations; political involvement was to be unobstructed and encouraged. Although it is difficult to judge accurately to what extent the traditional elitist culture has been replaced by the Maoist brand of populism, there is reason to believe that the common Chinese citizen has come to assume more participatory values and a more active, yet constrained political role. China has calmed down considerably in this respect in the 1980s as less emphasis is placed on mass mobilization and participation. Greater choice concerning political life is left to the individual. Although it is risky to generalize, given the differences between city dweller and peasant, worker and intellectual, it does seem fair to conclude that the role of the individual in political affairs is more meaningful than at any other time in modern Chinese history.

With Yugoslavia's break with Stalin and expulsion from the Communist Information Bureau (Cominform) in 1948 and the subsequent growth of the self-management form of industrial democracy, the traditional authoritarian political culture became outmoded. The

[27]The Soviet writer and historian Andrei Amalrik predicted a set of cataclysmic events leading to the disintegration of the Soviet state in his book *Will the Soviet Union Survive until 1984?* (New York: Harper & Row, 1971). Amalrik was jailed by the Committee for State Security (KGB) in 1970 and finally forced to emigrate in 1976. Solzhenitsyn was forced to emigrate in 1975. Sakharov, a leading spokesman for human rights, was banished to Gorki in 1979, a Russian city off-limits to Westerners, and continues to be harassed today.

[28]A study of Soviet attitudes based on questionnaires and interviews with 3000 Soviet refugees in the 1950s concluded that even during the years of Stalinism, the Soviet system enjoyed the support of popular consensus. (Alex Inkeles and Raymond A. Bauer, *The Soviet Citizen* [Cambridge: Harvard University Press, 1959].)

[29]See Franz Schurmann, *Ideology and Organization in Communist China* (Berkeley: University of California Press, 1966). Mobilization systems utilize government control to activate the people in the quest for high-priority goals.

basic task then confronting the leaders was to involve the broader society in political activity even though the general population tended to view the political realm with some fear and suspicion and was neither fully prepared nor equipped to participate in day-to-day social, economic, and political affairs. Through the 1950s and 1960s, the leaders attempted to transform these features of the traditional culture and expand the self-management concept to many areas of Yugoslav life. To do so, they passed laws and established constitutional guarantees providing (and requiring) the participation and involvement of all working people.

Although there is considerable evidence that Yugoslavia has succeeded in flattening the conventional power hierarchy, what has happened to the traditional political culture? Is it still authoritarian, elitist, and nonparticipant, or has it conformed more to self-management ideology?[30] Great strides have been taken in developing a "new citizen" and a participant political culture, yet remnants of the old value systems still persist. And, although middle-level political, social, and economic leaders tend to support the principles of self-managing socialism, they are still reluctant to place full policymaking power and responsibility in the hands of the people and relinquish their positions of primary control. They share and support the ideals of democracy and associate these ideals with a more just, more communist society, but they remain skeptical of the efficiency, effectiveness, and overall feasibility of mass democracy. The mass populace, on the other hand, tends to distrust the sincerity of the leaders and also has certain doubts about the desirability of mass democracy. Is it the most efficient and productive system? Do the masses have the knowledge, training, and general wherewithal to assume such integral responsibilities in political and economic life?

[30]For an interesting account, see Sharon Zukin, *Beyond Marx and Tito: Theory and Practice of Yugoslav Socialism* (London: Cambridge University Press, 1975).

These and other questions suggest that Yugoslavia has a diverse political culture, one that has undergone great change over the past 25 years, but still has a long way to go before becoming a democratic, participatory culture.

A comparative summary of the power dimension of the dominant political cultures in the Soviet Union, China, and Yugoslavia reveals not only certain similarities but also some important differences. The subject-participatory culture of the USSR closely reflects the prevailing power relationships in Soviet society. In the broadest terms, there are those who rule (the elites) and those who follow (the masses); the followers recognize the privileged position of the Party elites and seldom challenge it. The rank-and-file masses are typically content with their roles as subject-participants. They can and do participate in some constrained and narrowly defined political activities, but they are always cognizant that the leaders hold ultimate power and have the final say.

The dominant political culture concerning power in China is diverse. Many Chinese people remain extremely parochial and have little interest in or involvement in political affairs. Some Chinese exhibit even greater deference to Communist Party authority than do the Soviet people and have no aspirations or expectations about influencing what the Chinese leaders do. Yet, some others are true participants, widely involved, and eager to participate in the political process. Some of these maintain the revolutionary zeal of the Maoist tradition while others want to participate in the building of a more modern, less ideological China. Overall, this aspect of political culture in China reflects a changing, increasingly diverse Chinese society.

When viewing power in Yugoslav political culture, we must distinguish between political and industrial democracy. The Yugoslav people are being trained for industrial democracy, or what they call self-managing socialism, not for the political democracy known and practiced in Western Europe and North America.

The Yugoslav Party leadership continues to control political power at the national level and is reluctant to train and encourage the masses to assume a larger role in vital issues of national politics. On the other hand, Yugoslavs have been trained to assume a participatory role in their places of work and in their local communities. So while the Yugoslav people remain subject participants when it comes to the big issues of national-level politics, they are active participants at lower levels within their society.

RESPECT

In his opening remarks at the 24th Congress of the Communist Party of the Soviet Union in 1971, General Secretary Brezhnev spoke of the need for action "whereby trust in and respect for people is combined with principled exactingness toward them" to create a "business-like comradely atmosphere." What do trust and respect really mean in the Soviet context and why are they important in the building of communism? The qualities of which Brezhnev spoke are a vital element in communist construction because they pertain to the subjective feelings governing interpersonal and intergroup relations. Citizens in Communist Party states are expected to be comrades, which means that they are to have a common outlook and common interests. To promote comradeliness means to encourage a common class perspective. Soviet citizens are expected to possess similar attitudes and opinions and to relate to one another in a respectful, trusting way.

Communists from the Soviet Union, for example, believe that the problems of crime and racism in the United States are insoluble because Americans are unable to relate and work together humanely and on the basis of mutual respect. Divided by the class struggle and cleavages endemic in capitalist, bourgeois society, they claim the United States reaps fear, suspicion, and violence as the natural outgrowths of our social and economic system. Although some of these undesirable remnants of

traditional relations are obviously present in Soviet society, Communists expect them to dissolve with the further construction of communism.

As we observe the religious, ethnic, and class strife that pervades so many of the nations on the globe today, we can appreciate the great importance of a cohesive community of people who can work together and relate to one another on the basis of trust and respect. However, the diverse peoples of the Soviet Union are still unable to do this. One hears rude and ethnocentric comments and sees forms of discrimination throughout the USSR. The more advanced nationalities of the industrialized West (the Russians and the Ukrainians) sometimes see the less advanced Central Asians as primitive and backward. Although it is fair to say, then, that there is a certain sense of comradeliness, trust, and respect among the Soviet people that surpasses that found in some other First, Second, and Third World societies, it is unrealistic to assume that there is no suspicion, dishonesty, prejudice, or distrust in contemporary Soviet society. Even if one disregards the general rudeness Soviet people accord one another—pushing and shoving in queues and harsh and gruff service in stores and restaurants and the like—as a cultural trait that does not represent their true feelings about one another, there is still ample evidence to call into question the CPSU's complimentary assessments of Soviet culture. For example, there is a general distrust, cynicism, and suspicion of the "system," that is, of local officials, common bureaucrats, and so on. Everyone knows that petty officials who control such things as apartments, travel abroad, and the like are open to graft and that to get things done often requires the payment of small bribes to the "right" people. This is a widespread illness of Soviet society and one that appears to present a serious obstruction to the desired ideals of brotherhood and equality.

How are the Chinese doing in developing respectful and comradely relations among their people? In a revealing article, Ezra F. Vogel outlined the original Maoist objectives in this regard as well as the important changes that took place during the early period of Communist rule.[31] Vogel described a major movement away from what we know as friendship (a personal, private relationship between close companions) to the concept of comradeship. Comradeship in the Chinese context was to be based on a universal ethic in which individuals treat all other individuals as equal members of a political community. With the emphasis on collective rather than private relationships, comrades were obligated to mutually reinforcing roles within their society. The emphasis on the collective and helping was reflected in the common slogan and required reading: ''Serve the People.''[32] In attempting to establish comradely relations of this sort in China, the Western concept of private trust is lost. Under the system of comradeship, you would not tell a comrade a secret, something you wanted withheld from others. If a comrade knew, for instance, that you fudged on your income tax or that you took more than your allotment of rice from the storehouse, he or she would be expected to report you to the peoples' court. If you were found guilty of these transgressions, you would engage in self-criticism and admit to your crime against the people. In establishing a public surveillance system where few indiscretions avoided the public eye, Maoist China attempted to build a society free of corruption, crime, and graft. Although the personal costs might remind some of the cold-hearted efficiency of Orwell's ''Big Brother,'' the benefits were also of great merit in the Chinese context.

Overall, the comradeship movement in Mao's China did have an impact, although not always as intended. Personal relationships were changed; the role of the family was modified; the idea of personal friendships was altered. Although Mao did not fully succeed in ''wiping out the old,'' as he so often exhorted the people to do, he and his contemporaries did have an influence on the attitudes and values guiding interpersonal relationships in Chinese society. However, in the less ideological, more recent post-Mao period, it appears that the Chinese people are returning to the more traditional forms of interpersonal relations. True comradeship is not a dominant feature of Chinese political culture.

In Yugoslavia, the qualities of comradeliness, trust, and respect are particularly important in a setting where ethnic and religious enmity has characterized intergroup and interpersonal relations for centuries. With so many religious, ethnic, and lingual groups concentrated in this compact Balkan region, the propensity for intergroup conflict is dangerously high. Today, after over three decades of Communist rule, mass attitudes are still marked by strong doses of prejudice and discrimination. Intermarriage between different ethnic groups is infrequent, as is population movement between the different ethnic regions. The Yugoslav leaders acknowledge that their national problem has *not* been solved—the Soviet leaders claim the problem *has* been solved in their country—and have had their observations verified by nationalist movements and demonstrations (*e.g.*, Croatian and Albanian) in some of the Yugoslav regions recently. The question of comradeship also tells us something important about the political culture of Yugoslavs. It is clear that friendship has not been replaced by comradeship. To the contrary, interpersonal relations tend to be a carbon copy of those in most Western states. Greetings between people are made on a first name or a more formal Mr./Mrs./Miss basis; the designation of someone as comrade is seldom used except in official party or government activities.

To summarize, all the Marxist governments of the Second World have attempted to eradicate the class-based feelings of their presocialist periods and replace them with more respectful and fraternal orientations based on the concepts of brotherhood, equality, and unity. A close examination of behavior and be-

[31]Ezra F. Vogel, ''From Friendship to Comradeship: The Change in Personal Relations in Communist China,'' *The China Quarterly* 21 (1965): 46–60.

[32]''Serve the People'' was one of the three political writings that was required by the Chinese Government for all citizens.

lief systems in these countries shows definite gaps in these desired orientations, but it is fair to say that some changes have taken place. The more authoritarian system of government in the Communist Party states has something to do with the relative calm within their societies. A relaxation of government authority and an increase in civil rights might be followed by a dangerous upswing in intergroup animosity and violence.

Another form of respect is severely lacking in most Communist states and that concerns the way the leaders view and treat their citizens. The absence of governmental respect for basic human rights and personal freedoms results in a political culture rather far removed from the Marxist ideal.

Considerable distrust and animosity also characterize the feelings and relations among Communist Party states and their peoples. The continuing conflict in the war-torn states of Southeast Asia is a good example. The advent of communism in Laos, Cambodia (Kampuchea), and all of Vietnam in the 1970s obviously did not bring respect, peace, and prosperity to East Asia. And, respect and trust certainly do not exist between the Soviets and the Chinese or between the East Europeans and the Soviets. There appears to be a notable absence of respect for the Soviet Union throughout the Communist world, both at elite and mass levels. Although communism was to bring fraternal feelings among all worker states, one encounters considerable anti-Soviet sentiment in China, Yugoslavia, and in most of the countries of Eastern Europe.

WELL-BEING

What do the average people expect in the way of health care, social services, and consumer goods in Communist-run societies? What are their attitudes concerning a fair and proper distribution of these values? At the 24th Party Congress, Secretary Brezhnev announced: "The growth of the people's well-being is the supreme goal of the party's economic policy." At the 25th Party Congress five years later, in 1976, he noted that the most important goal remained "a further increase in the people's well-being." Brezhnev went on to say that this meant improvement in working and living conditions; progress in public health, culture, and education; and everything that facilitates "improvement of the socialist way of life." Similar pledges were given at the 26th and 27th party congresses. But do the people believe them?

First, we ought to be aware that the Soviet Union is a welfare state. It spends the equivalent of billions of dollars on education, health care, social security, and, at even greater cost, on the massive bureaucracy that coordinates these programs. However, in contrast to the leaders' hopes and perhaps good-willed intentions of upgrading the material and social well-being of the Soviet populace, the contemporary scene shows considerable shortcomings. There are critical shortages in housing and basic foodstuffs as well as poor service in many of those programs (e.g., medical and dental care) in which the regime prides itself most.

The dominant orientations of the Soviet populace reflect the contradiction between the communist ideal, where material goods are to be allocated on the basis of need, and the Soviet reality of reward on the basis of work. For the most part, the more poorly paid seem reconciled to their less privileged position on the income hierarchy, whereas the better paid tend to believe that a differential system of rewards is the only fair and reasonable way to handle income.

The American visitor views the living standard as one of general deprivation. To us, the most striking feature of this aspect of Soviet political culture is the passivity of the population in accepting the status quo. There are always some people intent (and sometimes successful) in ripping off the system and becoming millionaires in a proletarian state; still other people show a total lack of initiative and would prefer not to work if they are able to find some means of subsistence. But these two groups are almost invisible minorities in the enormous Soviet populace. The great majority are hardworking people who report daily to their jobs and seldom show signs of discontent. With a strong sense of history, they remember the difficult times of the past and generally agree that "we've never had it so good."

Some Western observers dispute this general picture of content and call attention to the unusually high level of alcoholism that continues to plague Soviet society. Party authorities have tried their best to alleviate this problem, including the encouragement of such soft drinks as Pepsi-Cola as preferred substitutes for vodka and wine, yet alcoholism continues to exist. The high percentage of personal income spent on liquor substantially reduces the general social and material well-being of the average Soviet family. Vladimir Treml, an American economist, estimates that the average Soviet family spends two months' salary a year on alcohol. However, the problem of vodka in Russia is far older than the Soviet state. Although we cannot conclude that communism has caused alcoholism, we can conclude that its Soviet proponents have done little to alleviate this historical problem.

An important component of this dimension of political culture concerns a society's expectations for the future. Soviet policy regarding material well-being has been very sensitive, almost paranoid, on the question of rising expectations. One of the reasons for the Party leadership's reluctance to loosen foreign travel is tied, no doubt, to their fear of increasing mass expectations, which the government will be unable to meet. Rising and unmet expectations have been more prevalent and, as a result, more of a problem among certain East European populations, such as Poland and Yugoslavia, where contact with the West is greater. In addition, the populations of these countries are less docile than the Soviet populace and frequently make their feelings known. Just before Christmas in 1970, for example, the Polish leaders instituted a major price increase in a variety of foodstuffs. Perceiving a substantial reduction in their level of material well-being, the Polish populace protested the government's policy, rioted in some coastal cities, stopped work, and burned down the Party headquarters in one major city. This action led to the removal of the Party leader, Wladyslaw Gomulka, and abolition of the price increases. The next party leader, Edward Gierek, attempted a new set of price increases in 1976 and also encountered mass dissatisfaction. The government was forced once again to rescind the increases. Gierek was ousted in 1980 during the workers' strikes when he, too, proved incapable of meeting the aspirations and demands of the Polish people. This calls attention to the power of a society's expectations and the importance that orientations concerning the fair and proper allocation of well-being can have on political life. As the awareness and sophistication of the Soviet populace increases with the normal and inevitable process of modernization, we can expect them to develop more discriminating attitudes and become involved in this important question of social and political affairs.

With the Maoist emphasis on equality and the collectivity, the Chinese people came to deemphasize, at least when compared with the West, private material interests and to work in the interests of society as a whole. To solve the problems of mass starvation and the general deprivation that characterized much of Chinese society at the time of the Communist assumption of power in 1949, a massive program of redistribution was adopted. Because egalitarianism was not then a dominant part of Chinese political culture, redistribution toward increased material equality did not meet with universal approval. During the radical 1966–1976 period, the Chinese moved decisively to promote the goals of equality. However, since 1976, the more radical egalitarian goals have been largely abandoned as the leaders have moved to establish a link between individual effort and individual reward. Today most Chinese accept the principle "from each according to his abilities, to each according to his contribution."

The Chinese compare their well-being with what was experienced in the past: almost without exception, they find it much improved and getting better. They have jobs and shelter, no one is starving, and most receive adequate medical and health care. But are these alone enough to command the support of the Chinese people? Recently, the Chinese leaders have been promising more consumer goods. In a 1985 policy statement, Premier Zhao Ziyang promised that such consumer goods as refrigerators, washing machines, and bicycles, once considered luxuries, would be easier to buy in the future. He went on to promise pay raises in many sectors of the economy. Later in 1985, however, the Chinese leaders were expressing concern about the rising expectations of the people. Could these rising expectations get out of control? Would the leaders be able to meet the peoples' demands? Where will it all end? These are among the many questions confronting the Chinese leaders today.

In contrast to the more centralized control over the distribution of well-being prevalent in the Soviet and East European systems, Yugoslavia allows individuals more freedom and opportunity to maximize their personal well-being. To be sure, Yugoslavia is a welfare state that provides a public system of social services, as do the Soviets. In contrast, however, more decentralized Yugoslav economic and political systems provide greater opportunities and incentives for increased personal welfare and consumption. In the late 1960s and early 1970s, many Yugoslavs proudly and openly displayed their material possessions, such as cars or private vacation homes on the Dalmatian Coast. The system was loose enough to allow the accumulation of a considerable amount of personal possessions. Many people were moonlighting, thousands were working abroad in Western Europe and sending home large amounts of hard currency,[33] and some were simply corrupt and absconded with public funds. Whatever methods were used, many

Yugoslavs were becoming rich even by Western standards, and the distance between the upper and lower income levels was growing excessively pronounced. After being generally tolerant of this feature of economic growth through the 1960s, Tito and the Party leaders aggressively attacked bourgeois materialism and corruption in the early 1970s and initiated policies that prevented the excessive accumulation of personal wealth. The action was only a partial success, however, and simply drove many of the striving Yugoslav entrepreneurs underground, forcing them to be a little more discreet in bragging about their material success. Although the government's hard-nosed policy lowered the level of prideful boasting, it had little influence on the deep-seated Yugoslav values of materialism and consumerism.

Such orientations in Yugoslavia represent a more individual-centered and consumption-oriented political culture than exists in either China or the Soviet Union. When a young Party member, dressed in the latest Italian fashion and excessively desirous of Western material possessions, was asked how the Marxist ideal of "to each according to his needs" would ever become a reality in view of the materialism so evident in her society, she said, "We are the babies of socialism. It may be 100 or even 200 years before we can free ourselves from the materialist values of our former society." Although this bit of honesty is a refreshing characteristic of the Yugoslavs, one wonders if Karl Marx would be so self-assured and flippant.

Overall, one gets the impression that self-interest still is the dominant feature of this aspect of political culture in Communist societies. Although there are differences among countries, people tend to place their personal interests before those of the collectivity. If the leaders of these states were suddenly to adopt the principle, "from each according to his abilities, *to each according to his needs*," people would probably react according to how this new policy would affect them. If they expected to raise their level of well-being, they would

---

[33]According to the 1971 Yugoslav census, there were 671,909 Yugoslavs temporarily living or working abroad; this amounted to 15.2 percent of the total registered non-agricultural work force. (Miloje Nikolić, "Some Basic Features of Yugoslav External Migrants," *Yugoslav Survey* 13 [1] [1972]: 4.)

tend to support the new policy. If they were engineers or successful writers and already making and enjoying more than they really needed, they would be likely to oppose it. In other words, attitudes and values in most Communist societies concerning well-being may not be all that different from those in the West. As the young Yugoslav said, it may take 100 or even 200 years!

ENLIGHTENMENT

The final dimension of political culture to be examined concerns the value, enlightenment. How "enlightened" are people living in Communist Party states? What are the values and characteristics of the "enlightened" citizen?

After the takeovers, Communist leaders knew they would have to develop a new set of values, new ideas, new skills, and new behaviors—in other words, a new socialist being—before they could succeed in building Communism. One way of examining the enlightenment dimension of political culture, then, is to examine the people in terms of a set of standards describing this new being. Using the following characteristics outlined by T. H. Chen, we can draw attention to both similarities and differences in the political cultures found in the Second World states.[34]

1. *Absolute selflessness.* The model Maoist citizen, according to Chen, was to hold no ambitions beyond serving the cause of the revolution and China. This characteristic, forced on the Chinese populace during the Maoist period, is in conflict with Western concepts of individualism and liberty. Although the Chinese and other Communist leaders have sought to instill this quality among their citizens, they have been largely unsuccessful. Most people living in Communist states are patriotic and may at times be willing to sacrifice their individual interests for what they perceive to be in

the best interests of their country.[35] But in everyday life, one gets the impression that they think first of themselves, then of their families and friends, and then perhaps remotely of their fellow citizens and country.

The political cultures of the East Europeans and Cubans also seem to approximate Western standards. The mass exodus of refugees from Cuba in 1980 suggests that these people placed personal interests and pre-Communist values over those of the Cuban Revolution. Although it is hard to characterize the Cubans who chose to stay or were unable to emigrate, one must conclude that at least a sizable minority have not assumed the characteristics of a selfless, model citizen as defined by Communist leaders.

2. *Obedience to the Communist Party.* Commitment to the leaders and to the party also is intended to be a dominant feature of Communist political culture. Chen quotes the words of the song "East is Red," which the Chinese children were taught to express their worship of the now-deceased Mao:

> *The East is red,*
> *The sun rises.*
> *China has brought forth a Mao Zedong.*
> *He works for the people's happiness.*
> *He is the people's great savior.*
>
> *Chairman Mao loves the people,*
> *He is our guide.*
> *He leads us onward*
> *To build the new China.*
>
> *The Communist Party is like the sun,*
> *Wherever it shines, there is light.*
> *Where there's the Communist Party,*
> *There the people will win liberation.*

[34]Theodore Hsi-en Chen, "The New Socialist Man," in C. T. Hu, ed., *Aspects of Chinese Education* (New York: Columbia University Press, 1969), pp. 88–95.

[35]A good indicator of selflessness is the willingness with which people come to the aid of their country. During World War II (renamed the "Great Patriotic War" by Soviet authorities), the Soviet people fought valiantly and selflessly against the Nazis. In 1968, the Yugoslav people rushed to the support of their government and were willing to take up arms against the USSR when it was rumored that the Soviets were going to follow their intervention into Czechoslovakia with an invasion of Yugoslavia.

Although adoration and respect for the Communist parties and leadership are desired features of Communist political cultures, they do not appear deeply ingrained. The Party leaders do command a certain amount of respect, and the Party is considered by some to be acting in the best interest of the people. However, there is a certain amount of cynicism and lack of respect displayed in the jokes that circulate in these countries, particularly in the East European countries, concerning the incompetence of the leaders and Party organizations. This cynicism is less widespread in the USSR and Yugoslavia, where the people are more likely to consider the Party leaders those of their own peoples' choosing, than it is in many of the East European countries, such as Czechoslovakia, Poland, and Hungary, where the leadership is perceived to have been picked by the Soviet Union. In these countries, the Party and leaders—especially the Soviet CPSU and its leaders—are the objects of some of the most caustic jokes ever told. These stories represent a good indicator of the legitimacy of the party as well as the obedience the population will accord it.

3. *Class consciousness.* The model Communist citizen should always be on guard against remnants of the class struggle, such as bourgeois ideas at home and abroad, the global threat of capitalist imperialism, and the like. Because of intense indoctrination by the schools, the arts, and the media during the Maoist period, the Chinese were immersed in the class struggle and were expected to assume a political consciousness as part of their belief systems.[36] Yet, one gets the impression that few Chinese really believe deeply in the significance of the class struggle today.

Again, there is evidence to suggest that class consciousness is even less deeply embedded in the beliefs of the Soviet and East European peoples. Every Soviet student can explain in class terms the Great Patriotic War or race relations in Africa; the same holds true for Yugoslavs and the East Europeans. However, in contrast to Mao's China, where class enemies were perceived to abound and where class warfare was said to rage endlessly, there is a much more relaxed atmosphere concerning the idea of class struggle in the European Communist Party states. The attitudes of the Soviet people concerning class consciousness are no doubt influenced by the official doctrine that says that the USSR has long since reached socialism and has eliminated antagonistic classes. Whatever the causes, the typical Soviet citizen, along with his or her counterparts in Eastern Europe, does not seem to be particularly conscious of the class struggle as Marxist theory would have it.

4. *Ideological study.* Ideological study in Mao's China meant the study of Mao Zedong's political writings; the works of Karl Marx, Friedrich Engels, and Joseph Stalin; and contributions by certain other Chinese party officials. Before Mao's death, schoolchildren and elderly adults alike were often seen reciting the thoughts of the Great Helmsman from his *Little Red Book*. The model Chinese citizen was to have the correct ideological outlook, which was to be derived from unceasing study of Chinese Communist ideology. However, the almost exclusive emphasis on ideological study has been sharply curtailed in the post-Mao period. Now, study of science, technology, and traditional academic disciplines is given more attention. The ideologically infused but poorly educated Chinese populace has a considerable amount of catching up to do to contribute fully to Chinese modernization.

Although revolutionary study was a pulsating enterprise very much a part of Mao's China, it has become passé in most Communist Party countries today. Rather than serving as an intimate part of one's everyday life, it tends to be a course one takes in school. When watching these courses being taught, one gets the impression that both teachers and students are simply going through the motions. In many respects, they resemble a course in American high school civics; there is some ma-

---

[36]The arts in China were viewed as a forum for heightening the class consciousness of the masses during Mao's time. The revolutionary operas and ballets were typically based on the class-struggle themes.

terial to be covered and a test at the end, but the most important concern to students is the grade one receives in the class.

In the early 1970s, Tito and the Yugoslav Communists feared that even this minimal amount of ideological study was fading further from the school curriculum. As a response, they inaugurated a campaign to bring Marx and Lenin back in the classroom and to renew the ideological indoctrination of the Yugoslav populace. Even after the campaign, however, one gets the impression—in Yugoslavia and elsewhere in Eastern Europe—that ideological study is something to be done but nothing about which to be overly committed.

5. *Labor and production.* The new Communist citizen in Mao's China was expected to thrive on, and enjoy, manual labor. All students during the Maoist period, for example, were required to engage in productive labor for the state in addition to their normal study. Schools and universities were to become centers of production as well as centers of learning. Mao's China was a picture of men and women at work: peasants marching in the fields, students and laborers working side by side in the factories.

Things have changed in contemporary China, and there is a stronger trend toward specialization. Requirements of manual labor for students and professionals have disappeared. The enlightened Chinese citizen of today is attempting to become an expert in computers or energy technology and is less likely to become involved in manual labor and production.

In 1958, Secretary Khrushchev proposed a set of far-reaching reforms for the Soviet educational system, part of which would establish a work/study program somewhat like those in Mao's China. Khrushchev's recommendations for a combined work/study experience for students were resoundingly defeated; a number of influential groups critically questioned the advisability of the proposals. "How can we compete with the United States in the development of science and technology when our best students are required to spend part of the day

in the factory?" the scientific leaders asked. "How can we meet our quotas," asked the factory directors, "when we have to put up with these immature students?" The defeat of Khrushchev's proposals and the continued separation of work and study in the USSR today does not mean that the leaders are unconcerned with labor and production. Rather, there is a feeling that modern economies require specialization and that it is unreasonable to expect trained professional or aspiring nuclear physicists to spend part of their day in a factory or on a collective farm. As a result, political cultures in contemporary Eastern Europe and the Soviet Union reflect growing divisions among workers and professionals. The "enlightened" citizen of these countries is likely to be well educated, highly specialized, and ill-disposed to taking part in manual labor.

6. *The Red/expert blend.* The enlightened socialist citizen in most contemporary Communist Party states is to be both committed to Communist ideology (*i.e.,* Red) and an expert with specific skills and talents that will contribute to the construction of communism. The different blends of Redness and expertness, however, illustrate some significant contrasts among the various Communist Party states. Mao's China invariably placed greater emphasis on the ideological side (Red) and less on the technical, scientific aspects (expert) of socialist construction. During the 1960s, Yugoslavia was at the other extreme on the continuum and had allowed expert to assume predominance over Red. This trend in Yugoslavia generated a highly educated technocratic sector that, although largely Communist, viewed the question of socioeconomic growth in developmental and scientific rather than ideological terms. More recently, however, they have become somewhat more alike. The Chinese are placing more emphasis on scientific training and less on ideology; the Yugoslavs are placing a little less on technocratic values and a little more on ideology. While these two systems have been changing, the Soviet Union continues to take a more conservative, middle-of-the-road position. Although the Soviet leadership has not

emphasized the value of extreme Redness, neither has it allowed the more unfettered development of the technocratic experts. What it has done is to emphasize both. That is, the new enlightened citizen should be not only ideologically committed but also trained and educated to bring the most advanced skills and training available to his or her work setting. Some individuals do indeed approximate this model citizen, but most have deficiencies in one or, more likely, both categories. It seems that the higher the level of training and education, the lower the level of Redness, and *vice versa*. If this relationship is indeed correct, the problem of assuring ideological purity and commitment will be an increasingly difficult one as the process of modernization and enlightenment continues. The recent Four Modernizations Program in China will provide an interesting test of this hypothesis.[37]

SUBCULTURES

We can think of Communist Party states in terms of their dominant political cultures, but we should recognize that this is a major simplification of reality. Because most Communist-run societies are complex and heterogeneous, they contain a variety of subcultures within their broader populations. Although these subcultures are likely to share certain values with the dominant political culture, they also hold many distinct values of their own.

Subcultures are based on a diverse set of characteristics. We can divide populations geographically (*e.g.*, the North and South in the United States) and find distinct subcultures; we can also divide societies by social or occupational attributes, ethnic differences, and so forth. Another meaningful and useful way to explore subcultures is by dividing societies into political elites and masses. The Chinese

masses, for example, hold values that are in some respect quite different from those held by the political elites.[38] In addition, workers in urban, industrial centers hold values that often contrast with those in isolated villages; and the political culture of the inhabitants of Beijing, the capital in the north, tends to vary in important respects from that of the populations in the more business-oriented south.

The dissidents in the Soviet Union—such as the noted physicist Andrei Sakharov, who was instrumental in developing the Soviet A-bomb; groups of courageous young people; Jewish and religious activists; and others—represent significant subcultures at odds with the official Party line. Because their ideas and values oppose the existing system, they are viewed as threats and have been harassed, banished, and imprisoned. When compared with the West, Communist leaders display a high level of intolerance toward groups in opposition to the desired culture.

Frederick C. Barghoorn has also distinguished different political subcultures in the Soviet Union on the basis of social structure.[39] Thinking of Soviet society in terms of intelligentsia, workers, and collective farmers, Barghoorn has identified attitudes and behaviors that distinguish each group from one another and from the dominant political culture as well. According to his study, different orientations toward politics are largely defined by one's position in the social structure. Because the intelligentsia are a somewhat privileged strata in Soviet society, they have higher levels of education and sometimes expect higher levels of power, respect, and well-being than do the less privileged "unenlightened" sectors. Different opinions, such as those about the proper distribution of values, have resulted in a variety of intense policy disputes over the years.

Nationality is also an important determi-

[37]For an examination of political socialization and educational policy in the post-Mao era, see Suzanne Pepper, "Chinese Education after Mao: Two Steps Forward, Two Steps Back and Begin Again," *China Quarterly 81* (1980): 1-65; also, see the recent articles written by various Chinese officials, observers, and scholars in the journal *Chinese Education*.

[38]For a study that uses the mass/elite distinction, see James D. Seymour, *China: The Politics of Revolutionary Reintegration* (New York: Crowell, 1976), pp. 25-66.

[39]Barghoorn, *op. cit.*, pp. 48-86.

nant of subcultures in the USSR. The Ukrainians, Jews, Crimean Tatars, the Baltic nationalities, and others sometimes evidence different attitudes and values having an impact on politics. Teresa Rakowska-Harmstone has written that nationalism in such groups challenges the central Soviet Government in three important areas: (1) pressure for broader political autonomy, (2) pressure for greater allocation of resources in local areas and more autonomy in managing local affairs, and (3) pressure for greater freedom to promote local national cultures.[40] Another leading expert on Soviet nationalities writes, ''Far from having solved the nationalities question, Soviet leaders must consider it as among the most salient issues on the political agenda.''[41]

The national differences among Serbs, Croats, and other national and ethnic groups define a diverse set of subcultures in Yugoslavia. Based on cultural, religious, lingual, and economic differences, these groups hold political orientations that contrast, and often conflict, with one another. Some of the groups (*e.g.*, the Macedonians and Albanians) who inhabit less-developed national areas of Yugoslavia feel that the state should do more to equalize the level of well-being among different national regions.[42] Because their levels of well-being are considerably below those in the developed regions, they feel funds should be taken from the developed regions and invested in their areas to aid social and economic development. These and other differences of opinion associated with ethnicity in Yugoslavia are reflected in both elite and mass political cultures and on many occasions have resulted in political conflict pitting one republic or a group of republics against another. Many Albanians

in the province of Kosovo demonstrated and rebelled in the early 1980s to indicate Albanian dissatisfaction with their situation in the Yugoslav union. Examples of this and other ethnic subcultures resorting to civil disobedience and violence in the Second World provide dramatic testimony to Communist shortcomings in building new, unified political cultures.

After having viewed the pre-Communist cultures, the desired political cultures, and the dominant political cultures and subcultures, we might conclude by assessing what it all means. Have the strategies of political socialization been successful? Have the Communists succeeded in creating new ideas and values, a new mentality, and a new socialist person? Although one does observe a certain level of conformity among the people throughout most of the Communist Party states and even some level of acceptance and support of the ideals and values of the regime, it seems apparent that there is no ''new socialist being.'' In their book on political culture and political change in Communist Party states, Archie Brown, Jack Gray, and others summarized the results of considerable research on this question.[43] In all of the countries examined, there is little evidence to suggest that human nature and political culture have been changed in a fundamental way. Although recognizing that the amount of time devoted to Communist change has been relatively brief in the course of human history and, therefore, recognizing that more fundamental changes may still come about, our conclusion raises some important implications for the question of politics to which subsequent chapters will now turn. Namely, because Communist leaders have been unsuccessful in creating a totally new political culture, they must make decisions in an environment blessed with less than total agreement on the distribution of such values as power, respect, well-being, and enlightenment. This means that policy will be made in a politicized

[40]Teresa Rakowska-Harmstone, ''The Dialectics of Nationalism in the USSR,'' *Problems of Communism* 33 (3) (1974): 12.

[41]Brian D. Silver, ''Soviet Nationality Problems: Analytic Approaches,'' *Problems of Communism,* 38 (4) (1979): 71.

[42]The autonomous province of Kosovo, inhabited primarily by Albanians, was rocked by rioting and demonstrations in the early 1980s as Albanians sought a greater share of resources in the Yugoslav federation.

[43]Archie Brown and Jack Gray, eds., *Political Culture and Political Change in Communist States*, 2nd rev. ed. (New York: Holmes & Meier, 1979).

environment where different groups and individuals will prefer different decisions and policy outcomes. Like the historical and socioeconomic forces reviewed in Chapters One and Two, the attitudinal and behavioral forces reviewed here are environmental determinants of considerable importance to politics and the political system.

Suggestions for Further Reading

Brown, Archie, and **Jack Gray**, eds., *Political Culture and Political Change in Communist States*, 2nd rev. ed. (New York: Holmes & Meier, 1979).

Change, Parris H., "Children's Literature and Political Socialization," in Godwin Chu and Francis Hsu, eds., *Moving a Mountain: Cultural Change in China* (Honolulu: University of Hawaii Press, 1979), pp. 237–256.

Chen, Theodore Hsi-en, *The Maoist Educational Revolution* (New York: Praeger, 1974).

Dewitt, Nicholas, *Education and Professional Employment in the USSR* (Washington, D.C.: U.S. Government Printing Office, 1961).

Fagen, Richard R., *The Transformation of Political Culture in Cuba* (Stanford, Calif.: Stanford University Press, 1969).

Grant, Nigel, *Soviet Education*, 3rd ed. (Baltimore: Penguin, 1972).

Harasymiw, Bohdan, ed., *Education and the Mass Media in the Soviet Union and Eastern Europe* (New York: Praeger, 1976).

Hollander, Gayle Durham, *Soviet Political Indoctrination* (New York: Praeger, 1972).

Hu, Chang-tu, *Chinese Education under Communism* (New York: Columbia University Press, 1962).

Lifton, Robert J., *Thought Reform and the Psychology of Totalism: A Study of "Brainwashing" in China* (New York: Norton, 1961).

Liu, Alan P., *Political Culture and Group Conflict in Communist China* (Santa Barbara, Calif.: Clio Press, 1976).

Matthews, Mervyn, *Education in the Soviet Union: Policies and Institutions since Stalin* (London: Allen & Unwin, 1982).

Metzger, Thomas A., *Escape from Predicament: Neo-Confucianism and China's Evolving Political Culture* (New York: Columbia University Press, 1977).

Mickiewicz, Ellen P., *Media and the Russian Public* (New York: Praeger, 1981).

———, *Soviet Political Schools: The Communist Party Adult Instruction Program* (New Haven, Conn.: Yale University Press, 1967).

Price, R. F., *Education in Communist China* (New York: Praeger, 1970).

Solomon, Richard H., *Mao's Revolution and the Chinese Political Culture* (Berkeley: University of California Press, 1971).

Volgyes, Ivan, ed., *Political Socialization in Eastern Europe* (New York: Praeger, 1975).

Welsh, William A., ed., *Survey Research and Public Attitudes in Eastern Europe and the Soviet Union* (Elmsford, N.Y.: Pergamon, 1980).

White, Stephen, *Political Culture and Soviet Politics* (New York: St. Martin's Press, 1979).

Zukin, Sharon, *Beyond Marx and Tito: Theory and Practice of Yugoslav Socialism* (London: Cambridge University Press, 1975).

CHAPTER FOUR

The Communist Parties: Structures and Personnel

Of what importance are Communist parties in the socialist states of the Second World? Are most citizens in these states members of the Communist Party? How does one become a party member, or a Communist leader? Who are the leaders of the Communist Party states we are studying?

It is the Communist Party and its dominating effect on the political process that most distinguishes Second World policymaking from that found in the two- or multi-party systems of the First World. Called by its leaders the "vanguard of the people" and the "fount of political wisdom," the Communist Party dominates the policymaking process in all Second World states. Characteristic of a one-party state is a policy process much more centralized and much less open to outside influence than that found in the United States or many of the West European democracies. This difference is, in part, a result of the historical origin and subsequent evolution of the Communist Party of the Soviet Union (CPSU).

HISTORICAL SETTING

Karl Marx and Friedrich Engels provided their heirs precious little guidance concerning the proper organization of the postrevolutionary Marxist state. "Now that we've won, what do we do?" Vladimir Ilyich Lenin and Leon Trotsky asked themselves after the Bolshevik victory in 1917. How should they organize political activity to solve the pressing social, economic, and political problems facing the Russian state?

Lenin was neither naïve nor unprepared when it came to the question of political organization. As one leading scholar puts it:

> One trait that made [Lenin] a pioneer of twentieth-century politics was his insight into the crucial role of organization. Lenin realized that . . . all human activities . . . are carried out in and through organizations and associations.[1]

In what is perhaps his most important work, *What Is to Be Done?*, Lenin recognized the need for a particular type of organization that could be used to speed work toward the revolutionary goal of socialist construction. Years before the Russian Revolution, Lenin's political organization, the Communist Party, evolved into a highly centralized, authoritarian, and militant "party of a new type,"[2] one that became the sole guardian of organized political rule.

Under Lenin's leadership, the Communist Party represented the key institution for con-

[1]Alfred G. Meyer, *Communism*, 4th ed. (New York: Random House, 1984), p. 46.

[2]For an excellent discussion of Lenin's "party of a new type," see Bertram D. Wolfe, "Leninism," in Milorad M. Drachkovitch, ed., *Marxism in the Modern World* (Stanford, Calif.: Stanford University Press, 1965), pp. 76–84.

solidating power and forging the subsequent construction of communism. Using great organizational and leadership skills and adhering to the pragmatic principle that "the ends justify the means," Lenin concentrated policy-making power within the organizational structure of the party. What was initially viewed by the Bolsheviks as the dictatorship of the proletariat became, for all intents, a dictatorship of the party. During Leninist and Stalinist stages of development, the party grew into a dictatorial bureaucratic organization that controlled the goals, actions, and policy outcomes governing the Soviet political process.

Lenin attempted, however, to combine democratic values with the party dictatorship by adopting the principle of democratic centralism. This formula represents an intended merging of both democratic and centralistic (or dictatorial) powers in which members of the party are encouraged to debate policy matters freely until the point of decision. Once a vote has been taken and a decision is made, however, centralism is required and further discussion and debate, outside normal party channels, are forbidden. Although this principle does allow some level of democratic debate within the party and although it is not clear to what extent subordinates are successful in challenging the policy preferences of superiors, it does not alter the underlying primacy of party rule, in which a small minority of the state's population monopolizes the primary institution of political power. One-party rule administered according to the principle of democratic centralism is the single most distinguishing characteristic of the Soviet and other Communist political systems.

Assuming a dominant position in the political system alongside the party is the state or government system itself, discussed more fully in Chapter Five. Early Marxist-Leninist doctrine posited that the state would "wither away" with the construction of communism and that "rule over men" would give way to the "administration of things." After 60 years of Soviet Communism and better than a quarter century of Communist rule in most other

Second World nations, the states seem to be growing rather than withering. As reflected in Leon Fischer's famous quotation, "What began to wither away was the idea of withering," contemporary Communist leaders seldom speak of the inevitable dissolution of the state. Dissolving the state would mean tearing down the elaborate bureaucracy on which Communist Party rule so heavily depends. Accordingly, the withering of the state appears to be a gamble Communist leaders are unwilling to take.

Another reorientation in doctrine in most Communist Party states that has to do with party rule involves the use of the phrase, "dictatorship of the proletariat." Because of the contradiction between the party monopoly of power and the "official" policy of a proletarian dictatorship, and because of the shrinking proletarian sector within the modernizing population, the proletarian-state concept slipped from usage in the USSR and was replaced in the 1977 Constitution by the "state of socialist toilers," in which the CPSU serves as "the leading and guiding force."

At the 25th Party Congress, then-General Secretary Leonid I. Brezhnev exclaimed:

> The Soviet people are aware that where the Party acts, success and victory are assured! The people trust the Party. The people wholeheartedly support the Party's domestic and foreign policy. This augments the Party's strength and serves as an inexhaustible source of energy.

With minor and generally insignificant exceptions, the leading roles of the Communist parties in the other Marxist-Leninist states are described similarly. One partial exception, however, is Yugoslavia; during the 1960s, the League of Communists of Yugoslavia (LCY) talked of "removing itself from power" by assuming a less central role in the political process.[3] In the resulting power vacuum, the frag-

---

[3]At the 6th Party Congress in 1952, the Yugoslav Communist Party changed its name to the League of Communists. This was a symbolic change related to the leaders' desire to alter the role of the party and, more importantly, to distinguish itself from the Soviet-dominated Communist parties of Eastern Europe.

ile political balance maintained by the LCY was upset when national (ethnic) conflict in the early 1970s threatened the unity and stability of the Yugoslav state. Fearing a factionalized and a possibly disintegrating state, Josip Broz Tito and the LCY leaders moved decisively to reassert the leading role of the Party in the government process.[4] The LCY is still less centralized and authoritarian than the CPSU and the Chinese Communist Party (CCP), but it has now assumed a considerably more orthodox "Leninist" position on the question of party rule.

In view of the high level of societal complexity and the growing diversity of political interests in most of these states, the monolithic dominance of the Communist parties is somewhat surprising and viewed by some Western observers as retarding political development. These observers contend that high levels of social pluralism and complexity require political expression and representation and that social and political development in modernizing industrial societies is facilitated by a more open, less controlled political process than that found among the Communist Party states. This point of view is widely held in the West, but it is heatedly challenged and denied in the Communist world.

Among the reasons for the Communist leaders' (particularly Soviet leaders') overriding concern with maintaining centralized party rule is their general distrust of foreign and internal hostile, anti-Communist forces. Externally, they view the capitalist West, particularly the United States, as an aggressive, imperialistic power that, if not challenged and checked, will exploit peoples and nations throughout the world. The best defense against this Western threat, in the eyes of the

Communist leaders, is strength at home; this is a capability that they believe can be guaranteed only through strict party rule.

There is also a distrust of forces at work within their own countries. Remnants of the pre-socialist system and signs of the continuing class struggle and bourgeois ideas are often considered present and require the vigilance of the Communist Party to keep them in check. There exists in this outlook a messianic vision that the party knows best, that it is really acting in the best interests of the working class; if the people will only give their unswerving support, the party will facilitate and hasten the eventual construction of communism. Although some party leaders occasionally register cynical, antiparty remarks in private, most are dedicated true believers convinced of the validity of this political philosophy and of their right to rule.

THE PARTY: MEMBERSHIP AND COMPOSITION

Who belongs to these Communist parties? As Table 4.1 indicates, only 6.7 percent of the Soviet people, 3.8 percent of the Chinese, and 10.9 percent of the Yugoslavs belong to the Communist parties in their countries. In other countries, membership ranges from a high of 15.2 percent in Korea to a low of 0.9 percent in Laos.[5] As one expert points out, the fact that only a minority of the populations in the Soviet Union and the other socialist states are party members does not mean that the majority are anti-Communist or opposed to the regime, rather:

> Party membership is demanding, and it is not easy to join. Nor does membership bring tangible rewards, although it does open some career opportunities that are virtually closed to non-Communists. Membership in the party may, indeed, bring with it some hardships. Theoretically, a member puts himself at the party's disposal when he joins; he may find himself sum-

---

[4]In a collection of speeches prepared for both domestic and foreign consumption, Tito and other LCY leaders outlined the LCY's revitalized policy role. High LCY official Stane Dolanc did so in particularly blunt terms: "We Communists are in power in this country. . . . This, comrades, must be openly stated, for there was a time [1960s] when it was shameful to admit this to anyone." (*Ideological and Political Offensive of the League of Communists of Yugoslavia* [Belgrade: Secretariat for Information, 1972], p. 46).

[5]As a result of the conflict in Cambodia (Kampuchea), Laos, and Vietnam in the early 1980s, the party figures for these states are either unavailable or approximate.

TABLE 4.1 Communist Party Membership

Country	Party Name	Total Communist Party Membership	Communist Party Membership as Percent of Population
China	Chinese Communist Party	40,000,000	3.8
USSR	Communist Party of the Soviet Union	18,500,000	6.7
Vietnam	Vietnamese Communist Party	1,730,214	2.9
Poland	Polish United Workers' Party	2,186,000	5.9
Yugoslavia	League of Communists of Yugoslavia	2,500,000	10.9
Romania	Communist Party of Romania	3,400,000	14.9
East Germany	Socialist Unity Party	2,202,277	13.1
North Korea	Korean Workers' Party	3,000,000	15.2
Czechoslovakia	Communist Party of Czechoslovakia	1,623,000	10.5
Hungary	Hungarian Socialist Workers' Party	232,000	2.1
Cuba	Communist Party of Cuba	434,143	4.3
Bulgaria	Bulgarian Communist Party	825,876	9.2
Cambodia	Khmer Communist Party	No current data	—
Laos	Lao People's Revolutionary Party	35,000	0.9
Albania	Albanian Party of Labor	122,000	4.2
Mongolia	Mongolian People's Revolutionary Party	76,240	4.0

SOURCE: Richard F. Staar, ed., *Yearbook on International Communist Affairs* (Stanford, Calif.: Hoover Institution Press, 1985).

moned to a political meeting or given some political assignment when he would rather do something else. Moreover, party members are supposed to provide a model for other Soviet citizens to follow; therefore, the Communist may find his private life scrutinized and his behavior called into account.[6]

Therefore, the low percentage of party membership may not be surprising at all. With the hardships involved, it is surprising that anyone belongs. There are a number of different factors, however, that lead people to join the party, and three are significant. First, some individuals are particularly achievement-oriented and have high aspirations for success. Joining the party, as Hammer noted, can open doors that might otherwise be closed. Others join the party because of the political influence it gives them. If one wants to pursue a career in politics or in some other line of government

[6]Darrell P. Hammer, *USSR: The Politics of Oligarchy* (Hinsdale, Ill.: Dryden, 1974), p. 166.

service, membership in the party is practically mandatory. Finally, there are those who join because of a spirit of conviction. Committed to the Marxist–Leninist doctrine, they perceive that their best opportunities for promoting communism and the betterment of the society are within the organizational structure of the party. In many respects, the motivations for joining are similar to those found for becoming involved in partisan politics in the United States.

Although citizens with such expectations continue to join, Communist parties are unlikely to become mass parties in the Western sense. One overriding reason for this results from the attitudes of the party leaders themselves. They prefer minority parties that include only the most dedicated, ideologically committed and "pure" citizens. This makes it easier to maintain party "correctness" and to ensure its role as the revolutionary vanguard of society. Because the parties are viewed as performing such a crucial and significant role in society, the leaders want to keep them small and to keep standards for party members high.

The Communist parties attempt to attract members from all sectors of their societies, although many states have difficulties keeping the peasant and workers' ranks sufficiently high to justify the toilers' or workers' orientation. At one time or another, most of the parties have undertaken campaigns to increase the number of peasants, workers, and minority nationalities among their members. The substantial increase (over 8 percent) in worker representation in the CPSU between 1957 and 1980 was the result of a campaign begun by Nikita S. Khrushchev and continued by his successors to increase proletarian involvement.

In all countries, the parties earnestly strive to ensure broad representation of all social classes. It is important to have communication channels linking the leadership to all sectors of society; this goal is best served by having party representatives drawn from all sectors of society.

Procedures governing entrance into the parties vary somewhat from country to country and, in some cases, from region to region. The procedures followed in the Soviet Union, however, are fairly representative and illustrate the strict standards that are maintained. When an individual wants to join the CPSU, he or she must be recommended by three persons, each of whom must have been a party member for five years and known the candidate well for one year. Once the application is prepared and brought before the local primary party organization, a two-thirds majority vote is required for admission as a candidate member. After serving for one year in this provisional status—a period when the candidate's work is closely monitored by peers—the application is again voted on by members of the local primary organization. If the individual receives a two-thirds vote, his or her file is sent to the next higher party level (usually city or district) where it is normally approved.[7]

[7]For a more detailed account of the Soviet selection procedures, see Hammer, *op. cit.*, pp. 176–177.

ORGANIZATIONAL STRUCTURE

PRIMARY ORGANIZATIONS

Figure 4.1 illustrates the typical organization of a Communist Party from the lowest level primary organization (what formerly were called the local party cells) to the highest-level party leader. The organizational structure of the party approximates a pyramid at the bottom of which are thousands of primary organizations based in factories, schools, collective farms, and the like. When an individual joins the party, it is this local organization that receives and processes the application. Recruitment of new members and ideological work (spreading official propaganda, political education, and so on) are major responsibilities of the primary organizations. These organizations also serve as ideological caretakers within factories, schools, and other institutions to ensure that attitudes and behavior correspond with the party's expectations. By linking with every social, economic, and territorial unit within the state, the primary organizations provide the central party with a communication network that reaches to the grass roots of their societies. There are over 400,000 primary organizations in the Soviet Union today.

The structure and organization of each cell varies somewhat according to the size of the organization and the country in which it is found. Typically, small organizations, such as those in stores or schools, elect a secretary who assumes a part-time role of directing the cell's party activities. Larger organizations, such as those in factories and universities, have a full-time secretary, an elected committee, and assorted assistants who serve the secretary in carrying out his or her work. To link these party cells to higher level organs, each primary organization elects a delegate (frequently the secretary) to represent the cell at the next highest level, usually the city or local district. This system of representation applies throughout the entire pyramid and has been called by some the dictatorship of the secretariat.

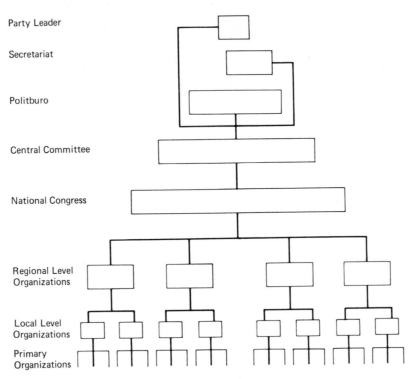

Figure 4.1 Communist Party organizational structure.

REGIONAL- AND LOCAL-LEVEL ORGANIZATIONS

The vast majority of party members work in part- and full-time capacities within the regional and local-level networks. The central party organization provides the regions with a relative degree of autonomy in the administration of party affairs. These regional organizations typically coordinate their own party conferences and have leadership organs that closely correspond with the national organization.

The regional-level party organizations in the Soviet Union are based on a federal structure. At the regional level, the parties of the 15 Soviet Union republics have the highest status. They hold party congresses once every two years. Next in order of importance are the regions and areas within the Soviet Union republics, followed by the towns, rural and urban districts, and so on down the list. Each of these organizational units has its own party networks, including full-time committees, offi-

cials, and elected delegates to represent the unit at the next highest level.

The CCP is also divided into regional and local party networks. The degree of regional party autonomy has been subject to the shifting desires of the central party leaders. During the Great Proletarian Cultural Revolution (GPCR) (1966–1969), for example, the provincial party structures were assaulted by both the national leaders and such grass-roots groups as the Red Guards. More recently, the provinces have regained some semblance of regional autonomy and are becoming a stronger force in making policy within their regions. Many of the new leaders emerging in the post-Mao era gained their experience in the regional organizations. Before assuming the post of premier in 1980, Zhao Ziyang was the head of the party organization in the province of Sichuan.

The Yugoslavs have the most formalized and autonomous regional party organizations. Each of the six republics and two autonomous provinces have regional congresses, central committees, and the usual executive party organs. Meeting regularly, these organs and their members have considerable power in determining regional party policy. In fact, when the central party organization withdrew partially from the political arena in the 1960s, the regional party organizations grew in status and power. Their vigorous pursuit of regional interests resulted in a high level of interregional conflict during this period, leading many to remark that Yugoslavia had a *de facto* multiparty system.

NATIONAL PARTY CONGRESS

In all Communist Party states, delegates from the regions and lower-level organizations tend to gather every four or five years to attend the national party congress. Called the All-Union Party Congress in the USSR and the National Party Congress in China and in Yugoslavia, these large and highly ceremonial meetings are filled with considerable party fanfare. As indicated in Figure 4.2, the meetings draw great crowds of delegates and, although they differ in many important respects from the national conventions of the Democratic and Republican parties in the United States, they hold some interesting similarities. In addition to the attendance of delegates from every section of the country and the pomp and circumstance (not to mention cocktails and parties) characteristic of the American conventions, the Communist Party congresses are also blessed with the speeches of the contemporary party dignitaries.[8] The ranking party leader typically opens the congress with a stirring call to arms that applauds the party's accomplishments and draws attention to its future goals.

Also bearing a certain similarity to American political party conventions is a statement of the party's platform, outlining the policy goals and directives that will guide the party's work until the next congress. To an even greater extent than in the United States, however, hammering out the platform is the right and responsibility of party leaders and is usually completed far in advance of the formal congress.

The most significant difference between Communist Party congresses and American political party conventions is the conspicuous absence of opposition, debate, and healthy political rancor. Generally, all proposals, all candidates, and all speeches are met with a uniform unanimity of opinion (and applause).[9] Although the rank and file's attendance at these meetings is an exciting event that few would want to miss, when it comes to political influence, they might as well have stayed home. The primary function of the delegates is to ratify the policy proposals of the leaders rather than to have any significant impact on the proposals themselves. Centralization of power is an undeniable fact of Communist political rule, and it is given clear expression in the functioning of the national congresses.

In theory, the delegates also come to the national congresses to elect the new central committee that will serve until the next congress. In fact, however, the slate of candidates is typically prepared in advance by the leaders themselves, which results in the unanimous election of the official slate. Rank-and-file delegates have little, if any, effect on the selection of their highest leaders. The content of the speeches, the selection of the central committee, and the congress in general is carefully orchestrated by the top party leadership.

CENTRAL COMMITTEE

Because of their great size, the infrequency of their meetings, and the general lack of expertise and information among the rank-and-file

---

[8]The congresses are colorful and festive occasions with workers and intellectuals, city dwellers and peasants, and members of national minorities in traditional dress rubbing shoulders in crowded reception halls. To emphasize the parties' worker orientation, welders, collective farmers, and other common folk grace the official program with presentations alongside those of the party leaders.

[9]There have been important exceptions to this trend. Yugoslav party meetings, and, for limited periods of time, those in Czechoslovakia and Poland, have been the scene of serious debate.

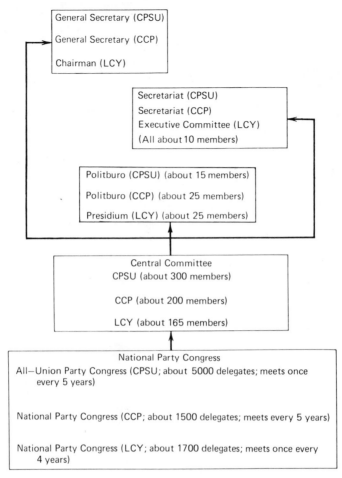

Figure 4.2 National Communist Party organizations, Soviet Union (CPSU), China (CCP), and Yugoslavia (LCY)—all figures are approximate and change periodically.

delegates, the national party congresses have little meaningful power as policymaking bodies. Although affected by some of the same factors, the central committee is a far more influential body. The central committees are large, generally ranging from 100 to 300 members within the different states, but not nearly so enormous as the bodies that supposedly elect them. Meeting periodically, usually every few months or so, the central committees are theoretically considered the most important party organization within their states. The Central Committee of the CPSU has its role outlined in the party statutes:

The Central Committee . . . directs all the activity of the Party, and of the local organs, selects and appoints leading personnel, directs the work of central governmental and public organizations of toilers through Party groups within them, creates various Party organs, agencies, and enterprises of the Party, and directs their activities, appoints the editors of the central newspapers and magazines operating under its control, allocates funds from the Party budget and controls their use.

In reality, however, the bulk of these responsibilities are reserved for higher organs within the various parties, organs to which we now turn.

POLITBURO, SECRETARIAT, AND PARTY LEADER

Although the central committees in theory hold enormous power, they delegate the bulk of it to the bodies and individuals they typically elect—the politburos, the secretariats, and the party leaders (see Figure 4.2).[10] The politburo is an exceedingly important decision-making institution with a great deal to say concerning who gets what in Communist Party states. Generally meeting at least weekly, this group of party members transacts the highest level and most important business on the nation's agenda. The sizes of these groups vary considerably over time and among the countries. Yet they are generally small enough to transact political business. Similar to cabinets in the First World states, the politburos are considered the most significant and powerful policymaking bodies in Communist Party states.

Formal power to make policy is given to the politburo, but the secretariats have considerable power and important responsibilities of their own. The Soviet Party statutes note that the CPSU Secretariat is ''to direct current work, mainly in . . . the organization and supervision over the fulfillment of Party decisions.'' As the organizational arm of the politburo, the secretariats supervise the implementation and execution of party policies. Meeting almost daily, these bodies have occasionally overshadowed the politburos, particularly in times of crisis, by making policy proposals, issuing decrees, and ensuring administrative execution.

The Chinese Central Committee Secretariat was abolished in 1967 and reestablished in February 1980. During that period, the Politburo Standing Committee—often thought of as the Secretariat but, in fact, a different body and much more than an administrative body—was even more powerful than the CCP Politburo and was, indeed, the topmost decision-making body in China. During the unstable period following Mao's death in 1976, for example, the Politburo Standing Committee convened an enlarged politburo session and undertook a number of important actions of great consequence to the future course of Chinese politics. Perhaps the most important was the purging of Mao's wife, Jiang Qing, and three additional members of the CCP Politburo, the so-called Gang of Four. Today the CCP Central Committee Secretariat is once again a major locus of power. Because of the relative absence of formal rules outlining the sharing and use of power in the upper party echelons as well as a general disregard for statutes and rules during times of crisis, the power relationships between these highest organs can become rather fluid.

As a result of their heavy supervisory, implementation, and execution functions, the Party secretariats control and rely on large bureaucracies to assist them in these tasks. The bureaucracies are divided into departments organized according to broad policy areas (defense, agriculture, etc.). Generally, each member of the secretariat is in charge of certain departments and specializes in these policy areas. In overseeing the policy implementation and execution in these different departments, the secretaries have a major impact on the policy process.

Also elected by the central committees, the party leaders have traditionally been the highest ranking officials in their states, outranking the top government officers, such as the president or the premier. The first among equals in their states and in their parties, the party leaders preside over the work of the politburos, control the central party apparatus, and act as the primary spokespersons for the party and for the state.

THE PARTY PERSONNEL

With approximately 40 million party members in China, over 18.5 million in the Soviet Union, and nearly 2.5 million in Yugoslavia, roles and personalities within the party structures are

---

[10]Because some of the counterpart institutions are named differently in the three countries, the Soviet designation is used when referring to the general institution.

numerous and diverse. Beginning at the top of the party hierarchy (illustrated in Figure 4.1), we consider some of the officials, ranging from the highest-ranking party leader in the nation's capital to secretaries of the primary organizations in the outlying hinterland.

PARTY LEADERS

Lenin was the supreme leader of Russia from 1917 to 1924.[11] After Joseph Stalin's assumption of power (he became General Secretary of the party in 1922), the position of party secretary soon overpowered all other political offices, including the leading government positions. In his so-called testament, Lenin warned his comrades that Stalin had already become too powerful and did not use his power with sufficient caution. Shortly before his death, Lenin added a postscript to his testament, suggesting that Stalin be removed from his post. As history shows, Stalin was not dislodged; rather, he moved decisively to increase his power within the role of General Secretary. Under his administration, this role of party leader became the dominant position in Soviet politics. This pattern is also reflected in all other Communist Party states through the present day.[12]

On Stalin's death in the spring of 1953, a power struggle between Nikita S. Khrushchev and a number of high CPSU officials ensued. Having a solid political base by virtue of being a member of both the Secretariat and the Politburo, Khrushchev soon became the dominant figure and had his title upgraded to First Secretary.[13] Unlike Stalin's leadership as General Secretary, however, Khrushchev's was never autocratic. Not only was he less powerful, but his reign of power was relatively short-lived. In the fall of 1964, while on vacation in the Crimea, Khrushchev was summarily summoned back to party headquarters in the Kremlin and ousted from his job. As Khrushchev learned, central committees elect party secretaries—but they also can fire them. Because of shortcomings in his agricultural policy, the embarrassment and failure of the Cuban missile episode, and other alleged shortcomings, the free-spirited, impulsive Khrushchev's career was abruptly brought to an end.[14] Replacing Khrushchev as head of the CPSU was Leonid I. Brezhnev, who headed the party for two decades, longer than both Lenin and Khrushchev. Beginning his stewardship of the CPSU under Khrushchev's former title of First Secretary, Brezhnev assumed Stalin's upgraded title of General Secretary in 1966 and the state presidency in 1977.[15]

In November of 1982, General Secretary Brezhnev succumbed to the frailties of advancing age and died at the age of 75. Who was to replace Brezhnev? Considerable attention focussed on the Kremlin as the Soviet leaders prepared to chose a successor. American Kremlinologist Myron Rush noted that the most striking feature of the Brezhnev succession was the absence of clearly qualified candidates who possessed not only good health but also broad political experience.[16] Many of the

[11]Lenin was referred to as premier, because he was chairman of the Council of People's Commissars and also a member of the Politburo, which at that time had no formal head.

[12]Stalin ruled in the dual position as head of both party and state. Although the tendency in most states during the post-Stalin era has been to divide these posts, General Secretary Leonid I. Brezhnev combined them once again in 1977 by assuming the ousted Nikolai V. Podgorny's role as President. Brezhnev's successors, Yuri Andropov, Konstantin Chernenko, and Mikhail Gorbachev, also assumed both positions.

[13]Georgi M. Malenkov initially replaced Stalin as head of both party and state. His leadership evolved into a triumvirate in which he shared power with Vyacheslav M. Molotov and Lavrenti P. Beria. Beria's arrest and Khrushchev's ascent to increased power in 1953 led to Khrushchev's election as First Secretary in September 1953.

[14]Khrushchev lived out the remaining years of his life in retirement on the outskirts of Moscow, in a *dacha* (''country home'') supplied by the state.

[15]For an excellent review of the Brezhnev era, see Jerry F. Hough, ''The Man and the System,'' *Problems of Communism* 25 (2) (1976): 1–17.

[16]Myron Rush, ''Succeeding Brezhnev,'' *Problems of Communism* 32 (1) (1983): 2.

candidates were older than Brezhnev; others had careers that were highly specialized. Brezhnev's apparent choice for a successor was Konstantin Chernenko, who had the unfortunate image of being Brezhnev's creature and an undistinguished staff man who had never been the responsible head of a high level party or government organization. Despite Brezhnev's apparent desire to make Chernenko his heir, Yuri Andropov, former head of the Soviet intelligence network (the KGB), moved decisively to assume the top party spot. Having capitalized on Brezhnev's physical frailties and political vulnerabilities during the final years of the former party leader's life, Andropov brought some strong qualifications to the job. Described by Kremlinologist Rush as highly intelligent, dispassionate and cool under fire, knowledgeable, and possessed of political courage, Andropov was impelled by a belief in himself as indispensable for the Soviet Union's salvation from increasing corruption and future economic and political decline.[17]

In the seven months following Brezhnev's death, the 68-year-old Andropov quickly took over the top party and government positions—recognition as "head" of the Politburo, chairman (or president) of the Supreme Soviet Presidium, leader of the Defense Council—something that had taken Brezhnev 13 years to accomplish. Once in office, Andropov moved decisively to wipe out corruption and turn around the Soviet Union's decline.

However, Andropov's reign was short-lived. By August 1983, nine months after assuming Brezhnev's mantle, Andropov had dropped from public view. According to official medical reports, Andropov had developed serious kidney problems in February of 1982; his condition deteriorated sharply in January of 1984, and he died the next month.

Many predicted that the Soviet Union would then turn to a younger successor—perhaps the 53-year-old Mikhail Gorbachev or the 61-year-old Grigori Romanov. However, the

After rapidly rising through the ranks of the Communist Party of the Soviet Union (CPSU), Mikhail Gorbachev assumed the top party position of First Secretary in 1985. Gorbachev's appointment appears to be ushering in a new generation of younger and better-educated Soviet leaders.

CPSU Politburo stuck with the most experienced generation and chose Brezhnev's original heir, 73-year-old Konstantin Chernenko. However, Chernenko also proved to be a short-term leader and 13 months later succumbed to ill health. Having long suffered from emphysema, Chernenko died in March 1985 of heart failure, following the deterioration of his lungs and liver.

Soviet leadership then underwent a swift, and what is proving to be a far-reaching, transformation in the course of a single day. Chernenko's death was announced in the afternoon of March 11 and by evening, Mikhail Gorbachev was installed as the new CPSU First Secretary. A native Russian, Gorbachev

[17]Ibid., p. 3.

was born in 1931 in the Stavrolpol region, an agrarian area, in the Russian heartland. According to his official biography, his parents were peasants and he worked on local collective farms as a youth. Bright, talented, and ambitious, Gorbachev went to study law at Moscow University in 1955. Unlike previous high CPSU officials, most of whom had little advanced education, Gorbachev earned a degree from Moscow University and another from a correspondence school in agricultural economics. Representing a new generation of Soviet leaders, he is the first leader to have come from a generation that did not take part in the Second World War and that received a full education in the post-war era.

After graduating from Moscow University, Gorbachev went back to Stavropol and began his rapid climb up the political ladder. He first became head of the Komsomol, later took charge of the collective farms in the region, and then, in 1970, became First Secretary of the Communist Party in Stavropol. In 1978, he was brought to Moscow to fill the vacant and powerful post of the Central Committee Secretary for Agriculture. The next year in a remarkable and meteoric rise, Gorbachev was catapulted into the CPSU Politburo, first as a candidate member, and, in 1980, as a full member. Although passed over for the top job when Brezhnev died in 1982, and again in 1984 when Andropov died, he took this time to acquire more experience and expand his power base. During this period, Gorbachev acquired considerable responsibility for matters concerning the economy, culture and ideology, personnel, and some aspects of world Communist and foreign affairs.

When Chernenko's health began to fail in 1984 and 1985, forcing him to drop more and more of his official activities, Gorbachev assumed a leading role in the work of the CPSU Secretariat and Politburo. Chernenko apparently supported Gorbachev's growing role and turned over considerable responsibilities to him. Although a power struggle was being waged behind the scenes at the highest levels of Soviet politics, the political momentum was very much behind Gorbachev. Working to his advantage were personnel changes made during Andropov's brief tenure. Andropov brought a number of younger people into the top party leadership who were natural allies to Gorbachev. By the time Chernenko's health failed, Gorbachev had assumed an almost unassailable position.

Gorbachev is likely to become a powerful, long-term Soviet leader. According to tradition established in the Brezhnev period, he is now entitled to the presidency of the Presidium of the Supreme Soviet (giving him the honorific title of "president" as Soviet Head of State) and the permanent chairmanship of the Defense Council. These are positions of considerable power and importance in the Soviet state. A man of substantial tactical skill, Gorbachev has already set about consolidating his political base. Two weeks after taking power, Gorbachev began a campaign to sweep out incompetent, corrupt, and aging party officials and replace them with younger, better educated, and more technocratic-minded successors. Among the first to go were the 74-year-old Minister for Power and Electrification and the 70-year-old First Secretary of the Kirov Region. In addition, at the April 1985 Central Committee plenum of the CPSU—the first to be held after Gorbachev assumed power—three staunch allies were brought into the Politburo. They were the 62-year-old head of the KGB, Viktor Chebrikov; 64-year-old Yegor Ligachov; and 55-year-old Nikolai Ryzhkov. Gorbachev is likely to extend his authority further at the 27th Party Congress, in the Central Committee to be elected at the Congress, and in the new five-year plan endorsed by the Congress.

It should be emphasized in summary, then, that the party leadership of the Soviet Union has been dramatically transformed in the 1980s. After the Brezhnev period of great leadership stability, the Soviet Union entered a period of rapid change. No longer can it be said that the Soviet Union is run by a gerontocracy. At the time of Brezhnev's death, the average age of the Politburo was over 70; but this was changed suddenly in 1985 once Gorbachev assumed power. At the beginning of 1985, 7 of 12 Politburo members were over 70; by mid-year, a majority of the 13 members were under 65, led by Gorbachev, who at 54 remained the youngest of them all.

Until September 1976, the People's Republic of China had known only a single leader of the CCP. As one of the founders of the CCP in 1921, Mao Zedong held a variety of positions in the Party before becoming its head during the period of the Long March (1934–1935). When the People's Republic was proclaimed in October 1949, Mao became chairman of the Republic as well as chairman of the CCP. The Chairman of the People's Republic is considered the head of state and is in charge of a number of executive and ceremonial responsibilities. Giving up the head of state role in 1959, Mao remained the reigning head of the CCP until his death. Although choosing Mao's successor was a favorite pastime of many Sinologists, most were surprised when Hua Guofeng, a rela-

tively unknown party official from the province of Hunan, assumed the party leadership on Mao's death. Hua, earlier designated as premier to replace Zhou Enlai, who had died in January 1976, assumed the dual roles of chairman of the CCP and premier of the State Council.

Hua was apparently Mao's personal choice for an heir; Mao was quoted as saying to Hua: ''With you in charge, I am at ease.'' However, Chairman Hua's leadership was short-lived. Deng Xiaoping and the so-called moderates in the CCP—those who opposed the ideological excesses of Maoism and favored more pragmatic reforms to modernize China— skillfully challenged and successfully dislodged Hua from his leadership posts. In September 1980 Hua resigned as premier in favor of Zhao Ziyang, a member of Deng's moderate coalition. Although Hua cited the party principle of collective leadership (to be discussed later in this chapter) as the reason for his resig-

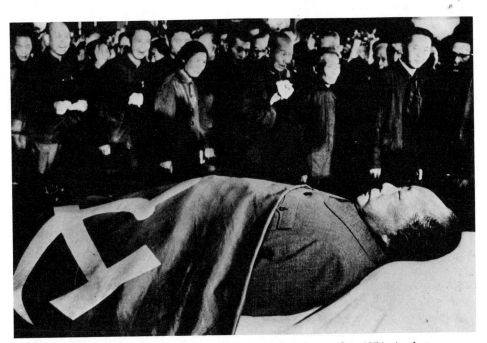

Chinese mourners file by Mao's body at his funeral in September 1976. At that very moment, an intense struggle for succession was underway. It resulted in the elevation of Hua Guofeng to take on Mao's mantle and the purging of the ''Gang of Four,'' which included Mao's wife, Jiang Qing.

nation, it was apparent that he was losing a struggle for power with the moderates. Two months later Hua also resigned the chairmanship of the CCP's Military Commission and, most importantly, the overall chairmanship of the party which went to another member of the moderate coalition, Hu Yaobang. These demotions were officially announced in June of 1981 when a lengthy party resolution critically assessed both Mao and Hua. Hua was charged with fostering a cult of personality, propagating erroneous policies and slogans and opposing correct ones, and committing other transgressions.[18] Finally, in September 1982, Hua was dropped from the politburo and relegated to a much more minor position in the Central Committee. The changes in the CCP leadership put the moderates Deng, Zhao, and Hu in a position of dominance in the Chinese political structure. Mao's designated successor, Hua, and those associated with Mao's rule, were clearly in decline.

The recent leadership changes and power struggles in the Soviet Union and China provide an important lesson about Communist Party rule in Second World states. We sometimes have the misleading impression that Communist leaders, once in power, are firmly in command. While they do have considerable power, we should recognize that power struggles often occur and that politics at the apex of the party pyramid has often been described as in a state of "constant conflict."[19] Furthermore, the many uncertainties surrounding changes in Communist leadership, and the absence of a formal, institutionalized succession process, sometimes result in surprises. When power-hungry leaders vie for the top spot, many things can happen.

In the same tradition as Mao, Tito was an organizer of the Yugoslav Communist Party and rose to the position of party leader before World War II. When the Yugoslav Communists assumed power in the postwar period, Tito became the head of both party and state. Tito had his special status written into the 1974 Constitution:

> In view of the historic role of Josip Broz Tito . . . and in line with the expressed will of the working people and citizens, nations and nationalities of Yugoslavia—the S.F.R.Y. [Socialist Federal Republic of Yugoslavia] Assembly may . . . elect Josip Broz Tito for an unlimited term of office.

Although Tito, like Mao, was not particularly active politically in the latter years of his career, he assumed a high level of official power through his dual role as head of the LCY and the state. On Tito's death in 1980, the LCY chairmanship was rotated on a yearly basis, and Yugoslavia moved to a more collective form of rule.

Table 4.2 shows that most party leaders have had an unusually lengthy term of office. It has proven exceedingly difficult, in most cases, to unseat a party leader in view of the leader's control over information, the military, and political power. Although Khrushchev's ouster, Hua's demotions, and Edward Gierek's and Stanislaw Kania's forced retirements in Poland demonstrate that it is not impossible, party leaders generally command widespread support among other high-level leaders and the mass populace; when they lose this support, the challengers still face considerable odds in mounting a movement that will successfully unseat the incumbent. The ouster of Khrushchev was successful because of his increasing unpopularity among the Politburo members and their ability to win the Central Committee's support of their anti-Khrushchev plot. The uncertainty of political succession, the lack of a regularized circulation of leaders at the highest party levels, and the general absence of any formal, constitutional provisions for replacing party leaders are unresolved shortcomings of Communist political rule.[20]

---

[18]See "The Resolution on Certain Questions of Our Party since the Founding of the People's Republic of China," *Beijing Review* 24 (27) (1981): 10–39.

[19]See, for example, Richard Thornton, "The Structure of Communist Politics," *World Politics* 24 (4) (1972): 498–517.

[20]Although the party statutes typically call for the election of a new party leader on the termination or death of the previous one, the struggle and jockeying for power within the highest level of the party makes this a rather contentious, conflict-ridden process.

Hu Yaobang and Zhao Ziyang sharing a light moment at the Twelfth National Congress of the Communist Party of China.

THE HIGH OFFICIALS:
POLITBURO AND SECRETARIAT

The highest party organs are staffed by individuals (usually men) who have generally worked their way up, step by step, from regional organizations to the national center of political power. Because of the great diversity of policy issues dealt with at this level of policymaking, members of the Politburo generally have greater expertise and special responsibilities in certain, specialized policy areas. Andrei A. Gromyko's considerable experience in international relations and his position as minister of foreign affairs make him a natural expert in the field of foreign policy. In policy discussions concerning relations with the West or Soviet involvement in the Third World, Gromyko's opinions are likely to have considerable weight even though all issues are decided through collective decision making. When the members of the Politburo assemble to discuss a particular issue, years of direct and extensive expertise in the various matters weigh heavily in the decision-making process.

High officials in Communist Party states tend to be quite old. Accordingly, the aging Soviet Politburo was struck by a succession of deaths (primarily from old age) in the 1980s resulting in the appointment of a number of younger Party leaders, led by the new CPSU Secretary Gorbachev. Some of the recent appointments, like the 64 year old Ligachov, have worked with Gorbachev to purge many of the older, more incompetent Party officials at all levels of Soviet government. Others, like the 55 year old Ryzhkov, an engineering graduate and former plant director of a huge engineering conglomerate, appear to represent a new role model for Soviet officials. Whether this trend will result in a significant and long term influx

	Initial Leader	Initial Leader's Fate	Present Leader	Years as Leader (1985)
	Enver Hoxha	Died in office	Ramiz Alia	0
	Georgi Dimitrov	Died in office	Todor Zhivkov	31
Cambodia	Pol Pot	Ousted[a]	Heng Samrin	4
China	Mao Zedong	Died in office	Hu Yaobang	4
Cuba	Fidel Castro	Still in office	Fidel Castro	27
Czechoslovakia	Klement Gottwald	Died in office	Gustav Husak	17
East Germany	Walter Ulbricht	Retired	Erich Honecker	14
Hungary	Mátyás Rakosi	Ousted	Janos Kadar	29
Laos	Kaysone Phomvihan	Still in office	Kaysone Phomvihan	13
Mongolia	Khorloin Choibalsan and Sukhe-Bator	Died in office	Zhambyn Batmunkh	1
North Korea	Kim Il Sung	Still in office	Kim Il Sung	40
Poland	Wladyslaw Gomulka	Ousted	Wojciech Jaruzelski	4
Romania	Gheorghe Gheorghiu-Dej	Died in office	Nicolae Ceausescu	20
Soviet Union	Vladimir Ilyich Lenin	Died in office	Mikhail Gorbachev	0
Vietnam	Ho Chi Minh and Truong Chinh	Died in office	Le Duan	25
Yugoslavia	Josip Broz Tito	Died in office	(rotates yearly)	—

[a]In late 1978, the Vietnamese Communist Party asserted control over large portions of Cambodia and, in January 1979, drove the Pol Pot regime from Phnom Penh. In 1985, guerrilla war between Pol Pot and his forces and those of the pro-Vietnam Heng Samrin (a Pol Pot deserter) continued.

of younger, more technocratic, and better educated leaders remains to be seen, but it is clear that the CPSU Politburo is much changed under Gorbachev's leadership.

The Secretariat, like the Politburo, has no fixed number of members. Although the number of party secretaries in the CPSU Secretariat has averaged about 10 in the last decade, there have been as few as three in the past. Unlike the nonsecretary members of the Politburo, who often hold high positions in the government, members of the Secretariat hold no other position than that of party secretary. Charged with supervising the work of the CPSU, these full-time professionals rely heavily on the departmental personnel under their administration. These individuals are professional administrators responsible for the implementation and execution of policies adopted by the national party and government organs.

The mid-1970s through the early 1980s were years of enormous turmoil and change within the highest leadership bodies of the CCP. Mao Zedong spent his last 10 years searching for a successor in hopes of preparing a stable succession that would follow his passing. Mao lost faith in two successors in the last decade—Liu Shaoqi and Lin Biao—and entered the mid-1970s with no clear heir apparent.[21] Although Mao did not consider Zhou Enlai (his second-in-command in the 1970s) as an heir to the chairmanship mantle, he did hope to have Zhou oversee an orderly succession after his death. However, on January 8, 1976, Zhou Enlai succumbed to the advances of old age and Mao's succession plans suffered another setback.[22]

[21]Liu was dismissed for being a "capitalist roader" during the GPCR in 1968 and Lin was reportedly killed fleeing to the USSR following an abortive anti-Mao plot in 1971.

[22]For a discussion of this period, see Parris Chang, "China's Politics and Policies: Mao's Last Stand?" Problems of Communism 25 (4) (1976): 1–17.

As the fall of 1976 approached, it was clear that the life of the fading Mao was nearing its end. Dignitaries who visited Beijing were permitted only brief sessions with the octogenarian and on September 9, 1976, the Great Helmsman died. Although silence initially surrounded the succession, news began to leak that called attention to a power struggle within the CCP Politburo and Standing Committee. Amidst the turmoil and within days after Mao's passing, the Politburo selected Hua Guofeng as Mao's successor. Moving decisively to consolidate his uncertain position, Hua and his moderate associates purged four of Mao's most ardent and prominent followers, the so-called Gang of Four. Accused of a variety of crimes against the Chinese people and Mao, the "four dogs" were vilified in wall posters that appeared throughout the country describing the culprits' antiparty plot. Some posters accused the zealots of "tormenting . . . vexing . . . and nagging" Mao to death. Others flatly referred to Mao's wife as his "killer." As noted previously, Hua's reign at the top of the party hierarchy was short-lived. Even though Hua engineered the coup that ousted the Gang of Four, many Chinese blamed Hua for collaborating with the radicals prior to Mao's death. This and other developments led to Hua's downgrading and to the rise of Deng Xiaoping and the moderates in the early 1980s.

The ascent to a position on the politburo or secretariat is usually a long and arduous process, yet a member's downfall can sometimes occur with surprising speed. After being revealed as two of the "persons in authority who are taking the capitalist road" during the GPCR, Liu Shaoqi and Deng Xiaoping lost Mao and the CCP Politburo's support and confidence and were dropped from its membership. Liu was banished from politics. Deng, on the other hand, made a comeback and was appointed vice premier and named to the CCP Politburo in 1973. Much to the chagrin of those who rehabilitated him, Deng proved to be an "unrepentant capitalist roader" after all, was purged from the political arena once again in 1976—only to return again in 1977 to become

the most powerful political actor during China's modernization program.[23]

Abrupt downfalls also have been experienced in both the highest CPSU and LCY leadership bodies. Tito's earlier heir apparent, Aleksandar Ranković, was ousted from his leading party and government positions in 1967 for committing a number of inexcusable transgressions, not the least of which was the bugging of Tito's private quarters. Two members of the CPSU Politburo, Pyotr Y. Shelest and G. I. Voronov, lost the support of their colleagues and were expelled in 1973 from their positions for assorted policy shortcomings. In 1977, Nikolai V. Podgorny, a member of the CPSU Politburo and president of the Soviet government, also lost the support of his comrades and was dismissed from both official positions.

Because the politburos and secretariats are collective bodies and have no formal procedures for rotating and replacing their members, it is the collective membership that determines the fate of an individual member. Although the party leader usually has somewhat more influence than the others, all members are of critical importance when it comes to leadership changes. If a certain individual loses the confidence of a majority of the body's membership, his or her future is cast in doubt. This leads to the inevitable in-fighting and contentious behavior associated with bureaucratic politics.

Finally, it should be noted that politburos and secretariats have had quite different relationships to the party leaders at different times and in different countries. Stalin intimidated members of the CPSU Politburo during the 1930s and 1940s and clearly dominated the meetings and the general policymaking process. Members of the Politburo were often summoned to Stalin's home in the middle of the night where the pathological leader would criticize and ridicule them. John A. Armstrong and Darrell P. Hammer note that Stalin was

[23]Under Deng's leadership, Liu Shaoqi was also rehabilitated posthumously in the post-Mao period.

even able to have some Politburo members shot during his leadership of the CPSU.[24]

THE UP-AND-COMERS: THE CENTRAL COMMITTEE

If we were to gather the leading national and state government officials as well as the officials of the political parties in the United States and if we were to include a sampling of leading representatives of the diplomatic, military, labor, and scientific communities as well, we would have a body fairly similar to the central committees found in Communist Party states. The central committees are diverse groups that draw representatives from virtually every social and geographic sector in the country. The convening of the central committee is a gathering of the power elite of the state, a meeting of powerful figures who, to a great extent, have the formal (not *de facto*) responsibility for making policy decisions for the entire populace.

Because the central committees elect the politburos and secretariats from among their own ranks, representatives of these two bodies are automatic members of the central committees. The largest bloc of members in the central committees are the party secretaries from the territorial party organizations. In the early 1980s, approximately one-third of the CPSU Central Committee were secretaries of the republic and *oblast* ("regional") party organizations. The next largest bloc typically comes from the central government institutions discussed in Chapter Five. These members represent heads of the central ministries, various departments, and committees.

In some Communist systems, a large group of central committee members are drawn from the military. This is particularly true in China, where the People's Liberation Army (PLA) has played a central role in politics. As Yugoslavia prepared for the Tito succession in the 1970s and became more concerned with the problems of continuity and political stability, the number of representatives from the Yugoslav People's Army (YPA) swelled within the LCY Central Committee.

Also represented in the central committees are members of the diplomatic corps, the highest officials from the provincial governments, and a number of special groups. Typically included are representatives of the scientific communities and intelligentsia, heads of trade unions and other official national organizations, and a few token representatives from blue-collar and peasant communities.

This collection of individuals usually works closely with the Politburo and Secretariat. There have been exceptions, however, as represented by Stalin's purging of the CPSU Central Committee in the 1930s. Khrushchev once played the Central Committee against the CPSU Politburo, only to have it side some years later with the Politburo to bring about his removal. Theoretically, the central committees could play a much more influential role vis-à-vis their party leaders and leading organs. Possessing the power to hire and fire, they could pressure the leadership into accepting policy positions they might not otherwise support. This is an infrequent phenomenon, however, and unlikely to be followed much in the future. The central committees meet only infrequently, are not as well organized as the politburos and secretariats, and find it difficult from an organizational viewpoint to challenge these higher bodies. In addition, the up-and-coming status of a majority of their members might be ruined in an unsuccessful assault on the leaders who control their destinies.

THE PARTY PROFESSIONALS: *APPARATCHIKI*

Proceeding down the party hierarchies, we encounter an important sector (approximately 2 to 3 percent of all party members) who are engaged in full-time party work. These are the so-called *apparatchiki*, the paid party functionaries who serve in the central, regional, and local party offices. Although they do not possess decision-making powers at the national level, they often have influential positions in the areas of policy implementation and execution.

[24]John A. Armstrong, *The Politics of Totalitarianism* (New York: Random House, 1961), pp. 14, 48, 200; Hammer, *op. cit.*, p. 193.

These officials are also up-and-comers in the sense that many aspire to, and may attain, higher levels within the party network. Holding ministerial and cabinet positions in the nation's bureaucracy or in other organizations such as the party newspapers, journals, and publishing houses, these officials are often a step away from the central committee. At the regional and local levels, the *apparatchiki* have powerful positions within their respective political jurisdictions.

The *apparatchiki* represent a variety of social and occupational backgrounds. Although the bulk of these officials in the immediate post-revolutionary years were individuals who fought in the revolution and were awarded their positions as a result of their participation, there is now a trend toward increased professionalism among the middle-class *apparatchiki*. Now, most have attended special party training schools; in addition, most have completed secondary educations and many have earned a university degree.

THE RANK-AND-FILE ACTIVISTS

The largest bloc of party members are at the bottom of the hierarchy and represent those millions of rank-and-file volunteers at the disposal of the party. Although some may receive part-time pay for their party activities, the majority volunteer for work out of a sense of civic duty. Drawn from all sectors of the population, they are decidedly less "middle class" than the *apparatchiki* and higher level party officials. In China and the Southeast Asian Communist Party states, the majority of these volunteers are peasants; in the USSR and Eastern Europe, many are industrial workers drawn from the skilled and unskilled ranks. Some are apathetic and unenthusiastic, but the majority attend the meetings of the primary organizations and carry out the responsibilities expected as a part of their membership. These rank-and-file activists represent a local power elite who predominate in the leadership roles within their communities, work places, and social organizations. But, with increased influence and status come the risks of increased responsibil-

ity and political accountability. Those who would rather spend their evenings watching television or talking with friends and family avoid joining the party because they are aware of the many burdens of membership. As in states throughout the world, these represent the great mass of the population, the silent majority who are willing to leave politics in the hands of others.

PARTY RULES AND PRACTICES

Unlike American political parties, Communist parties require more from their members than occasional financial contributions, verbal support, and turnout at key elections. What is expected of party members is made abundantly clear in the CPSU rules:

1. To fight for the creation of the material and technical base of communism, to serve as an example of the Communist attitude toward labor, to raise labor productivity, to take the initiative in all that is new and progressive, to support and propagate advanced experience, to master technology, to improve his [the party member's] qualifications, to safeguard and increase public, socialist property—the foundation of the might and the prosperity of the Soviet homeland;

2. To carry out party decisions firmly and undeviatingly, to explain the policy of the party to the masses, to help strengthen and broaden the party's ties with the people, to be considerate and attentive toward people, to respond promptly to the wants and needs of the working people;

3. To take an active part in the political life of the country, in the management of state affairs, and in economic and cultural construction, to set an example in the fulfillment of public duty to help develop and strengthen Communist social relations;

4. To master Marxist–Leninist theory, to raise his [the party member's] ideological level and to contribute to the molding and rearing of the man of Communist society. To lead a resolute struggle against any manifestations of bourgeois ideology, remnants of a private-property psychology, religious prejudices, and other survivals of the past, to observe the principles of Communist morality and to place public interests above personal ones;

5. To be an active proponent of the ideas of so-

cialist internationalism and Soviet patriotism among the masses of the working people, to combat survivals of nationalism and chauvinism, to contribute by work and deed to strengthening the friendship of peoples of the USSR and the fraternal ties of the Soviet people with the peoples of the socialist countries and the proletariat and working people of all countries;

6. To strengthen the ideological and organizational unity of the party in every way, to safeguard the party against the infiltration of persons unworthy of the lofty title of Communist, to be truthful and honest with the party and the people, to display vigilance, to preserve party and state secrets;

7. To develop criticism and self-criticism, to boldly disclose shortcomings and strive for their removal, to combat ostentation, conceit, complacency, and localism, to rebuff firmly any attempts to suppress criticism, to speak out against any actions detrimental to the party and the state and to report them to party bodies, up to and including the Central Committee of the CPSU;

8. To carry out unswervingly the party line in the selection of personnel according to their political and work qualifications. To be uncompromising in all cases of violation of the Leninist principles of the selection and training of personnel;

9. To observe party and state discipline, which is equally binding on all party members. The party has a single discipline, a single law for all Communists, regardless of their services or the positions they hold.

10. To help in every way to strengthen the defensive might of the USSR, to wage a tireless struggle for peace and friendship among peoples.[25]

This is obviously a formidable set of rules, far more than is expected of Democrats in the United States or Social Democrats in Italy. Those who do not fulfill their responsibilities and obligations are subject to dismissal. Hough surveys CPSU admission and dismissal policy over a 60-year span and illustrates that the leaders are committed to ensuring a party membership supportive of regime goals.[26] For

example, the Brezhnev regime "cleansed" the CPSU ranks a number of times in the 1970s to ensure a cadre of dedicated and responsible party members. Brezhnev announced at the 25th Party Congress in 1975 that around 347,000 persons "did not receive new party cards" as a result of these exchanges (the leaders emphasized this was an exchange of party documents and not a purge). Hough quotes *Pravda* in noting that these were persons "who had deviated from the norms of party life, infringed discipline, or lost contact with party organizations."[27]

The CCP is also guided by certain rules and obligations. In 1980, the Central Committee reissued the following basic principles for CCP members:

1. To adhere to the party's political and ideological line of Marxism–Leninism–Mao Zedong thought.

2. To uphold collective leadership and oppose the making of arbitrary decisions by individuals.

3. To safeguard the party's centralized leadership and strictly observe party discipline.

4. To uphold party spirit and eradicate factionalism that undermines the party's unity.

5. To speak the truth, match words with deeds, and show loyalty to the cause of the party and to the people.

6. To promote inner-party democracy and to take a correct attitude toward dissenting views.

7. To guarantee that the party members' rights of criticism, policy formulation, and implementation are not encroached upon.

8. To provide genuine democratic elections within the party and give full expression to the voter's wishes.

9. To criticize and fight against such erroneous tendencies as factionalism, anarchism, and extreme individualism and evildoers such as counterrevolutionaries, grafters, embezzlers, and criminals.

10. To adopt a correct and positive attitude toward comrades who have made mistakes.

11. To accept supervision from the party and the masses and to see that privilege seeking is not allowed.

[25]*The Current Digest of the Soviet Press* 13 (47) (1961): 1–8; *18* (15) (1966): 9, 43; cited in Jerry F. Hough and Merle Fainsod, *How the Soviet Union Is Governed* (Cambridge: Harvard University Press, 1979), pp. 320–322.

[26]Hough and Fainsod, *op. cit.*, pp. 323–340.

[27]*Ibid.*, p. 336.

12. To study hard and become both Red and expert in order to contribute to the four modernizations.[28]

Just because the above are called Communist Party rules does not mean they are realities. Although there are certain principles suggested by the rules, one needs to examine them in the light of practical experience. Both the Soviet and Chinese parties reveal important practices, and some interesting similarities and differences.

Collective leadership is a fundamental practice of both Soviet and Chinese Communist Party rule and, with a few marginal exceptions, of all other contemporary Communist Party states. Decision making in party organs at all organizational levels is a collective exercise that usually involves more than a few people. Although party secretaries may be the first among equals, they still must gain the support of their peers. The so-called one-man rule under Stalin, Mao, or Tito was never really a reality; and, in the absence of such powerful leaders, all three countries have more fully embraced the principle of collective rule.

Democratic centralism is another important practice at work in the Communist parties of the Second World states. Developed by Lenin to reconcile both freedom and discipline, democratic centralism is based on the following principles: (1) election of all party bodies, (2) accountability of party bodies to their organizations and higher bodies, (3) strict discipline of the minority to the majority on all decisions, and (4) decisions of higher bodies are binding on lower bodies. As one can see, there are both democratic and centralistic elements in these principles. Some interesting differences exist among Communist parties, both between states and over time, concerning the blend of these two elements. The Communist parties under Stalinist and Maoist rule emphasized the centralistic elements. The parties in the 1970s under Brezhnev, Hua, and Tito gave the

democratic principles more importance. And, the CCP in the late 1970s and early 1980s flirted openly with much higher levels of inner-party democracy than had been previously known. The bottom line is, however, that the party never loses ultimate control. If democracy goes too far and threatens the dominating role of the party, as it did in Yugoslavia at the end of the 1960s, the party can move to tip the balance toward centralism. Although there are elements of both democracy and centralism, or freedom and unity, in Communist Party life today, the emphasis is decidedly on the side of centralism.

Another practice or set of practices is noteworthy, partly because of the general absence of party rules. This concerns the problems of *circulation and rotation* of party leaders, and the issue of *succession* once leaders die or are removed. The Yugoslavs have done the most in formalizing both rotation and succession of party leaders. In the immediate post-Tito period, the process by which successors were named to Tito's party and government roles went smoothly and as had been constitutionally established prior to his death. In the post-Tito period, the two most powerful LCY positions, the party chairmanship and secretaryship, were to rotate on a yearly and biyearly basis, respectively.[29] Efforts of most other states to formalize turnover within party organs have been ineffective or short-lived. For example, at the 23rd Congress of the CPSU in 1966, Brezhnev and his colleagues abolished the requirement (adopted at the previous Congress in 1961) that there would be a regular, specified turnover in party leadership bodies. The requirement was intended to avoid the election of the same leaders time after time and to bring some new blood into decision-making circles. This Soviet principle of systematic renewal, or anything like it, has not been ob-

[28]"Guiding Principles for Inner-Party Life," *Beijing Review* 23 (14) (1980): 11–20.

[29]In 1978, Tito suggested that yearly rotation should be applied to almost all LCY organs from the commune to the SFRY. In 1979, the Central Committee endorsed the practice. See Stephen L. Burg, "Decision-Making in Yugoslavia," *Problems of Communism* 29 (2) (1980): 1–20.

served in the USSR or most other Communist Party organizations. What often results is what some have called ossified or petrified leadership bodies that are isolated and insensitive to the constituencies that elect them. Although party leaders recognize the problem and criticize its negative features, they have done little to resolve or reform it.

The question of *political succession* within party bodies raises similar problems. There is considerable uncertainty and political conflict once a leader dies or is removed. The succession periods can generate considerable turmoil, as the Mao succession, described previously, revealed. The lack of formal rule for the circulation, rotation, and succession of elites, then, is a glaring shortcoming in Communist Party practice.

Another significant practice, proclaimed by all and practiced by few, concerns the principle of *criticism and self-criticism*. The CPSU rules require such behavior, but Soviet party leaders from the Politburo in Moscow down to local party secretaries often seem reluctant to engage in critical assessments of their own or their body's performance. About the only criticism one sees is that of higher bodies directed toward lower bodies, or toward ousted colleagues who have been purged from the leadership ranks. In contrast to the Soviets, the Chinese Communists (initially under Mao and now under Hu) seem much more prepared to recognize their mistakes and try to improve through self-criticism. A major thrust in the four modernizations program is to recognize shortcomings and to learn from one another as well as from other countries.

The final practice we will address here is called *nomenklatura. Nomenklatura* refers to a list of positions, both in the party and in society at large, that the party maintains and for which party approval is necessary before personnel changes, removals, or replacements can be made. The *nomenklatura* list in the USSR includes such diverse high positions in the military, in scientific organizations, and in the mass media. This practice allows the CPSU to control appointments to key positions throughout Soviet society. CPSU party officials have actively used the *nomenklatura* practice to remove undesirables and select officials who meet party standards. Although less is known about this practice in China, available evidence calls attention to its importance there as well. Finally, the importance of the *nomenklatura* practice is much less and is still decreasing in much of Eastern Europe and particularly in Yugoslavia. In environments with weaker parties and stronger social institutions, the power of the party's *nomenklatura* practice is reduced. The consequence in these countries is a lower level of party control.

THE PARTY: PAST, PRESENT, AND FUTURE

Although the Communist Party is one of the most significant political inventions of the twentieth century, a variety of disputes have arisen concerning its proper role and functions. Even before the Bolshevik takeover, Leon Trotsky expressed fears concerning the Leninist conception of the party: ''The party takes the place of the working class; the party organization displaces the party; the Central Committee displaces the party organization; and finally, the dictator displaces the Central Committee.'' Under Lenin and Stalin, the revolutionary, militant, centralized party evolved in a fashion surprisingly parallel to Trotsky's prediction.

In all contemporary Second World states, the Communist Party performs a number of common functions. First, the Communist Party organizations perform an important role regarding international organization and control. Although the nonaligned Yugoslavs and nationalistic Chinese have tended not to participate, the CPSU has established close communication links with other Communist Party organizations, particularly those in Eastern Europe. The Soviet party leaders utilize these links to coordinate and sometimes dictate on such policy matters as defense, relations with the West, trade and revolutionary strategy in the Third World, and so forth.

The Communist parties also perform some important domestic functions. Perhaps most important, the party has served to preserve the political system and to protect the incumbent regime. From the immediate postrevolutionary days through the current period, the party has controlled power in a manner that disallows both domestic and foreign challenges. Although internal rebellions have developed on occasion and although outside forces have threatened the existence of some systems, none of the Communist Party states have been overturned. In an age of great domestic and international turmoil, this is indeed a significant fact.[30]

Communist parties have also performed the important function of social control. In large and diverse countries, such as the Soviet Union and China, the propensity for internal conflict and civil strife is great. Occasional eruptions have dotted the years of Communist rule, but few have been of major significance. Of course, assuring domestic order and stability has often meant considerable infringements on civil liberties and personal freedom. Communist leaders apparently feel these are necessary policies at this stage of development. To preserve their own rule as well as to provide social services, domestic and international security, and other desired values, these leaders have chosen to use authoritarian Communist parties to direct or administer their societies—an approach to social control we often consider in conflict with basic human rights.

Finally, Communist parties have been used to order and organize the political process in a manner that the leaders consider in the best interests of the general society. The leaders have vested the most important political functions (policy initiation, policymaking, and policy implementation) within the structure of the party. Chapter Five illustrates that government organs participate and share in these functions. Yet, we should recognize that the government is staffed primarily by Communist Party members. This means that political processes in Communist Party states are carried on in an arena relatively free of the organized political opposition found in the two- or multi-party systems of the First World. Obviously, there are different interest groups and government organs that sometimes disagree and challenge party policy; however, there is little freedom to mount a serious political challenge to the ruling position of the incumbent Communist Party and even less opportunity to replace it with another.

The privileged and unassailable position of Communist parties has been criticized from both within and outside the Second World. The most stunning critique of all, however, came from a dedicated revolutionary and former Communist leader in Yugoslavia. In 1953, Milovan Djilas, president of the Yugoslav National Assembly, vice-president of the Republic, and ranking party official, denounced the dictatorial role and privileged practices of Communist Party officials. After being relieved of his official duties and quitting the party, Djilas published his famous indictment, *The New Class*.[31] This exposé argued that although the Communist elite had struggled to end class exploitation, they themselves had become a new class, placed in a privileged position over the rest of society.

Djilas's critique was followed in the 1960s by considerable discord among the leaders of the Soviet Union, China, and Yugoslavia. Mao Zedong and other CCP officials were the most

---

[30]The 1973 toppling of the Salvador Allende Gossens regime in Chile is an exception resulting from both domestic and foreign (United States) involvement. At the same time, it should be noted that there might have been major changes in Eastern Europe (*e.g.*, Czechoslovakia in 1968 and Poland in the early 1980s) if it had not been for Soviet involvement under the terms of the Brezhnev Doctrine.

[31]Milovan Djilas, *The New Class* (New York: Praeger, 1957). Djilas suffered several periods of imprisonment for his persistent criticism of the party. Throughout the 1970s, however, he was free and living comfortably on a government pension in Belgrade. While harassed by the Yugoslav authorities in the 1980s, he continues to live in Belgrade.

outspoken and accused both the USSR and Yugoslavia of phony communism and of fostering the exploitative new-class character of their parties.[32] Khrushchev responded by defending the historic and orthodox role of the CPSU and denigrating the revisionist character of both the CCP and the LCY. Although tending to be less acrimonious than the Chinese and Soviet leaders, the Yugoslavs defended their party and the Yugoslav approach to building communism. Soviet criticism of the Chinese has softened somewhat, yet the Chinese continue to rebuke the Soviet leaders and the CPSU. The Sino-Yugoslav acrimony of the 1960s seemed to fade by 1980 as the contentious Mao and Tito passed from the political scene and the Yugoslavs moved their LCY back into a more orthodox, Leninist position. The peculiarities and unique features of the Communist parties may evolve in slightly different ways, but none are likely to relinquish their leading political roles.

In conclusion, do Communist parties have any significant impact on human dignity? They certainly do, although the weighing of costs and benefits and the overall record is not easily established. Many observers contend that although the party leaders have done much to develop their countries economically and to provide education, health care, and other social services for their people, the authoritarian way in which they have gone about it has involved great cost to the human spirit. How one weights these costs and benefits is a question we will return to in Chapter Seven.

In conclusion, then, the Communist parties are the dominant institutions in the Second World states. Using Hough and Fainsod's description of the CPSU, we can apply it to all Communist Party states and say the real prime minister is the party General Secretary, that the real cabinet is the Politburo, and the real Parliament is the Central Committee.[33] In all Second World states, the parties dominate the allocation of values and have a powerful impact on the level of human dignity.

Suggestions for Further Reading

Armstrong, John A., *The Soviet Bureaucratic Elite: A Case Study of the Ukrainian Apparatus* (New York: Praeger, 1959).

Barton, Allen H., Bogdan Denitch, and **Charles Kadushin,** eds., *Opinion Making Elites in Yugoslavia* (New York: Praeger, 1973).

Beck, Carl, et al., *Comparative Communist Political Leadership* (New York: McKay, 1973).

Bialer, Seweryn, *Stalin's Successors: Leadership, Stability, and Change in the Soviet Union* (Cambridge: Cambridge University Press, 1980).

Breslauer, George W., *Khrushchev and Brezhnev as Leaders: Building Authority in Soviet Politics* (Winchester, Mass.: Allen & Unwin, 1982).

Bunce, Valarie, *Do Leaders Make a Difference? Executive Succession and Public Policy under Capitalism and Socialism* (Princeton: Princeton University Press, 1981).

Djilas, Milovan, *The New Class* (New York: Praeger, 1957).

Farrel, R. Barry, ed., *Political Leadership in Eastern Europe and the Soviet Union* (Chicago: Aldine, 1970).

Fischer-Galati, Stephen, ed., *The Communist Parties of Eastern Europe* (New York: Columbia University Press, 1979).

Gelman, Harry, *The Brezhnev Politburo and the Decline of Detente* (Ithaca, N.Y.: Cornell University Press, 1984).

[32]*On Khruschchev's Phoney Communism and Its Historical Lessons for the World* (Beijing: Foreign Languages Press, 1964).

[33]Hough and Fainsod, *op. cit.*, p. 362.

Hough, Jerry F., *Soviet Leadership in Transition* (Washington, D.C.: Brookings Institution, 1980).

Houn, Franklin W., *Short History of Chinese Communism,* rev. ed. (Englewood Cliffs, N.J.: Prentice-Hall, 1973).

Janos, Andrew C., ed., *Authoritarian Politics in Communist Europe* (Berkeley: University of California Press, Institute of International Studies, 1976).

Lewis, John Wilson, ed., *Party Leadership and Revolutionary Power in China* (Cambridge: Cambridge University Press, 1970).

Rush, Myron, *How Communist States Change Their Rulers* (Ithaca, N.Y.: Cornell University Press, 1974).

Rusinow, Dennison, *The Yugoslav Experiment, 1948–1974* (Berkeley: Univers Press, 1977).

Ryavec, Karl W., ed., *Soviet S munist Party* (Amherst: Uni chusetts Press, 1978).

Scalapino, Robert A., ed., *l Republic of China* (Seattle: University of Washington Press, 1972).

Schapiro, Leonard, *The Communist Party of the Soviet Union* (New York: Random House, 1971).

Schulz, Donald E., and **Jan S. Adams,** eds., *Political Participation in Communist Systems* (New York: Pergamon, 1981).

Terrill, Ross, *Mao: A Biography* (New York: Harper & Row, 1980).

Chapter Five

Government and Institutional Actors in Communist Party States

If Second World societies are ruled by Communist parties, what are the functions of their governments? Are the party and government organizations distinguishable in any important ways? Which is more important in shaping the overall policy process and in influencing policy outcomes? This chapter considers the part played by formal government structures and other institutional actors in Communist political systems.

Although Communist constitutions recognize the leading role of the Communist Party, they also outline a complex set of government structures of significance to the policy process. For example, all states have representative assemblies that have constitutionally prescribed legislative authority. All have a collegial or collective head of state, usually called a presidium, that also possesses legislative authority in addition to its presidential functions. Finally, all have executive or ministerial bodies, typically called the council of ministers, which are entrusted with the functions of policy implementation and execution. Although the Communist Party organizations outlined in Chapter Four overshadow these government bodies, a discussion of the policy process would be incomplete if it did not include the government sector.

Perhaps the most important role of the government organs in the policy process involves the legitimation of party actions. If one assessed the influence of legislative assemblies on the initiation and formulation of policy decisions and programs in Communist Party states, one would be forced to conclude that their power is minimal. This leads to the oft-cited rubber stamp description of Communist assemblies. However, if one were to assess the importance of the assemblies in legitimating the party's policies in the eyes of the people, the role of the legislatures would be considerably more significant. These and other government institutions do a great deal to gather mass support for party decisions concerning the allocation of values and, in so doing, ensure more compliant, supportive citizenries.

Generally speaking, although the Communist Party can be viewed as the source of policy, the government is its constitutional executor. The government bodies take the policy directives of the party and translate them into the rules and regulations that organize socialist life. Having rejected the idea of the separation of powers as a bourgeois theory, the responsibilities of the party, assemblies, presidiums, and councils are often intermeshed and ill defined.

To better understand the poorly defined setting in which the policy process takes place, we begin by describing the basic government structures and institutional actors in these states. Then, we explore their relationships with the Communist parties to determine the ways in which the highest party and government organs interrelate and overlap in the execution of their political functions. Last, we will examine the roles of other important institutional actors in the political process. The leaders of these states have meticulously prepared constitutions and party statutes to delineate the rights and responsibilities of the various organs, yet we will learn that the boundaries and relationships between them are very murky indeed. Before exploring these more complex issues, however, we begin with a basic overview of key government institutions.

THE SOVIET UNION

In 1977, the Soviet Union adopted a new constitution replacing the Stalinist version of 1936. Perhaps the most surprising feature of the new constitution, the fourth since the Bolshevik uprising, is its close resemblance to its Stalinist predecessor. Serving a number of functions, including the legitimation of party policy and propaganda, the constitution also outlines basic law and the government structure of the Soviet state. The body that approved the new constitution, the Supreme Soviet, is the nominal legislative organ of the Soviet government.[1]

THE SOVIET ASSEMBLY: THE SUPREME SOVIET

As indicated in Figure 5.1, the Supreme Soviet is a bicameral legislature consisting of the Soviet of the Union and the Soviet of Nationalities. Neither of these two Soviets is a significant policymaking body that initiates and independently decides on legislation.[2] Rather,

[1]For an analysis and the text of the constitution, see Robert Sharlet, *The New Soviet Constitution of 1977* (Brunswick, Ohio: Kings Court, 1978).

[2]The word *soviet* means *council* in the Russian language.

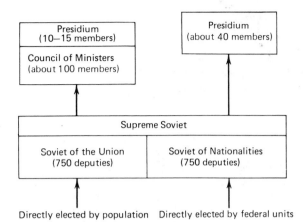

Figure 5.1 The Structure of the Soviet Government.

the Supreme Soviet is a government organ whose primary function is to enact the legislation sent to it by more powerful policymaking bodies. The political impotence of these two Soviets is indicated by the unusually short time they are in session; each house meets twice yearly, usually for only two to four days during each session.

The Soviet of the Union is elected according to the population density of territorial administrative units, with 1 deputy elected per 350,000 inhabitants. The second chamber, the Soviet of Nationalities, is comprised of deputies elected by the federal units. The 15 union republics are each allotted 32 deputies, the 20 autonomous republics 11, the 8 autonomous regions 10, and the 10 national areas 1 each. The system of representation results in chambers of about 750 deputies, bringing delegates from all sections of the country and representing all national and ethnic groups.

The two houses of the Supreme Soviet are constitutionally prescribed equal status and rights. Although they normally conduct their business jointly, unlike the U.S. House of Representatives and Senate, they do vote separately by a simple show of hands. If differences between the houses arise, the Soviet constitution prescribes their arbitration and resolution by a joint conciliation commission; failing that, the Presidium can dissolve the Supreme So-

Deputies of USSR Supreme Soviet unanimously pass a resolution on ''The International Situation and The Foreign Policy of the Soviet State'' at a joint sitting of The Soviet of the Union and The Soviet of Nationalities.

viet, send the delegates home, and call for a new election. In fact, however, all votes are unanimous; the two chambers never disagree on any matter of legislation. These facts, taken together with the unusually short legislative sessions, illustrate that the Supreme Soviet is not an important, independent policymaking body. Rather, its chief functions are to ratify policy proposals of the smaller, more powerful party organizations, such as the Politburo, to legitimate the actions of the Communist Party of the Soviet Union (CPSU) in the eyes of the Soviet people as well as influence future policy.

Hough provides some insights into the work and role of the Supreme Soviet. Describing the activity surrounding a bill concerning the Soviet educational system, he calls atten-

tion to the appeals and policy recommendations of the various deputies.[3] Some deputies appealed for more funds for their own localities or for various educational programs. Other deputies raised more basic policy issues concerning the very nature of the Soviet educational system. Still others attacked an important CPSU decision, an earlier Central Committee/Council of Ministers decree on educational financing. Although the various appeals, suggestions, and attacks within the Supreme Soviet had almost no impact on the law under consideration, Hough contends that the important function and objectives of the exer-

[3]Jerry F. Hough and Merle Fainsod, *How the Soviet Union Is Ruled* (Cambridge: Harvard University Press, 1979), pp. 368–369.

cise was to affect future policy and appropriations. At the conclusion of the session, an official said, ''all these proposals and remarks will be attentively examined by the government, and also by corresponding ministries and departments.''[4]

Deputies are elected to the Supreme Soviet every four years on the basis of universal suffrage (over 18 years) and secret printed ballots. Even though only one name appears on the ballot for each official position, 99.9 percent of the Soviet population votes in national elections, a surprising figure that remains relatively constant year after year. One might wonder why so many Soviet citizens go to the polls when no meaningful choices are afforded. Soviet doctrine considers voting an obligation as well as a right; everyone is expected to go to the polls regardless of health, income, or preoccupation. To ''get out the vote,'' criminals are required to vote in their prisons; the infirm vote from their hospital beds; ocean-going passengers cast votes on their ships; and so forth. Societal pressures are great and everyone votes as a matter of civic responsibility and national pride. Voters can cross off names on a ballot, although a candidate for the Supreme Soviet has never been denied election as a result of such votes. On the other hand, some candidates at the provincial and local levels have been so denied on occasion.

The more important stage in selecting deputies, however, occurs *before* the election. Selection of the official slate that appears on the ballot begins with the nomination of candidates by public organizations, such as schools, factories, and the like. These nominees are subsequently discussed at public pre-election meetings where choices are made on the candidates to be supported. Although the rank-and-file citizen can have some input at this stage of the process, the nomination is not entirely open and democratic; names forwarded to the electoral commission to be placed on the ballot

are still very much determined by the appropriate CPSU officials.

Deputies to the Supreme Soviet represent an interesting cross section of Soviet society. Although far more of the deputies are party members (around 75 percent) than are found in the society at large and although approximately 40 percent are professional party bureaucrats (all members of the CPSU Central Committee are Supreme Soviet members), the remainder represent almost every conceivable occupational and ethnic group in the country. Approximately one quarter of the Supreme Soviet members are workers of one sort or another; another quarter are from collective farms. The most typical occupation of American representatives and senators is the law, yet less than 1 percent of the deputies of the Supreme Soviet are lawyers. In addition, the USSR has a far greater representation of women in its national legislative chambers (around 25 percent) than does the United States. It also has a strong sampling of ethnic and racial minorities.

Being a deputy in the Soviet Union is not a lucrative enterprise, because delegates receive an allowance barely covering their official expenses. Turnover is high and most deputies who do not have some other career office do not serve a second term. Although this has the benefit of providing more citizens with the opportunity of participating in the national government, it also means that the nonprofessional deputies lack the experience, contacts, and information developed by additional terms in office. These less-experienced representatives find it difficult to participate effectively and competently with those experienced party professionals who spend term after term in the halls of the Kremlin.

Considerable evidence suggests that the Supreme Soviet is controlled by powerful personalities who hold high positions in the CPSU hierarchy. For example, high party leaders control appointments to two important bodies, the Presidium and the Council of Ministers. The Supreme Soviet is constitutionally

[4]*Ibid.*, p. 370.

prescribed to make such appointments.[5] Darrell P. Hammer quotes the official text of a Supreme Soviet meeting in 1966; this provides a rather clear picture of how the Soviet's appointments are handled.

1. General Secretary Brezhnev took the floor, said he was speaking "in the name of the Central Committee," and proposed the election of Podgorny as chairman of the Presidium. Podgorny was elected unanimously.

2. Podgorny then was recognized. Announcing that he was acting "on the instructions of the party group," he nominated the other members of the Presidium, who were likewise elected.

3. The next speaker was Premier Kosygin, who presented a list of proposed members of the Council of Ministers. He noted that the list has been "approved by the Central Committee of the Communist Party." The list was then approved by the Supreme Soviet.[6]

The power of the CPSU party leadership was brought to bear unexpectedly once again in 1977. Wanting to enhance his own power at the top of the government, party leader Leonid I. Brezhnev engineered a movement that stripped Nikolai V. Podgorny of his chairmanship of the Supreme Soviet Presidium (which Brezhnev assumed one month later) as well as his seat on the CPSU Politburo. The Supreme Soviet had no prior knowledge and nothing to do with the ouster. Therefore, real appointment power to the Presidium and Council of Ministers remains in the hands of the CPSU leaders.

Unlike the Supreme Soviet, the Presidium is a relatively influential policymaking body within the Soviet government. Much more professional and less heterogeneous than the

Soviets, the 40-member Presidium, likely to be headed in the future by new party leader Gorbachev, has the right to conduct legislative affairs and make decisions while the Supreme Soviet is not in session. As a result of the short and infrequent meetings of the Supreme Soviet, this provides the Presidium with considerable policymaking responsibility and power for most of the year. Throughout this period, the Presidium undertakes a variety of policy actions, including issuing decrees later approved by the Supreme Soviet and promulgated as official statutes. The Presidium also has the power to interpret what the statutes mean, a right reserved for the Supreme Court in the American system of government.

THE EXECUTIVE: THE COUNCIL OF MINISTERS

The executive arm of the Soviet government, the Council of Ministers, includes the heads of all Soviet ministries, chairpersons of the Union of Republic Councils of Ministers, and chairpersons of important state committees. Ministries are the functionally organized departments in charge of foreign affairs, agriculture, and so forth. The chairman of the Council of Ministers, Nikolay A. Tikhonov, is legally head of the Soviet government. The frail, 80-year-old Tikhonov is likely to be replaced soon by a younger, more technocratically minded chairman more to party leader Gorbachev's liking. Because the body Tikhonov heads, the Council of Ministers, totals around 100 members, a smaller body, the 10-to-15 member Presidium of the Council of Ministers (not to be confused with the Presidium of the Supreme Soviet) often acts in the council's name.

The Council of Ministers is an extremely important government institution, both in theory and reality. It is constitutionally prescribed the powers and responsibilities for issuing decrees in a fashion similar to the Presidium of the Supreme Soviet, that is, directing and coordinating the work of the All-Union ministries and carrying out the economic plan of the CPSU. Hough examined the most important

[5]The Soviet Constitution also gives the Supreme Soviet the right to appoint members of the Supreme Court, the Procurator General (a national administrative and legal agency that has no counterpart in the United States), and other national commissions. Because these institutions are of little relevance to the policymaking process, they receive no attention here.

[6]Pravda, 4 August, 1966, cited in Darrell P. Hammer, USSR: The Politics of Oligarchy (Hinsdale, Ill.: Dryden, 1974), pp. 261–262.

collection of Soviet laws and decisions, *The Handbook of the Party Official*,[7] to determine who issued policy concerning the economy, living conditions and wages, education, law and order, and so forth. Of those promulgated between 1964 and 1976, 21 were laws of the Supreme Soviet and 86 were decrees of the Supreme Soviet, whereas 207 were Council of Ministers decisions. Another 139 were decisions of the Council of Ministers in conjunction with other bodies.[8] Most Council of Ministers decisions were probably taken by the body's Presidium. In addition to these policymaking functions, the Council is entrusted with the responsibility of maintaining law and order, conducting foreign affairs, organizing the armed forces, and setting up and coordinating the work of important state committees. In its role as both a policy maker and chief executor of the party's policy, it has the capacity to shape policy outcomes significantly. The Council has been referred to as a collective head of government, a title it justly deserves in view of its many important functions.

Although we usually conceive of the Council of Ministers as the bureaucratic and executive arm of the Soviet government, its legislative powers are also of considerable importance. David Lane calls attention to these powers when he notes, ''In practice, the council and its ministries are the main sources of legislation and issue decrees and regulations governing the whole of economics and social life.''[9] As we will see when examining the policy process in Chapter Six, the boundaries of policymaking power become extremely fuzzy when the functions of the party Politburo and Secretariat, the government Supreme Soviet and its presidium, and the Council of Ministers and its presidium are considered with respect to specific policy issues and programs. Although in theory these institutions have specific powers and functions, in practice the realities of power politics have made their jurisdictions subject to change and influence by the party elite.

CHINA

The People's Republic of China is a clear example of how individuals can shape, and even eclipse, the roles of formal political institutions. The institutional fabric of the Chinese political system has been very much influenced by the strong personalities of such leaders as Mao Zedong and Deng Xiaoping. These men viewed political institutions as necessary administrative tools, but when institutions obstructed revolutionary politics or became archaic they were simply ignored. Liu Shaoqi, for example, was chairman of the People's Republic from 1950 to 1966, and then he fell into the party's disfavor and was ousted at the outset of the Great Proletarian Cultural Revolution (GPCR). Liu's official position was ignored and went unfilled for over nine years until it was finally dropped from the government structure with the adoption of the new constitutions of 1975 and 1978. It is hard to imagine the presidency of the United States or even the chairmanship of the Soviet Presidium remaining vacant for almost a decade. But although the importance of Chinese government institutions should not be overemphasized, neither should they be ignored. If China continues its policy of modernization and adopts a more orthodox political strategy in the post-Mao years, as appears to be happening, the role and significance of government institutions in the Chinese political process are likely to increase.

NATIONAL PEOPLE'S CONGRESS (ASSEMBLY)

In constitutional terms, the National People's Congress (NPC) represents the highest organ of state power. The 1954, 1975, and 1982 constitutions accorded it this same status, but it had been dormant for a decade until its meeting in

---

[7]*Spravochnik partiinogo rabotnika [The Handbook of the Party Official]*, 6th to 16th eds. (Moscow: Politizdat, 1966–1976).

[8]Hough and Fainsod, *op. cit.*, pp. 380–381.

[9]David Lane, *Politics and Society in the USSR* (New York: Random House, 1971), p. 149.

1975! Although it is supposed to convene yearly, the constitution provides the nation's leaders with considerable flexibility for canceling or postponing meetings of this highest legislative organ. The NPC meets less frequently than the Supreme Soviet in the USSR, but its sessions are somewhat longer, normally running two or three weeks.

Representatives to the NPC are elected for five-year terms by the provincial-level congresses, the armed forces, and the overseas Chinese (see Figure 5.2). The NPC elections are indirect in the sense that rank-and-file citizens do not cast ballots for specific candidates. The nomination, selection, and election of delegates in China is handled through organizations even more party-dominated than in the Soviet Union. What has resulted in the past has been a nonprofessional congress easily

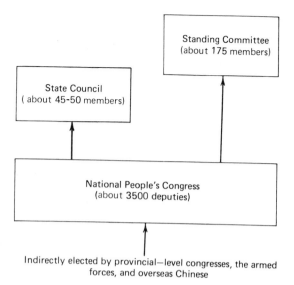

Figure 5.2 The Structure of the Chinese Government.

A meeting of the Standing Committee of The Sixth National People's Congress in 1984. Members of the Committee are examining documents outlining the new agreement with the United Kingdom that will return Hong Kong to Chinese administration.

dominated by the party leadership. A Chinese publication noted that of the 2864 deputies attending the 1975 Congress, 72 percent were workers, peasants, and soldiers; 22 percent were women; and 54 minority nationalities were represented. This diverse group, however, has no real power in the policymaking process. Like the Supreme Soviet's Presidium, the People's Congress elects a smaller standing committee empowered to act on behalf of the NPC when not in session.

STATE COUNCIL (EXECUTIVE)

The head executive body, and the most important body, in the Chinese government is the State Council. Since its inception in 1954, this counterpart to the Soviet government's Council of Ministers had been headed by Premier Zhou Enlai. On Premier Zhou's death in January 1976, Hua Guofeng became the new premier and leader of the State Council. In 1980, Hua passed the premiership on to Zhao Ziyang, the energetic and effective protégé of the pro-modernization leader, Deng Xiaoping. The State Council consists of the premier, four vice premiers, half a dozen state councillors (with the rank of vice premier), and the 45 heads (as of 1984) of ministries and commissions.

Above the State Council is the chairman of the Republic (head of state), a post which is different from chairman of the Standing Committee of the National People's Congress. Since June 1982, the chairman of the Republic post has been held by Li Xiannian, a member of the Politburo Standing Committee. Mao held this post during 1954–1959 and passed it on to Liu Shaoqi, who held it from 1959–1966, when he was purged. The post was abolished, but restored again in 1982, when Li Xiannian assumed this head-of-state role.

As the highest executive body, the State Council directs and supervises the Chinese administrative structure. Assuming many of the same functions as the Council of Ministers in the USSR for fleshing out the party's policy proposals and for coordinating the economy

and foreign and domestic affairs, the State Council shares political power with the CCP Politburo and Standing Committee. Many of the high party leaders simultaneously hold positions on the State Council. Composed of the premier, about 13 influential vice premiers, and approximately 30 heads of ministries in the early 1980s, the council performs the primary function of policy implementation and execution in the Chinese government.

YUGOSLAVIA

In February 1974, the Yugoslav assembly adopted the fifth constitution in the country's short life span of less than 30 years. Showing a flexible attitude toward constitutional revision, the Yugoslavs' most current constitution is a far cry from the 1946 version modeled after Stalin's 1936 Soviet Union constitution. Designed to formalize the unique system of one-party rule and self-managing socialism, the 1974 constitution is one of the longest and most complex in the world. Outlining an intricate system of constitutional rights and responsibilities, the Yugoslavs have moved farther in the direction of constitutionalism, a movement toward legal/judicial rule, than any contemporary Communist Party state.[10]

THE FEDERAL ASSEMBLY

As indicated in Figure 5.3, the bicameral Yugoslav Assembly is composed of the Chamber of Republics and Provinces and the Federal Chamber. The Chamber of Republics and Provinces is based on the concept of territorial or federal representation, much like the U.S. Senate. With indirect election by the republic and provincial assemblies, this system of delegate selection demonstrates the powerful and important role played by the republics and provinces in the federal Yugoslav system. An accepted fact of Yugoslav politics is that the

---

[10]Winston M. Fisk, "The Constitutional Movement in Yugoslavia: A Preliminary Survey," *Slavic Review* 30 (2) (1971): 277–297.

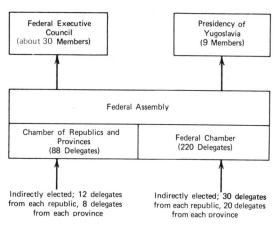

Figure 5.3 The Structure of the Yugoslav Government.

federal government cannot act without the advice and consent of its territorial jurisdictions.

The Federal Chamber, on the other hand, demonstrates the equally strong position of the local units (municipal, community, and work organizations) in the political system. The 220 delegates in this chamber are chosen from local self-managing organizations and communities and are elected by local assemblies; 30 delegates are elected from each of the republics and 20 from each province.

Elections to the two federal chambers and to the regional and local assemblies are controlled by the Socialist Alliance, a broad-based mass organization sponsored by the League of Communists of Yugoslavia (LCY) and designed to mobilize and encourage popular participation in sociopolitical affairs. Although the majority of delegates in the Federal Assembly are members of the LCY, most delegates to local assemblies are *not* Communists. Elected to serve four-year terms, but limited to two consecutive terms, the local-level delegates are characteristically rank-and-file members of society. In 1974, over 700,000 Yugoslavs— *approximately 1 out of every 20 voters*—served in an assembly at some level in the political system.

In contrast to the situation in the Soviet Union and China, the Yugoslav Federal Assembly is a relatively influential branch of the federal government. Programs and proposals are vigorously debated, amendments to government policies are frequently made, and legislation relatively free of party control is produced within the chamber halls. Although the assembly does not have sufficient stature to block official LCY policy, it plays a meaningful participant role in the policymaking process. Without a doubt, the Yugoslav assemblies, from the federal to the local levels, are the most influential legislative institutions in the Second World.

In addition to his role of party leader, Josip Broz Tito (1892–1980) was president of the Yugoslav Republic throughout his career. On his death in 1980, he was replaced by a collective executive, as called for in the 1974 constitution. The Presidency of Yugoslavia is composed of representatives from the six republics and two autonomous provinces, elected by secret ballot from their regional assemblies, and an ex officio member from the LCY Presidium. They are elected to five-year terms and can serve no more than two consecutive terms. The positions of President and vice president rotate annually among the eight representatives of the state presidency.

The idea of constitutionally establishing a collective head of state is a unique and risky experiment. Collective leaderships often degenerate into highly competitive power struggles in which one participant normally emerges as the victor. The Yugoslav planners were willing to take this chance, however, because of their unique situation. With no successor to Tito who has widespread support from all of the national and ethnic groups that comprise Yugoslavia, they were forced to compromise with a collective executive comprised of representatives from all these different groups. The collective leadership body is a very important key to the future of Yugoslavia. If it works well, the country may have found an answer to the difficult leadership problem it faces in the post-Tito era. If it fails and the collective arrangement degenerates into partisan squabbles among the regional leaders or results in a situation where one regional leader emerges who can win the

The Presidency of Yugoslavia met on March 5, 1980 to discuss the country's foreign activity and efforts to affirm the principles of nonalignment in international relations. Pictured from left to right are: Josip Vrhovec, Federal Secretary for Foreign Affairs; Veselin Djuranovic, President of the Federal Executive Council (Premier); Vidoje Zarkovic and Fadilj Jodza, members of the presidency; and Lazar Kolisezski, Vice President of the presidency, who presided over the meeting.

support of neither the other members nor the nationalities they represent, then the Yugoslav future may be bleak.

Delegated by the constitution with a host of important government functions, the collective presidency could become a powerful government institution in the Yugoslav political arena. It is entrusted with the typical head-of-state functions, including the conduct of international security and foreign affairs, command of the armed forces, and the proclamation of law by decree.

FEDERAL EXECUTIVE COUNCIL

Like the State Council in China and the Council of Ministers in the Soviet Union, the Yugoslav Federal Executive Council is the chief executive organ of the government. Elected for four-year terms by the assembly in conformity with the principle of equal representation

among the republics and provinces, the premier of the Federal Executive Council, his vice premiers, and the federal secretaries are in charge of such federal administrative agencies as defense, foreign affairs, and justice.[11] Serving as key advisors to the presidency, premier, and other national leaders, the ministers oversee the bureaucratic hierarchies in their specialized areas. Unlike their counterpart councils in China and the USSR, members of the Federal Executive Council serve four-year terms in office. Although they are permitted to serve an additional term if reelected by the assembly, the Yugoslavs' emphasis on the rotation of public office holders insures a higher

[11]The Yugoslavs refer to the premier and vice premiers of the Federal Executive Council as president and vice president. To avoid confusion, we will reserve these designations for the presidency.

circulation of officials than found in most other Communist Party states.

COMPARATIVE OVERVIEW

When we compare the basic government institutions of the three states, we find a high degree of structural similarity among them. All three have: (1) an assembly, (2) a collegial head of state, and (3) a ministerial council entrusted with the administration of government policy. Examining the different institutions more closely, however, reveals a number of noteworthy contrasts.

The assemblies in the USSR and China are extremely large, meet infrequently for very brief periods, and are not the independent legislative institutions we know in the West. The two chambers of the Yugoslav Federal Assembly, however, are considerably smaller (roughly the size of the U.S. House of Representatives and Senate), meet frequently and sometimes for extended sessions, and have become active and reasonably powerful legislative bodies. Yugoslavia is a notable exception from the general rule of rubber stamp legislatures in Communist Party states. Although the constitutions of these states uniformly call the assemblies the ''highest organ of state authority,'' most are in fact very weak in policymaking power.

Because of the infrequent meetings of the Supreme Soviet and the NPC, the assemblies ''elect'' organs to act in their names while they are not in session. Even this body in China—the Standing Committee—has little political power and is no test for the stronger Chinese Communist Party (CCP) organs. The Presidium in the USSR is more powerful, and the collective state presidency in Yugoslavia seems to be the most powerful of all.

Finally, each assembly appoints an executive council to supervise and control the national bureaucracy and to oversee the execution of party policy. As the administrative sector of government grows with the development of the state, the role and importance of this executive branch has increased. The Council of Ministers in the USSR, the State Council in China, and the Federal Executive Council in Yugoslavia are all vital organs that ensure the functioning and coordination of the bureaucracy. Headed by high party officials with strong administrative experience, these councils make sure that the government operates effectively and in a manner that corresponds with the desires of the party elite.

The governments of other Communist Party states correspond with the general descriptions outlined above. Most East European governments have national assemblies that approximate the influence and roles of the Supreme Soviet. Like their Soviet counterpart, these assemblies also have executive committees and administrative councils that assume many of the functions constitutionally prescribed to the assemblies. Relatively little is known about the government structures of the new Southeast Asian Communist Party states or, for that matter, even about those of North Korea and Albania. What we do know is that all assume some features of both the Soviet and Chinese government systems and that the party tends to dominate the government institutions in all.

OTHER INSTITUTIONAL ACTORS

There are other institutions of significance to policymaking in addition to the Communist Party and the government structures we have outlined. Among the most important are the state ministries and committees (the bureaucracy), the military, and the scientific, intelligence, and security communities.

Communist bureaucracies are big. Convinced of the leading role of the Communist Party in social and economic development, the leaders have established massive bureaucracies to carry out their messianic vision. There are many commissions, councils, ministries, and committees under the umbrella of the Soviet Council of Ministers. All of these bodies have their own bureaucracies with hundreds and often thousands of additional offices, committees, and assorted bodies. Many employ hundreds of thousands of civil servants and have administrative structures that stretch throughout the country.

The Soviet Council of Ministers has a number of important commissions, such as the Military-Industrial Commission (VPK), which cut across ministry or departmental lines. The VPK is in charge of the defense industry, a very high priority sector in the Soviet economy, and must work with other ministries and bodies to ensure Soviet preparedness in the defense sector. The interagency commissions on Foreign Economic Questions and the Council for Mutual Economic Assistance (CEMA or COMECON) have similar responsibilities in coordinating government activities to ensure international economic cooperation.

In addition, the Council of Ministers includes many ministries with their own areas of responsibility and specialization, e.g., Foreign Affairs, Defense, Agriculture, and Health. Each is headed by a highly trained and specialized minister—for example, Andrei A. Gromyko is the Minister of Foreign Affairs—and a thousand or so officials. There is little mobility from ministry to ministry as there is among departments and agencies of the United States. Government officials such as Gromyko are usually knowledgeable specialists who work their way up the bureaucratic ladder within a particular ministry. The primary function of these ministries is to coordinate policy in their specialized areas and supervise activities at the regional and local levels.

A particularly important ministry in the USSR is GOSPLAN, or the Ministry of Planning. GOSPLAN's primary responsibility is much like that of the Office of Management and Budget (OMB) in the United States, that is, to balance and meet ministerial needs and requests for resources in view of national goals. A large ministry with nearly 20 deputy ministers, GOSPLAN has a heavy responsibility in planning and coordinating the complex and cumbersome centrally controlled economic system.

Although China has a substantially smaller bureaucracy and fewer ministries, the State Council also includes numerous ministries comparable to those of the Soviets. One of them, the State Planning Commission, was established in 1952 as the Chinese counterpart to GOSPLAN. The Chinese bureaucratic system has been characterized by much higher levels of provincial power than has the Soviet system. During various Maoist movements, such as the Great Leap Forward, the GPCR, and the anti-Deng campaigns, decentralization to the provincial levels made some provinces and municipalities into what were called independent kingdoms.[12] Both the national ministries and provincial organs, then, can serve as powerful actors in the Chinese policymaking process.

Yugoslavia also has delegated considerable political and bureaucratic power to the regional levels of government. In the 1970s, however, the Federal Executive Council in the capital city of Belgrade and the various ministries within it increased their power at the expense of the regional levels. Stephen L. Burg notes that this results in the federal bureaucracy's "near monopoly over the scientific, technical, and bureaucratic resources of the state and over the agenda of federal decision-making."[13] Although the republics and provinces of these Communist Party states can be important actors within the political process, they tend to be less powerful than the federal institutions and bureaucracies in the state capitals.

The military can also be a significant actor in Communist political systems, if for no other reason than that it is the only institution with the power to overthrow the government and regime. Although the military is a powerful participant in Soviet politics, the CPSU has taken care to keep the military establishment,

---

[12]The January 14, 1977 issue of the *People's Daily* spoke of the Gang of Four and their supporters usurping power in the municipality of Shanghai and the province of Liaoning.

[13]Stephen L. Burg, "Decision-Making in Yugoslavia," *Problem of Communism*, 29 (2) (1980), p. 15.

including the Ministry of Defense, under party control.[14] The military is likely to remain active and powerful in Soviet politics in view of the high priority on defense in contemporary Soviet policy. Military leaders are well represented in the party bureaucracy (the Minister of Defense is generally a member of the Politburo), the size of the military bureaucracy is vast, and the money allocated to defense continues to rise.

The Chinese military, the People's Liberation Army (PLA), has traditionally played a more important role in Chinese politics than has the Red Army in Soviet politics. During the civil war years, the CCP and the PLA were indistinguishable; during Mao's reign, the PLA was clearly the most powerful bureaucracy in politics. More recently, however, the PLA has been deemphasized politically, made clearly subordinate to the party, and assumed what most experts call a pressure group role. In 1985 party leader Hu Yaobang announced that China was going to reduce the 4.2 million-man PLA by 1 million! This was viewed as another move inspired by Deng Xiaoping to reduce the political influence of the army. It is likely that it was also an effort to cut military expenditures, which took about 14 percent of the Chinese budget, in 1985.

The highest military decision-making body in Chinese politics is the Military Affairs Commission of the CCP. In 1983, a state military commission was also set up, but its leadership is identical with that of the CCP Commission. Deng Xiaoping is the acknowledged leader in China today, partly because he heads these two bodies and is commander-in-chief of the PLA. Interestingly, as a result of the attempts to disperse power in the post-Mao era, China's three major institutions—the party, state, and the military—have three different leaders. A situation of potential rivalry among these institutions and leaders looms large in

the Chinese future. Because of their role in protecting national security, the military establishments will remain influential actors in all Communist political systems.

The scientific communities are playing increasingly important roles in the politics and policy of Communist systems. Scientific personnel are found within universities and within various ministries, committees, and scientific academies. The Soviet Academy of Sciences, with nearly 300 different institutes, represents a vast network of specialists expected to improve the scientific basis of Soviet development. Involved in such diverse areas as earth sciences, space technology, and foreign policy, scientific personnel play an important role in Soviet planning. Both party and government bodies make use of their expertise by requesting and drawing on position papers and studies that address issues of technical and scientific importance. In addition, although the scientific communities are diverse and represent a variety of opinions, groups within the larger establishment are purported to serve as pressure groups influencing party and government policies.

The role and influence of the scientific community is changing quickly in contemporary China. With the rapid expansion of the modernization program, more expertise is required in making decisions concerning Chinese development. Party leaders in the post-Mao era have called attention to the important role to be played by the scientific community and have shown greater attention to the reports and recommendations of scientific personnel.

Other institutions, such as trade unions, mass organizations [like Komsomol (Communist Youth League)], and security organizations play significant roles within the political process. Owing to Communist sensitivity to internal security, such organizations as the Soviet's Committee for State Security (KGB) have a special role in Soviet politics, certainly greater than that of the Federal Bureau of Investigation (FBI) and the Central Intelligence Agency (CIA) in the United States. As Chapter

---

[14]Roman Kolkowicz refers to the Communist Party and the military as the two most powerful bureaucracies in the USSR. Roman Kolkowicz, *The Soviet Military and the Communist Party* (Princeton, N.J.: Princeton University Press, 1967).

Six on the policymaking process points out, under certain conditions these and other institutional actors can take on important roles in the formulation and implementation of policy.

GOVERNMENT/PARTY RELATIONS

Many observers have called attention to the close relationship between the party and government in Communist systems and have described them as interlocking directorates. According to Darrell P. Hammer, two principles govern party/government relations in the USSR. The first concerns the paramount position of the party and the subordination of the government and the bureaucracies to its official line. Hammer quotes an authoritative Soviet text: "No important decision is ever taken by an organ of government, or by an administrative organ, without corresponding instructions from the Party."[15] The second principle is that, although the party provides guidance, it does not replace the government organs or totally dominate their administrative work. Hammer cites another Soviet source: "The central Party organs give guiding instructions to the ministries . . . while not restricting their operational independence."[16] These principles underline the fact that, in the Soviet Union, the party leads and the government executes.

To ensure proper execution from the party's point of view, the CPSU places high-level party officials in the various government institutions. At the national level, for example, members of the Politburo head the Supreme Soviet Presidium and the Council of Ministers. As high-level officials in the CPSU and as the top officials (chairman and premier) in their government organs, the party leaders are able to assure a close working relationship between party and government.

This interlocking relationship (illustrated in Figure 5.4) applies at all levels of Soviet gov-

ernance. From the all-union level down through the local villages, party officials simultaneously staff the organs of government and administration. As noted in the diagram, however, there is much more overlap at the highest levels and less overlap further down the hierarchy. This means that, although party leaders dominate the highest government levels, there is considerably more separation of function and power at the provincial levels and even more at the local levels of government.

The overlapping party/government relationship applies also for China, Yugoslavia, and other Communist Party states. Organizational charts listing the members of the Standing Committee of the Chinese NPC and the State Council and its ministries contain many names that appear in the CCP Politburo and Central Committee. As one proceeds downward from the national through the provincial to the local levels, the dual roles continue although, as in the Soviet case, they become less frequent.

The LCY leaders attempted to end the interlocking directorate and divorce themselves from government power in the 1960s by prohibiting the simultaneous holding of party and government positions.[17] In the early 1970s, however, the LCY leaders perceived that the party was losing political control and decided to reassert their leading role. In the early 1980s, the Yugoslav system once again had a relatively small number of elites holding the highest level party and government posts.

A brief look at how the Soviet Union puts together its economic five-year plans provides some idea of the interrelationship between party and government organs. To begin the preparation of the plans, members of the Politburo usually commission their economic advisors and government planners to prepare a set of studies and guidelines for the future course of Soviet development. Then, a draft plan is eventually brought before a session of the Polit-

[15]V. A. Vlasov, *Sovetskii gosudartvennyi apparat* (Moscow, 1959), p. 361, cited in Hammer, *op. cit.*, p. 278.

[16]I. N. Ananov, *Ministerstva v SSSR* (Moscow: 1960) p. 22; cited in Hammer, op. cit., p. 277.

[17]See the article by the former leading LCY official Krste Crvenkovski, "Divorcing the Party from Power," *Socialist Thought and Practice 69* (7) (1967): 40–49.

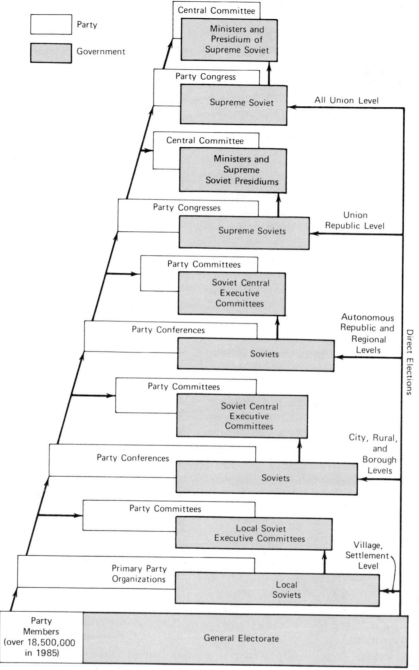

Figure 5.4 Interlocking party and government structures in the USSR. [Adapted from V. Aspaturian, "The Soviet Union," in R. C. Macridis and R. E. Ward, eds., *Modern Political Systems: Europe*, 2nd ed. (Englewood Cliffs, N.J.: Prentice-Hall, 1963).]

buro for discussion and debate, often over a series of long and difficult meetings. The heads of the relevant government ministries (e.g., defense and agriculture) are brought in to discuss what resources they need to fulfill their responsibilities. Other governmental planners may be consulted to determine what they think should go in the new plan. Finally, a set of economic guidelines is prepared by the government planners under the direction of the highest party officials. These guidelines then go to the CPSU Politburo, where they are reviewed, amended, and generally approved. The Politburo then recommends its plan to the party's Central Committee and the government's Supreme Soviet for their stamp of approval. After this predictable ratification, the new five-year plan is given the force of law and becomes the responsibility of the Council of Ministers to implement. The CPSU Secretariat evaluates the implementation of the plan and intermittently reports to the Politburo on the execution of the plan.

The handling of a new five-year plan portrays the way in which party and government bodies and personnel interrelate in the making of Soviet policy. Their respective functions result in a back-and-forth, cooperative sort of relationship where the functional divisions among party, government, and other institutions become extremely blurred. Although the general principle of party determination and government execution applies in most policy matters, leeway exists that allows personnel from both hierarchies to step outside the normal lines of responsibility. Furthermore, because most high officials perform both party and government roles, the structural division between party and government can become extremely blurred.

The formal separation of party and government functions is even less pronounced in China. During many phases of Chinese development, institutional responsibilities were simply ignored as the top CCP leaders moved to decide and implement their directives. During the GPCR, for example, Mao and a few close advisors disregarded both party and government organs as they sought to rekindle the revolutionary spirit of Chinese society. In the aftermath of this chaotic period, which often approached a state of general anarchy, both party and government organs had to be rebuilt as China moved into the more orderly and moderate developmental phase of the 1970s and 1980s. In this period, party and government organs have interacted in a more cooperative and predictable way.

As in the Soviet example, the power of initiation and establishment of general policy guidelines in China rests with the party leadership. In the Soviet case, the Politburo usually is the primary initiating institution at this phase of the policy process; in Mao's China, however, where power was more fluid and concentrated among a few key officials, the smaller Standing Committee of the Politburo assumed a more influential role. The nature of the Standing Committee/Politburo relationship in the post-Mao era is still unclear, but it appears that the role of the Politburo and Secretariat have been enhanced under Chairman Hu's leadership.

Once the top CCP organs establish the general policy guidelines, the State Council expands them into programs and policies that are eventually formalized into government statutes and directives. As the key executive arm of government, the State Council supervises their execution through the central economic ministries and provincial and subprovincial layers of government and administration. Both the party's Standing Committee and the government's State Council intermittently evaluate implementation at all levels to ensure execution in accordance with the CCP's intent.

Although we tend to know more about both party and government organs in Yugoslavia, their relationships also are clouded because of the ongoing change and reform in the Yugoslav system. We do know, however, that there are four key government organs—the state presidency, the Assembly (with its Federal Executive Committee), the provincial governments, and the LCY Executive Committee—whose interrelationships have defined the policy process in the post-Tito phase of Yugoslav development.

In the post-Tito period, the LCY Executive Committee remains the central policymaking body in the Yugoslav system. Functioning on a day-to-day basis, the Executive Committee is in a better position to remain abreast of policy matters than the leading government bodies that meet less frequently and regularly. However, the interrelations between party and government bodies in Yugoslavia exhibit a higher level of sharing and cooperation than do their Soviet and Chinese counterparts. The National Assembly meets more frequently, for longer sessions, and conducts more policy-relevant business than either the Supreme Soviet or the NPC. Although it lacks some of the independence of Western parliaments, the Yugoslav Assembly is nonetheless an important and influential political institution.

As the primary executor of government policy, the Federal Executive Council exhibits considerable autonomy as it goes about its work. The interagency and government working relations approximate those with which we are familiar in the West. In Yugoslavia, the executive arm of government has a base of power and a set of policy responsibilities independent of the domain of the party organs.

SUMMARY

It should be clear that government organs and institutional actors do play indispensable roles in the policy process. In the area of economic planning and policymaking, for example, government officials work with the party leaders in preparing guidelines, formulating plans, and executing policy decisions. Although the party heads may initially prepare and debate policy guidelines among themselves and their advisors, the heads of government planning in the relevant ministries provide extensive comments and review and redraft the guidelines with the help of their own expert staffs. The party heads consider the revised drafts, amend them, and pass them on to the national assem-blies for ratification. It is therefore the responsibility of the government ministries to execute the plans that have been arrived at by this long and intricate process of give and take between party and government hierarchies. There are certain variations on this general party/government relationship in different issue areas (for example, the party organs tend to be even more influential in the area of foreign policy), but the pattern is one that tends to hold across issue areas in all of the Second World states.

Because of their close and overlapping relationship, trying to determine which hierarchy is more important at a particular stage of the policy process is a very difficult task. It is fair to say, however, that the party tends to make policy in all Communist Party states and that the party organs at the summit—the politburo and the secretariat—are the most influential political bodies at the stages of policy initiation and formulation. This is not to say that they make policy in a vacuum and disregard the advice and counsel of others. Rather, they tend to have final authority in initiating policy proposals and deciding on those that come before the decision-making bodies.

Once these crucial decisions are made, the government organs tend to take over and assume their primary roles of ratification, implementation, and execution. After the CPSU Politburo decides the basic guidelines of a new five-year plan or a set of policies toward the Third World, it is up to the government actors to put them into practice and to see that they are properly executed. A loyal, dedicated government bureaucracy, from the highest national executive down to the local commune, is an extremely valuable political asset. In addition to legitimating public policy, a loyal government can promote decisive, effective action. In the next chapter, we will examine to what extent such governments and bureaucracies exist in Communist Party states. Because the policy process is such an important key to the question of value distribution, and to the cause of human dignity in general, we examine it in greater detail in the pages ahead.

Suggestions for Further Reading

Armstrong, John A., *Ideology, Politics, and Government in the Soviet Union,* 4th ed. (New York: Praeger, 1978).

Barnett, A. Doak, *Cadres, Bureaucracy, and Political Power in Communist China* (New York: Columbia University Press, 1967).

Bialer, Seweryn, and **Thane Gustafson,** eds., *Russia at the Crossroads: The 26th Congress of the CPSU* (Winchester, Mass.: Allen & Unwin, 1982).

Carter, April, *Democratic Reform in Yugoslavia: The Changing Role of the Party* (Princeton, N.J.: Princeton University Press, 1982).

Cocks, Paul, *Controlling Communist Bureaucracy* (Cambridge: Harvard University Press, 1977).

Colton, Timothy J., *Commissars, Commanders, and Civilian Authority: The Structure of Soviet Military Politics* (Cambridge: Harvard University Press, 1979).

Harding, Harry, *Organizing China: The Problem of Bureaucracy, 1949–76* (Stanford, Calif.: Stanford University Press, 1981).

Hazard, John N., *The Soviet System of Government,* 5th ed. (Chicago: University of Chicago Press, 1980).

Hinton, Harold C., *An Introduction to Chinese Politics,* 2nd ed. (New York: Praeger, 1978).

Hough, Jerry F., and **Merle Fainsod,** *How the Soviet Union Is Governed* (Cambridge: Harvard University Press, 1979).

Lindbeck, John M. H., *China: Management of a Revolutionary Society* (Seattle: University of Washington Press, 1971).

Nelsen, Harvey W., *The Chinese Military System: An Organizational Study of the Chinese People's Liberation Army* (Boulder, Colo.: Westview, 1977).

Oksenberg, Michel C., and **Frederick C. Teiwes,** eds., *The Chinese Communist Bureaucracy at Work* (New York: Praeger, 1972).

Pye, Lucien, *The Dynamics of Chinese Politics* (Cambridge: Oelgeschlager, Gunn & Hain, 1981).

Schapiro, Leonard, *The Government and Politics of the Soviet Union* (New York: Random House, 1965).

Schurmann, Franz, *Ideology and Organization in Communist China,* 2nd ed., (Berkeley: University of California Press, 1968).

Sharlet, Robert, *The New Soviet Constitution of 1977: Analysis and Text* (Brunswick, Ohio: King's Court Communications, 1978).

Skilling, H. Gordon, *The Governments of Communist East Europe* (New York: Crowell, 1966).

Staar, Richard F., *Communist Regimes in Eastern Europe,* 4th ed., (Stanford, Calif.: Hoover Institution Press, 1982).

Vanneman, Peter, *The Supreme Soviet: Politics and Legislative Process in the Soviet Political System* (Durham, N.C.: Duke University Press, 1977).

Waller, Derek, J., *The Government and Politics of Communist China* (Garden City, N.Y.: Doubleday, 1971).

CHAPTER SIX

The Policy Process in Communist Party States

If Communist parties are so powerful and if governments and bureaucracies are structured to assure their rule, is the policy process a highly rational and organized effort based on carefully studied goals? Or have the increasingly complex and bureaucratized party and government structures resulted in the same sort of "muddling through" policymaking process so characteristic of the developed states in the West? Are Communist Party states well equipped to cope with the pressing challenges of the contemporary age? More generally, in other words, what do we know about policymaking in the one-party systems of the Communist world?

MODELS OF COMMUNIST POLITICS

The question of power and policy in Communist Party states has long intrigued Western scholars. Does the party leadership share power as a collective decision-making body? Is the party head first among equals? What power do other groups and actors have? Are these groups able to influence the policy process? To help address such questions, political scientists often use models, that is, simplified representations (e.g., a diagram or a verbal description) of reality.

Until the 1960s, the *totalitarian model* guided most studies of Communist systems. This model drew attention to a highly organized, dictatorial political process where individuals and groups outside of the top party leadership had no significant political power. Two early proponents of this model, Carl Friedrich and Zbigniew K. Brzezinski, argued that the totalitarian system involves an unavoidable compulsion on the part of the rulers to absorb or destroy all social groups obstructing its complete control.[1] Although this widely used model drew attention to some very important features of Communist political systems, an increasing number of scholars began to feel that it also obscured some equally important aspects. H. Gordon Skilling, for example, contended that the totalitarian model focused too much attention on outputs (the decisions made by the party leadership) and too little on inputs.[2] Skilling argued that

[1]Carl Friedrich and Zbigniew K. Brzezinski, *Totalitarian Dictatorship and Autocracy* (Cambridge: Harvard University Press, 1956). The authors outlined the five essential features of a totalitarian system as: an official ideology, a single mass party, a monopoly of control of all means of armed combat, a monopoly of control of mass communication, and terroristic police control.

[2]H. Gordon Skilling, "Interest Groups and Communist Politics," *World Politics* 18 (3) (1966): 435–451.

groups and actors outside the formal party leadership can and do influence inputs (the structure of demands and supports) that affect the political process.

This viewpoint resulted in new concern with the input side of the policy process and brought increasing attention to the competing interests and bargaining that goes on prior to the formal making of decisions. Scholars with these interests began to use *group or pluralist models* to study power and policy in Communist systems. For example, utilizing a group model, Joel J. Schwartz and William R. Keech explain how a number of significant interest groups—teachers and administrators, higher education and scientific personnel, parents and factory managers—in Soviet society overrode First Secretary Nikita S. Khrushchev's suggestions for education reform in 1958.[3] Many other scholars began to use the group model to draw attention to the important roles that groups play in the Communist political process.[4] Other studies illustrate the importance of political participation, conflict, and competition.[5]

By the 1970s, most scholars felt that increasing numbers of groups and political actors both inside and outside the party hierarchy were becoming influential in the policy process. With the decline of terrorism following Stalin's death; the increasing complexity of social, political, and economic decisions; and the growing expertise of different sectors of society, the conditions were set for a more open, sometimes pluralistic process. Jerry F. Hough contended, for example, that these tendencies had become so prevalent that a new pluralist model of Communist politics was needed.[6] Although many scholars continued to use the totalitarian model and although some were critical of the group and pluralist models,[7] nevertheless, these newer approaches brought attention to the presence of interest group competition and to at least some measure of political pluralism in Communist-run societies.[8]

At the same time, some scholars expressed concern that the new models and approaches were detracting attention and study from the critical features of Communist politics. Franklyn Griffiths noted, for example, that "it seems apparent that interest group activity cannot be regarded as the central phenomenon in Soviet policymaking."[9] Although bringing attention to a host of interesting and, in some respects, significant phenomena concerning pluralism and interest group activity, the newer approaches tend to lose sight of the most important feature of Communist policymaking—the dominant role of the party hierarchy. Griffiths goes on to suggest a *systems model* that stresses the importance of the hierarchical party system and its role in the articulation of values as well as in the formation and execution of policy. Paul Cocks also supports the systems model and notes, "Though generally not used by Western analysts of Soviet af-

[3]Joel J. Schwartz and William R. Keech, "Group Influence and the Policy Process in the Soviet Union," *American Political Science Review* 62 (3) (1968): 840–851.

[4]See, for example, the different studies reported in H. Gordon Skilling and Franklyn Griffiths, eds., *Interest Groups in Soviet Politics* (Princeton, N.J.: Princeton University Press, 1971).

[5]Barbara Jancar, "The Case for a Loyal Opposition under Communism: Czechoslovakia and Yugoslavia," *Orbis* 11 (2) (1968): 415–440; D. Richard Little, "Mass Political Participation in the US and USSR: A Conceptual Analysis," *Comparative Political Studies* 8 (4) (1976): 437–460; Richard C. Thornton, "The Structure of Communist Politics," *World Politics*, 24 (4) (1972): 498–517.

[6]Jerry F. Hough, "The Bureaucratic Model and the Nature of the Soviet System," *Journal of Comparative Administration*, 5 (2) (1973): 134–167; and "The Soviet System: Petrification or Pluralism?" *Problems of Communism* 21 (2) (1972): 25–45.

[7]William E. Odom, "A Dissenting View on the Group Approach to Soviet Politics," *World Politics* 28 (4) (1976): 542–568; and Andrew C. Janos, "Interest Groups and the Structure of Power: Critique and Comparisons," *Studies in Comparative Communism* 12 (1) (1979): 6–20.

[8]Some observers have described Soviet policymaking in the Brezhnev era as one of corporatism, that is, the incorporation of interest groups and specialists into a policy process coordinated and controlled by the Communist Party. See, for example, Valarie Bunce and John M. Echols III, "Soviet Politics in the Brezhnev Era, 'Pluralism' or 'Corporatism'?" in Donald R. Kelley, *Soviet Politics in the Brezhnev Era* (New York: Praeger, 1980), pp. 1–26.

[9]Franklyn Griffiths, "A Tendency Analysis of Soviet Policymaking," in Skilling and Griffiths, eds., *op. cit.*, p. 335.

fairs, the systems approach is equally if not more useful than group theory as a guide and aid in understanding recent developments in the politics of oligarchy in the USSR."[10] Before deciding which of these models might be most useful in our study, it will be instructive to consider how Communist leaders see the question. For example, how would they like to make policy?

POLICYMAKING MODES

In his illuminating essay on the policy process in the Soviet Union, Cocks argues that Soviet leaders would like to make policy according to the *synoptic* or rational-comprehensive mode.[11] On the basis of this mode:

1. The policymakers review all information and specify the needs confronting their system.

2. The policymakers identify goals related to the resolution of these needs and rank them according to a thorough listing of priorities.

3. All possible actions, or policy alternatives, for meeting social needs and fulfilling the specified goals are examined.

4. The costs and benefits of each alternative are carefully reviewed and compared with those resulting from other policy options.

5. The probable outcomes of each policy alternative are evaluated.

6. Finally, the policymakers select that action or set of actions that maximize the probabilities of achieving the desired goals.

The synoptic policymaking process involves careful and thorough planning and the analysis of all available information. Although this process is comprehensive and rational and preferred by policymakers throughout the world, it is difficult to apply.

The *incremental* mode of policymaking, considered a more accurate description of what really happens in most political systems, is described in terms of the following features:[12]

1. The policymakers consider only a limited range of goals that differ only marginally (i.e., incrementally) from previous goals.

2. The policymakers consider only some of the actions for attaining the specified goals, which will differ only marginally from existing policies.

3. The specification of goals and selection of policies are closely intertwined, with selection sometimes determining specification.

4. The total costs and benefits of each alternative action are not carefully evaluated, and probable outcomes are not clearly understood.

5. The policymakers select that action with which they can agree, a policy not necessarily the one that is most probable (scientifically speaking) to achieve the desired goal.

Incremental policymaking, often called the process of muddling through, deals with policy matters as they arise on a more or less *ad hoc* basis and results in decisions that deviate from present policy only marginally. This form of policymaking is essentially short-term, or remedial, and does not place much emphasis on long-range planning and analysis or the foresight necessary to promote future social and ideological goals.[13]

Which mode of policymaking—incremental or synoptic—is preferred by Communist policy makers? How do they assess policy processes in their own systems? Do they see a rational comprehensive approach to attaining high priority goals or do they perceive a process of muddling through? Like the Soviets, other Communist leaders would prefer to make policy according to the synoptic mode.

---

[10]Paul Cocks, "The Policy Process and Bureaucratic Politics," in Paul Cocks et al., eds., *The Dynamics of Soviet Politics* (Cambridge: Harvard University Press, 1976), p. 157.
[11]*Ibid.*

[12]The discussion of the synoptic and incremental modes draws on Charles Lindbloom's *The Intelligence of Democracy* (New York: Macmillan, 1964) and *The Policymaking Process* (Englewood Cliffs, N.J.: Prentice-Hall, 1968).

[13]For a discussion of incrementalism in Communist systems, see Valerie Bunce and John Echols, "Power and Policy in Communist Systems: The Problem of Incrementalism," *Journal of Politics* 40 (4) (1978): 911–932.

Michel C. Oksenberg describes the frustration of the synoptically oriented Mao Zedong as he battled with the short-sighted bureaucrats motivated by incrementalist goals and actions.[14] Although the Chinese bureaucrats considered only a limited range of policy alternatives designed to serve the interests of their government sectors, Oksenberg contends that Mao was guided by the following principles:

> A stress upon investigation of actual conditions; the necessity of remaining attuned to public opinion; the value of clarity, conciseness, and precision of expression; a distrust of highly institutionalized decision-making mechanisms; the need for open debate within Party committees followed by discipline after decisions were made; a belief that policy formulation and implementation are intertwined and hence the wisdom of fusing these two phases of the policy process.[15]

Oksenberg concludes that during Mao's rule, China combined elements of both the synoptic and incremental policy process. Like Mao, leaders throughout the rest of the Communist world are also disturbed by tendencies toward incrementalism. Despite the efforts of the party leadership to coordinate the planning process and their attempts to dominate decision making to move the society toward high-priority goals, the tendency has been toward incremental bargaining and negotiations. The political process is marked by a diversity of interests that result in clashes and compromises among the different leaders and agencies. Under these conditions, in the words of Jerry F. Hough, incrementalism has become the "hallmark of the system."[16]

What happened? How has the tightly controlled highly centralized leadership of Stalinist Russia evolved into a group of political brokers who mediate the competing demands of the different government and bureaucratic sectors? Changes have definitely occurred in Communist systems over the last few decades

and they have had a major impact on the way policy is made. With the death of Joseph Stalin and the deconcentration of power that Khrushchev's rule ushered in, political power has devolved to a certain extent from the highest party bodies to different bureaucratic and state organs.[17] Although Khrushchev was an impulsive policymaker who would often take adventurous action to attain high-priority goals, his policies of liberalization and decentralization dispersed considerable autonomy and policy-relevant authority in the Soviet system.

Khrushchev's successors, Leonid I. Brezhnev and Aleksei N. Kosygin, moved the USSR even further in the direction of incrementalism. Basing their leadership on a system of collective rule, the post-Khrushchev leaders provided the specialized state, party, and scientific complexes with considerable policymaking autonomy in their fields. To avoid the loss of support that had led to Khrushchev's ouster, the leaders usually gave the various departments an incremental budgetary increase each year.[18] Although many terms have been used to describe Soviet politics over the past few decades—institutional pluralism, bureaucratic pluralism, participatory bureaucracy, and so on[19]—most draw attention to a sharing of political power in which ideas and actions flow up as well as down the traditional power hierarchy.

The 1970s witnessed further change in Soviet decision making. The leaders became increasingly concerned and frustrated with their brokerage roles and decided that something would have to be done to stop the trend toward

[14]Michael C. Oksenberg, "Policy-Making under Mao Tsetung, 1949–1968," *Comparative Politics* 4 (2) (1971): 327–328.

[15]*Ibid.*

[16]Hough, "Soviet System," p. 29.

[17]T. H. Rigby, "The De-concentration of Power in the USSR, 1953–1964," in John D. B. Miller and T. H. Rigby, eds., *The Disintegrating Monolith: Pluralist Trends in the Communist World* (Canberra: Australian National University, 1965), pp. 17–45.

[18]Jerry F. Hough, "The Brezhnev Era: The Man and the System," *Problems of Communism* 25 (2) (1976): 1–17.

[19]Hough, "Soviet System," pp. 27–29; Darrell P. Hammer, *USSR: The Politics of Oligarchy* (Hinsdale, Ill.: Dryden, 1974), pp. 223–256; Robert V. Daniels, "Soviet Politics Since Khrushchev," in John W. Strong, ed., *The Soviet Union Under Brezhnev and Kosygin* (New York: Van Nostrand Reinhold, 1971), pp. 22–23.

incrementalism. Cocks reports that the Soviet leaders may have reflected on the experience of the United States and borrowed a capitalist technique (modern systems theory) to move their policymaking process closer to the synoptic mode:

> Indeed, modern systems theory with its sophisticated analytical methodology, managerial technology, and centralizing bias has increasingly attracted Moscow's attention. . . . Like Washington in the sixties, the Kremlin in the seventies exhibit[ed] a peculiarly keen fascination with "technological forecasting," "scientific management," and the "systems approach." . . . Forces aiming at strengthening the capability of central authorities to plan, coordinate, and implement national policies and program priorities have grown steadily since 1970.[20]

Although it is difficult to assess the full impact of these techniques, it is clear that they were adopted to inject greater rationality and planning into the cumbersome and fragmented Soviet policy process.

If the Soviet Union and China are both characterized as representing a blend of synoptic and incremental policymaking processes Yugoslavia has moved considerably further in the direction of the latter. With the movement toward decentralization in the 1950s and 1960s, power was devolved both vertically and horizontally from the party center to regional and administrative complexes. Simultaneously, the role of national planning was severely curtailed, resulting in an unavoidable tendency toward *ad hoc*, remedial policymaking. More and more, the Yugoslav leaders assumed the roles of political brokers in which they would mediate the competing demands of the various regions, different government bureaucracies, or interest groups.

Like the Soviets, the Yugoslav leaders also became concerned about the continuing trend toward incrementalism in the early 1970s. Viewing the lack of national planning and program development, along with increasing interregional and government conflict, as unde-

sirable costs of incrementalism, the League of Communists of Yugoslavia (LCY) leadership decided to reemphasize centralization in planning, decision making, and policy implementation within the Yugoslav system. Placing greater emphasis on party leadership, democratic centralism, and government planning, the new policies represented what Dennison Rusinow so aptly called "a return to Leninism."[21] Although these policies were continued in the post-Tito period, the multiethnic composition and more decentralized political structure of Yugoslavia makes her particularly susceptible to incrementalism.

What kind of policymaking process do we find in Communist systems? Because of the trends toward pluralism in the post-Stalin era, the deconcentration of power, and so forth, incrementalism has become a predominant feature of all Communist systems. At the same time, the continuing presence of centralized party rule with its emphasis on planning, coordination, and management assures the presence of some elements of the synoptic process.

If the policy process is characterized by both group activity and centralized party rule, by pluralism and by centralism, the model we use to study the process must draw attention to all these important phenomena. In addition, it should help account for changes in the various Communist systems and allow us to compare one with another. Unfortunately, no one model satisfies all these criteria. In the pages ahead, we utilize elements of both the *group* model, with its emphasis on bargaining and competing interests, and the *systems* model, with its emphasis on party control, to describe three important phases of the policy process.[22]

PHASES OF POLICYMAKING

The policy process is a series of activities that can be viewed in different phases. For pur-

---

[20]Cocks, *op. cit.*, pp. 157, 163.

[21]Dennison Rusinow, *The Yugoslav Experiment, 1948–1974* (Berkeley, Calif.: University of California Press, 1977), p. 338.

[22]Cocks recommends using both models in viewing the Soviet policy process. (*Op. cit.*, p. 175.)

poses of our study, it is divided into three major parts. *Setting goals* refers to the formulation of policy proposals as responses to ideological guidelines, political interests and exigencies, and social needs. *Taking action* embodies the decision phase where proposals are either approved or vetoed by the relevant authorities. *Producing outcomes* involves the implementation and execution of the policy decisions.

SETTING GOALS

Goals can be derived from an ideology, such as Marxism-Leninism; from social needs that arise in a society in the course of national development; and from the sociopolitical experiences of leaders and masses. In Communist states, goals have all these origins.

The monumental study of Soviet politics by Barrington Moore, Jr., deals with the impact of ideology on social and political change and *vice versa*. Moore outlines the complex interplay between ideology and policy in the following way:

> Once an ideology has been determined it enters in as a determining factor in its own right in subsequent social situations. It has an effect, sometimes slight, sometimes considerable, on the decisions taken by those who hold it. In its turn, it is modified, sometimes slightly, sometimes considerably, by the impact of subsequent considerations.[23]

Historical events in the Soviet Union altered the goals of classical Marxist thought. For example, the equalitarian goals were modified as a result of Stalin's emphasis on variable income because of the need for rapid industrialization; the democratic goals were modified in favor of the authoritarian rule the leaders considered necessary for socialist construction. Moore refers to these more pragmatic ideas and considerations as an ideology of means. He contends that the Soviet ideology of means, as exemplified in the words and deeds of its leaders, has had a greater impact on policy than has the classical Marxist ideology of ends.[24]

Yet the ideology of ends continues to influence policy—at least, so the leaders would have the people believe. The Soviet leaders continue to speak of equality, democracy, respect, and well-being and to act as if these were among the ideological goals that guide Soviet policy. Although it would be naïve to say that such idealistic goals are foremost in the leaders' minds, it would be equally naïve to contend that they have no effect whatsoever. Soviet goals result from both political exigencies (ideology of means) and idealistic goals (ideology of ends). This blend also is reflected in policy. Concerning political power, contemporary Soviet society shows both signs of a one-party dictatorship and a grass-roots democracy; concerning equality, we see both boring uniformities and glaring disparities; concerning respect, both brotherhood and a tragic disregard for human rights. This strange amalgam of policy outcomes reflects the conflicting goals guiding Soviet policymakers. Some result from the expedient ideology of means and others from the idealistic ideology of ends.

The ideology of means is related to the leaders' perceptions of the needs of the people and the state. Vladimir Ilyich Lenin and Joseph Stalin ignored the democratic goals of classical Marxism because they felt authoritarian rule within the party hierarchy was the best way to ensure Communist rule and national development. The Chinese Communists shared this basic assumption although they also recognized the great resources that could be provided by the hundreds of millions of Chinese people. Mao's emphasis on mass involvement and participation resulted from his perception that this was a way to bind the people to the collective and, simultaneously, to mobilize the masses to attain otherwise impossible goals.

The Yugoslavs' turn toward self-management and participatory democracy also grew out of political exigencies and the leaders' perceptions of social needs. After the break with

---

[23]Barrington Moore, Jr., *Soviet Politics—The Dilemma of Power* (Cambridge: Harvard University Press, 1950), p. 412.

[24]*Ibid.*, p. 403.

the Soviet Union in 1947, Josip Broz Tito realized that the Yugoslav regime would have to develop a high level of mass support to preserve its rule in the face of Soviet opposition. The Yugoslav leaders' emphasis on democracy, independence, and a more humanistic road to socialism served that purpose, changed the course of Yugoslav development, and, in the eyes of many observers, took the Yugoslavs closer to the ideals of classical Marxism. So, although it is true that ideology influences the setting of goals, it does not determine them in a vacuum. Sometimes the impact is great, at other times it is slight. Sometimes it is the more utopian ideology of ends, at other times, the more pragmatic ideology of means.

Finally, policy goals also result from the complex interplay between leaders and masses. Mao observed that it is the leadership's responsibility to turn the "scattered and unsystematic ideas of the masses into concentrated and systematic ideas" and to "synthesize their experience into better articulated principles."[25] Conventional wisdom in the West often assumes a shocking insensitivity among the Communist leaders to the needs and demands of their people, yet this feeling seems excessively harsh. Leaders realize that they must maintain the support of their people and that the chances of doing so are greater when they can provide the values the masses desire. They also recognize on occasion that some good can come from the ideas of the masses and that a two-way flow of communication can have valuable benefits. The history of a number of Communist Party states indicates that breakdowns in this communication flow and mass frustration among the populace can result in serious political difficulties for the leaders.[26] While perhaps not the major determinant, nevertheless, the needs of the society,

as perceived and interpreted by the party leaders, have considerable impact on setting goals.

How are the different ideological, social, and personal considerations incorporated into an overall plan? Do the leaders set goals on a short-term, *ad hoc* basis or do they synthesize all the competing goals into a comprehensive plan? In the area of economics, where comprehensive planning appears most feasible, Communist Party states have shown remarkable difficulties. The five-year plans adopted throughout Soviet history and within most of the other Second World states seem unable to match societal needs with productive capacities. Either the plan falls short of the need or supply far exceeds demand.

Considerable effort is made to plan in other areas of government activity. Giant bureaucracies are engaged in the study of regional development, housing, education, health care, energy, the environment, and so on. The significant Soviet advance in space, defense, and some fields of science indicates that long-range planning has freed some areas from the incrementalist muddling characteristic of most bureaucracies. Where goals have been clearly specified and agreed on, as they have in these few areas, major accomplishments have been recorded. Yet past experience has generally been far less than satisfactory and illustrates a long record of overly optimistic plans and unfulfilled goals.

The problems of long-range planning have become even more difficult in the past few decades. With the partial devolution of power to various ministries and regional networks, more individuals are given a role in the planning process. In addition, different groups, often with competing interests in common policy areas, also want to participate in the goal-setting process. Goals desired by one ministry or group often conflict with those of another. Increased funding for space exploration or for defense investment must come at the expense of social programs. These are the guns-versus-butter issues important to the people and over which the party leaders must preside. The re-

[25]Mao Zedong, *Selected Works*, vol. 3 (Beijing: Foreign Languages Press, 1961), pp. 119, 158.

[26]For example, demonstrations of mass discontent in Poland led to the ousters of the party leader Wladyslaw Gomulka in 1970; his successor, Edward Gierek, in 1980; and his successor, Stanislaw Kania in 1981.

sultant bargaining indicates the forces of incrementalism, a trend that narrows the flexibility of the party leaders and limits their overall power and influence in the goal-setting process.

The extent to which the specification of goals is the right and responsibility of the party leaders is an issue of considerable and continuing importance in these states. Today, the general pattern is one in which the national leadership is struggling to maintain final control in the identification of developmental priorities and policy goals. At the same time, the leaders rely heavily on lower-level agencies and complexes, including government organs, party committees, research offices, and so forth, to provide them with reports and recommendations on alternative courses of action. If a Soviet research institute on higher education recognizes certain difficulties in scientific education, for example, it will inform the CPSU Central Committee's Department on Science and Educational Institutions of its concern and findings. These party officials, in turn, may report to members of the CPSU Politburo. Likewise, if a Yugoslav institute in charge of the study of self-management finds certain trends that will be of interest to the LCY leadership, it too will inform them of its specialized knowledge. The party leadership is then in a position to synthesize this more specialized information and include it in its consideration and ranking of national goals.

In contrast to the case of United States and First World states, national priorities and goals are usually established at the highest party and government levels. Although middle-level bureaucrats and private and social groups are often successful in placing items on the American political agenda, the process is more restricted and controlled in Communist Party states.[27] Inputs from these groups are sometimes articulated in Communist Party states,

but they typically are made at lower levels and then incorporated into written reports prepared by research or government agencies before being forwarded to the appropriate party authorities. If the relevant authorities consider the issue sufficiently important, they will bring it to the attention of the party secretariat or politburo where it will be discussed and debated.

TAKING ACTION

Once goals have been identified, they must be transformed into policy proposals. This also tends to be a function of the party leadership. Normally, the party leaders discuss policy options and alternatives with associates and advisors before they formally present them for debate and decision within the politburo. Often they will first make reference to the issues and policy options in public speeches to initiate newspaper coverage and some public debate of the issue. Questions of agriculture or educational reform, for example, may be addressed in the newspapers and discussed for some period outside the official party organs before official action is taken within the politburo. During this period of debate and discussion, such special groups as interest associations, labor unions, research institutes, and so forth, can make their own preferences known. The exchange of ideas is not as open and freewheeling as in the United States; nevertheless, interested parties are likely to express their opinions either by consulting directly with the party authorities or by going through lower-level organs or advisors. For example, a member of the politburo may request to meet personally with the head of a research institute to discuss policy options in some area of domestic or foreign affairs. Scientific institutes of all kinds do specialized government research and are at the disposal of the party leaders. Before the politburo or a close advisor meets to take some policy action, many hours of specialized research and consultation are conducted.

As the issues are clarified and options be-

[27]See Zbigniew K. Brzezinski and Samuel P. Huntington's comparison of policy formation in the Soviet and American systems, *Political Power: USA/USSR* (New York: Viking, 1965), pp. 202–223.

come better defined, coalitions within the politburos often develop. It is at this time that the high concentration of power within the Communist policymaking process becomes most apparent. Although hundreds of individuals would still have considerable influence at this phase of the policy process in First World states, in Communist Party states it resides in the hands of a much smaller number of party members, most of whom hold positions within the politburo. At this stage, politburo members begin the process of persuasion and coalition building. To have their point of view supported, they lobby informally with one another and attempt to secure a voting majority within the politburo's membership.[28]

After this period of discussion and debate, alternative policy actions are formally brought before the members of the politburo. In the Soviet Union, China, Yugoslavia, and all other Second World states, ultimate decision-making power resides within the politburo. When members of these bodies seat themselves at the long tables within their party headquarters, they discuss, debate, and attempt to decide the course of action most likely to achieve their desired goals. Often debate on an important policy matter will carry far into the night or even over a series of long, interminable meetings. Sometimes an issue is dropped or postponed when the party leaders are unable to agree to a satisfactory action or resolution. Ultimately, most policy alternatives come to a vote and the politburo sets forth its official action.

The final decision process tends to correspond with the Leninist principle of democratic centralism. According to this principle, open discussion and debate take place until the point of decision; then, the democratic nature of the process ends and centralism begins. Once the politburo members have voted and made a final decision, expression of alternative points of view is to cease. The principle of democratic centralism assures that different ideas are given expression before a vote is taken, but, once the decision is made, most politburo members abide by the principle of centralism and avoid publicly criticizing decisions with which they may disagree.

Although final decisive action is taken by a small number of people within the top party committee, a successful action still requires the support of a large number of other people. Ross suggests that key institutional actors in the hierarchy must be minimally satisfied before major decisions can be reached.[29] A policy action benefits from having the approval and support of officials from various government agencies and the central committee department most directly concerned with that particular area of policy. A successful action should also have the support of the government presidium.[30] If a particular policy program does not have the support of these people, it is likely to encounter difficulties and could be vetoed. Although the politburo membership can ultimately force an unpopular action through the policymaking process, it must remain sensitive to the preferences of these other individuals and groups. To maintain the support of their broader constituencies, the leaders attempt to operate in an atmosphere of cooperation and consensus.

PRODUCING OUTCOMES

Once a decision has been taken within the high party organs, it is sent to certain party and government bodies for ratification and approval. The most important party organ is the central committee that normally meets every few months to review national party activity and the work of the politburo. Constitutionally recognized as the leading government organs, the Supreme Soviet in the USSR and National People's Congress (NPC) in China are also expected to ratify the politburos' decisions and

[28]Dennis Ross, ''Coalition Maintenance in the Soviet Union,'' *World Politics* 32 (2) (1980): 258–280.

[29]*Ibid.*

[30]See Brzezinski and Huntington's discussion of the necessary support, *op. cit.*, pp. 217–218.

legitimize them by stamping them with the peoples' approval. Because they meet so infrequently, however, many decisions are made and implemented without their ratification or with the approval of the smaller executive bodies (e.g., presidiums or standing committees) of the assemblies.

After a policy action is taken and ratified by the appropriate bodies, the government bureaucracy is responsible for seeing that it is implemented. Government agencies under the chief executive and administrative branch of government, the council of ministers or its counterpart, use a vast bureaucracy to ensure policy execution. Traditional ministries within the council are in charge of executing the party's decisions in their areas of responsibility, including foreign affairs, defense, agriculture, education and culture, and so forth. Relying on their own bureaucracies, the ministers expect, but seldom get, prompt and efficient implementation down the administrative hierarchies. As we will shortly see, executing an idealistic decision is often more difficult than making it.

Although there is considerable party oversight, the government has great authority of its own at this stage of the policy process. The stereotype of paunchy, dim-witted bureaucrats inflexibly carrying out party orders in the isolated hinterlands is a description not without fact. From the nation's capital to the outlying periphery, the Second World states have organized an elaborate but cumbersome and often inefficient network to carry out the party's directives.

In executing party policy, the government bureaucracies have policymaking powers of their own. Brzezinski and Huntington put it simply: "Those who execute policy can also make it."[31] Party directives are typically issued in imprecise and ideological language. The executors must attempt to interpret the meaning and intent of the party leaders. Usually, of course, they feel some compunction to apply

the policies as they perceive the leaders intended them. However, they often have sufficient autonomy and independence of action to register their own preferences or those of the constituency they represent.

As a result, most observers agree that the bureaucracy has become extremely powerful and sometimes dominates the policy process. In evaluating the Soviet experience in which he originally participated, Leon Trotsky contended that bureaucracy assumed this dominant role as early as the 1920s when it "conquered the Bolshevik party [and] defeated the program of Lenin."[32] A leading American scholar speaks of the USSR as a large complex bureaucracy and calls attention to the power of bureaucratic interest groups within the policy process.[33] Overall, the power and importance of the government bureaucracy in shaping outcomes is a widely accepted fact.

The elaborate bureaucratic structure provides the party with certain advantages in producing desired policy outcomes. As a result of the interlocking hierarchies of the party and government organizations illustrated in Figure 5.4, the party can maintain fairly close control over the execution function. The interlocking structure aids communication processes and allows the party direct input into the executive organs. Under these circumstances, the party can quickly mobilize the bureaucracy to carry out policy with a speed and ideological fervor that Western democratic systems with nonpartisan bureaucracies can seldom muster.

Another important factor that contributes to the potential efficiency of Communist administrative branches is what many scholars have referred to as a politicized bureaucracy.[34] Administrative officials in Communist Party states, particularly in the more authoritarian

[31]Brzezinski and Huntington, op. cit., p. 220.

[32]Leon Trotsky, The Revolution Betrayed (New York: Doubleday, 1937), p. 93.

[33]Meyer, op. cit.

[34]Ezra F. Vogel, "Politicized Bureaucracy: Communist China," in Lenard J. Cohen and Jane P. Shapiro, eds., Communist Systems in Comparative Perspective [Garden City, N.Y.: Doubleday (Anchor Books), 1974], pp. 161–170.

and ideological ones, are expected to demonstrate a high level of commitment to the ideology and to the regime. Promotions and forms of monetary and symbolic rewards are often provided on the basis of political consciousness and commitment rather than on professional merit. Accordingly, a politicized bureaucracy might be expected to carry out policy in a more efficient and commited way than the less politicized bureaucracies of the non-Communist West. Of course, commitment is sometimes suspect and problematical and varies considerably among administrative officials and among the various countries. Yet Communist Party countries have a closer fusion of politics and bureaucracy than most of the world and, therefore, can more effectively utilize their politicized bureaucracy to ensure proper execution of the party's policy.[35]

At the same time, Communist bureaucracies in the execution process reveal certain disadvantages compared with the political systems of the West. The socialist public sector is so massive that the policy process in Communist Party states encounters inevitable problems of coordination and control. The state tries to do too much in administering the society. The huge bureaucracy this task requires encounters administrative overloads as it attempts to administer everything from space exploration to day care centers, from business trips to family vacations. Another factor that complicates the implementation and execution of policy involves the problems of regionalism and provincialism so prevalent in China, the Soviet Union, and Yugoslavia. Getting lower-level, regional-oriented bureaucrats to execute national policy uniformly throughout the country is a difficult task that has no easy solution. Although new ideas are now being used to combat the problems of overload, coordination, and so forth, they are no panacea to the

communication barriers that permeate these heterogeneous systems.[36]

A rather different disadvantage of the Communists' efforts to produce rational and effective policy outcomes involves the lack of autonomy and resistance within the politicized bureaucracies. If bureaucrats do disagree with party policy, they sometimes repress their feelings or sabotage the execution process in an underhanded, damaging way. Instead of openly discussing the party's unreasonable expectations concerning industrial output in the five-year plans, for example, an official in charge of steel output might allow the production of a lower quality of steel simply to meet the production quota. The lack of full and open upward communication in the administrative networks of these states is a widely recognized cost of the politicized bureaucracy.

EXAMPLES OF POLICYMAKING

We must remember when examining the policy process that to some extent what you find depends on where you look. The constellation of actors and structure of the process can vary significantly over time, between states, and across policy areas within the same state. Peter H. Solomon, Jr., has provided considerable insight into the area of criminal policy in the USSR.[37] By undertaking a number of case studies stretching from the late 1930s through the 1960s, Solomon uncovered a significant growth of the participation and influence of specialists in policymaking during the post-Stalinist years. Solomon's work provides some valuable insights into the roles of scientists and specialists in the policy process, a phenome-

[35]Party control over the bureaucracies varies over time as well as among countries. See Trong R. Chai, ''Communist Party Control over the Bureaucracy: The Case of China,'' *Comparative Politics* 11 (3) (1979): 359–370.

[36]The USSR is utilizing new hardware (*e.g.*, computers) and software (*e.g.*, managerial methods) in attempting to meet these organizational and structural problems. See Paul Cocks, ''Rethinking the Organizational Weapon: The Soviet System in a Systems Age,'' *World Politics* 32 (2) (1980): 228–257.

[37]Peter H. Solomon, Jr., *Soviet Criminologists and Criminal Policy: Specialists in Policy-Making* (New York: Columbia University Press, 1978).

non that apparently is growing in other Communist states as well.[38]

One of Solomon's case studies deals with the issues of alcoholism and hooliganism. (*Hooliganism* is defined in the Soviet criminal code as "intentional actions violating the public order in a coarse manner and expressing a disrespect for society."[39]) These two issues correspond with two distinct approaches for dealing with the problem of increasing crime in Soviet society. One approach attacks the root of the crime problem, alcoholism. The second addresses the consequences of excessive drinking, hooliganism. The story begins in the winter of 1965 when the Soviet Supreme Court, at the urging of the head of its criminal division, proposed to the Presidium of the Supreme Soviet a compulsory treatment program for alcoholics. Solomon found that the Supreme Soviet reacted favorably to the Supreme Court's proposal but also decided that it was time for a comprehensive consideration and treatment of the issue. Accordingly, the Presidium established an investigative commission, including representatives of many government agencies and scholarly institutions, to study the issues.

During the summer and spring of 1965, the commission collected studies and other submissions from the relevant ministries and academic institutions. In the summer, a major public discussion of the issues took place. Among other things, *Izvestia* printed stories, commentaries, and letters, and there was a series of round-table discussions. In the fall, the Presidium of the Supreme Soviet asked for a draft law on the fight against alcoholism. The law was drafted by the Procuracy Institute, approved by the commission, and forwarded to the Presidium of the Supreme Soviet. Subsequently, the draft law received favorable discussion and press. It appeared that the leaders were going to adopt the alcoholism strategy as a response to the problem of Soviet crime.

Early in 1966, however, the alcoholism proposal was apparently in trouble; there was a mysterious silence about the legislation. Indeed, in April, *Izvestia* published an article by the Minister of Defense of the Social Order, V. S. Tikunov, calling for increased repression of hooliganism. This was a clear hint that someone was considering the antihooliganism strategy rather than the alcoholism response as the way to deal with the problem of Soviet crime. Suddenly, in June, with little public discussion, the Presidium of the Supreme Soviet appointed another commission (actually, a subcommission of the Commission on Legislative Suggestions of the Supreme Soviet) to prepare a finished legal draft of antihooliganism legislation. On July 26, 1966, the Supreme Soviet passed a new law on hooliganism.

Solomon asks what happened. Why did Tikunov's proposal on hooliganism prevail over the carefully prepared and publicly acclaimed legislation on alcoholism? Apparently, three major reasons exist: (1) the high personal stature of Tikunov, (2) the political clout of his ministry, and (3) a conservative backlash against the post-Stalinist liberalization of law, which the alcoholism legislation was considered to be. In retrospect, it appears that the Soviet leadership was vacillating between two possible responses to the problem of crime. Just as it appeared that alcohol prevention would prevail, Minister Tikunov intervened with his attack on hooliganism and the political leadership went along. Solomon's study indicates that the policymaking process can be quite fluid, can involve diverse actors with conflicting interests, and can be influenced by those outside the immediate party leadership. However, when political interests and scientific recommendations come in conflict, political considerations generally prevail. In this context, incrementalism prevails over rational, comprehensive decision making.

A critical area where this fact has been obvious concerns Soviet economic policy. The period of rapidly accelerating economic growth in the USSR has ended. The Soviet economy is

[38]The following discussion draws heavily on Solomon, *op. cit.*, pp. 81–90.

[39]*Ibid.*, p. 194.

now characterized by decelerating growth; while the economy is still growing, it is growing at a slower rate than previously and much more slowly than the Soviet leaders desire. Under present economic trends, it will be very difficult for the Soviets to achieve some of their high-priority goals. Some observers believe that while the Soviet economy will not collapse, it may deteriorate even further in the future in view of labor shortages, low productivity, and an impending energy crisis. These economic pressures confront the Soviet leaders with some very difficult challenges. What are they to do to improve the Soviet economic future?

A leading American economist has outlined four alternatives that may realistically be considered by the Soviet leaders for adoption.[40] The "conservative" alternative would consist of the present system projected into the future with minor incremental changes. The "reactionary" approach would represent a return to the highly disciplined economic system of the Stalinist period. This alternative would place a high priority on discipline and order and mean an even greater assertion of centralized CPSU control of the economy. The "liberal" alternative would maintain traditional planning methods while liberalizing restrictions on private initiative and competition. Finally, the "radical" approach would represent the most significant change and emphasize the decentralization of planning and management found in the Yugoslav and Hungarian economies.

Although Western scientific evidence suggests that fundamental changes—that is, the liberal or radical approaches—are required to right the Soviet economy, past CPSU leaders have opted for the conservative alternative. The choices made and changes pursued have been incremental and technical rather than synoptic and comprehensive. Why is this so? Berliner argues that it is because politics rather than ec-

onomics dictates the choices.[41] The leaders opted for the conservative strategy because it is most in line with the vested interests of the Soviet leaders and governing institutions. Scientific, rational analysis might suggest radical solutions, but short-run political considerations in the USSR rule them out. While there is considerable support within the Soviet leadership for the "conservative" and even the "reactionary" approaches, there is very little for the liberal, and even less for the radical, alternatives. The Soviet economy continues to require innovative and fundamental reform. However, rather than undertake such reforms, the Soviet leaders have tried to muddle through incrementally by making choices on the basis of short-run political considerations rather than on the basis of rational and comprehensive economic considerations and norms. One might argue, however, that within the Soviet context rational comprehensive analysis has also ruled out the liberal and radical alternatives. That is, if Soviet leaders begin with the assumption, as they apparently have in the past, that fundamental change of the economic system cannot be tolerated, then synoptic decision making will also disallow the liberal and radical options. Clearly, past Soviet leaders have been ill disposed to fundamental economic reform under both modes of decision making. Gorbachev's response to the economic challenge will be a topic of considerable importance and interest in the years ahead. Although it is too early to forecast with confidence, the available preliminary evidence suggests that the more technocratically minded Gorbachev regime may be more inclined toward genuine reform than its more cautious, conservative predecessors.

Examining five policy issues in China during Mao's reign—the Twelve-Year Agricultural Program, administrative decentralization, the commune movement, the Socialist Education Campaign, and the ideological rectification campaign—Parris H. Chang made substantial progress in determining how policy was made

[40]See Joseph S. Berliner, "Managing the USSR Economy: Alternative Models," *Problems of Communism* 22 (1) (1983): 40–56.

[41]*Ibid.*, p. 54

and who was making it in the 1950s and 1960s.[42] Chang found a variety of important actors in the decision-making process in addition to Mao, the Chinese Communist Party (CCP) Politburo, and the CCP's Standing Committee. Other actors included the party's Central Committee; party officials at the provincial and local levels; the People's Liberation Army (PLA); bureaucracy; and extraparty forces, such as the Red Guard and revolutionary rebels. The actors involved, of course, varied according to the policy area. For example, Chang noted that those institutions involved in setting goals, taking action, and producing outcomes in the area of rural policies at the national level included at least the Ministry of Agriculture, the Agricultural and Forestry Staff Office, the CCP Central Committee Rural Work Department, and the CCP Secretariat, Politburo, and Central Committee.[43]

How, then, was policy made in Mao's China? Chang contends that:

> Policy in Communist China was not made by a few leaders alone; actors possessing different political resources participated, directly or indirectly in each stage of the policymaking process and affected in a variety of ways, the decision-output of the regime.[44]

At the same time, Chang cautions, it is necessary to recognize the enormous power wielded by Mao. When Mao was most active—for example, during the second half of the 1950s—the policymaking process was more personalized and totalitarian and less routine. Mao used the other institutions and actors to initiate, accept, and carry out the policies he preferred. For example, when other party leaders favored a go-slow approach toward organizing collectivization in 1955, Mao argued vehemently for stepping up the tempo in a secret speech to provincial party secretaries. By skillfully using others, Mao was able to overcome the go-slow opposition and launch an intense nationwide campaign to accelerate agricultural collectivization.[45]

The policymaking process became more open and less totalitarian in the post-Mao period. American Sinologists Oksenberg and Bush describe China as having moved from "revolutionary totalitarianism" to "reformist authoritarianism."[46] They see the Maoist "totalitarian revolutionaries" as having attempted a rapid, violent, and comprehensive transformation of China. In contrast, the "authoritarian reformers" of the 1980s appear to be committed to more gradual and peaceful change within a more stable political framework. Although Deng, Zhao, Hu, and the other reformers remain authoritarian and tolerate no organized opposition to their rule, they adhere to a more open, institutionalized form of collective rule. Decision making is more likely to involve the relevant party and governmental bodies and be based upon compromise and consensus. The authoritarian reformers have shifted the policymaking process away from Maoist totalitarianism and mobilization to a more institutionalized process of governing through the party and governmental bureaucracies. The power of individuals and factions has been reduced; the power of governmental institutions and scientific bodies increased. The reformers are allowing more scientific input and broader discussion of policy alternatives. They have established the Chinese Academy of Sciences and reestablished many professional associations in order to promote a more scientific policy process. Chinese policymaking in the 1980s has become more open and incremental.

COMPARATIVE OVERVIEW

To an extent unparalleled in most other political systems, the Soviet leaders have attempted

[42]Parris H. Chang, *Power and Policy in China*, 2nd enlarged ed. (University Park, Pa: Pennsylvania State University Press, 1978).

[43]*Ibid.*, pp. 186–187.

[44]*Ibid.*, p. 181.

[45]*Ibid.*, p. 189.

[46]Michel Oksenberg and Richard Bush, "China's Political Evolution: 1972–82," *Problems of Communism* 31 (5) (1982): 1–19.

to articulate their plans for the future. In the visions they outlined at their recent party congresses and through other forums, three long-range goals have special significance: continued party leadership, continued industrialization and development of the defense sector, and a rise in the standard of living. Concerning the first goal, after considering the options to the authoritarian form of CPSU rule, the party leaders decided that centralized policymaking dominated by the Communist Party is a necessary prerequisite to other Soviet goals. In attempting to build a strong socialist state, the leaders chose to follow an ideology of means, with its centralizing bias, rather than the classical Marxist ideology of ends, with its emphasis on more democratic rule. Given their dominant role in policy formation, the CPSU leaders were able to select other goals in governing the Soviet future; e.g., continued industrialization and heavy defense spending. These represent more of the same, a continuation of the policies of the past.

Proceeding with single-minded dogmatism in following the specified plan, policymakers have disallowed either internal dissidents or Western critics to detract them from their objectives. Stressing technological forecasting and systems theory, the Soviets would like to follow a "scientific" process of decision making and management to fulfill the Soviet vision. Yet, Communist planners in the Soviet Union and other Marxist-Leninist systems often acknowledge that they have not achieved the synoptic planning and policymaking they so strongly desire.

The goal-setting process in Maoist China showed a greater emphasis on ideology, both the means and ends varieties, than in either the USSR or Yugoslavia. The Chinese Communists approached the task of national development through a perspective very different from our own. Mao and his associates studied the Chinese dilemma and decided on a revolutionary, peasant-oriented strategy of development. Ignoring the Soviet model of heavy industrialization as well as the more consumption-oriented approach of the West, Mao attempted to forge a distinctively Chinese road to socialism.

In this process, Mao played the roles of a revolutionary totalitarian. After evaluating alternative courses of policy, Mao attempted to take actions he judged were in the collective interest. It is here, Michel C. Oksenberg notes, that Mao encountered the incrementalist intrusions of the self-interested bureaucrats.[47] According to Oksenberg, Mao strove to operate according to the synoptic mode, whereas specialized interests drove China toward incrementalism. This leads Oksenberg to observe: "The [Maoist] policy process combine[d] elements of two separate models . . . the 'synoptic' and the 'incremental' policy processes."[48]

In the post-Mao period, there has been a further trend toward incrementalism. Lacking the personal stature of Mao, the new leaders (Hu Yaobang, Deng Xiaoping, Zhao Ziyang, and their colleagues) are involved in the more pedestrian adjustment of interests with all of the conflict, compromise, and consensus building that implies. The overriding theme of politics in the more recent period has been the continuous and often intense conflict beneath the facade of leadership unity. However, if the more pragmatic leaders can reach a higher level of agreement on the specifics of Chinese modernization and gain the widespread support of an increasing number of actors, the possibility for more rational comprehensive policymaking exists.

One of the features that has distinguished the Yugoslav form of decentralized socialism over the last few decades has been the relative absence of long-range planning. Although the result has been the most pluralistic system in the Communist world, it is also the site of considerable incrementalism. Alternative courses of action are examined, but rarely is the policy that is most likely to serve the overall Yugoslav interest selected. Decisions are made to reach agreement in the contentious and conflict-

[47]Oksenberg, op. cit., pp. 323–360.
[48]Ibid, p. 324.

ridden state rather than to select the optimal policy. Policy programs are rarely executed in correspondence with a long-term plan, because either a plan does not exist or, if it does, it tends to be so ill-defined and vague that administrative discretion is inevitable. The leaders attempted to recentralize the fragmented system and reassert the leading role of the party in the 1970s and 1980s, but the politics of incrementalism is continuing in the post-Tito era.

Relative to First and Third World states, one might consider the Communist-run states of the Second World better equipped to make policy according to the synoptic mode. Centralized political leadership within an authoritarian system of government facilitates long-term planning, coordinated decision making, and more effective implementation and execution. A small group of decision makers is relatively free to weigh competing goals, study alternative actions to attain them, and decide on those that appear to be in the collective interest. At the same time, excessive centralization can rule out valuable information and contribute to the process of ''group think,'' that is, a situation where individuals are reluctant to challenge prevailing opinions.

Another significant trend is pushing the Communist countries toward incrementalism and away from the synoptic decision-making mode. This trend involves the continuing growth of government. The Communist states have big governments and they are getting big-ger. With the growth of government come the bureaucratic fiefdoms that the leaders find difficult to control. Making special interest demands on the top decision makers, these bureaucracies discourage the radical actions that many policy problems require. The Soviet economy cries out for fundamental reforms. Synoptic, rational comprehensive decision making suggests the need for economic decentralization and change. Motivated by conservative political interests, the economic bureaucracies do not want to relinquish their traditional controls. New CPSU leader Gorbachev has shown early signs of taking greater command of the Soviet system. Whether he will succeed is still open to question.

In summary, which systems make policy according to the preferred synoptic mode and which tend toward the incremental? Of the three comparative cases, although the Soviet Union is the most synoptic, considerable incrementalism prevails. China has represented a blend of both decision-making modes, but, in the post-Mao era, has moved considerably in the direction of incrementalism. Yugoslavia, traditionally the most open and democratic system, has the most incrementalist policy process.

Now that we have some understanding of the way political actors behave and how they formulate, make, and execute public policy, we can consider what power and policy mean to the people. This is the theme of Chapter Seven.

Suggestions for Further Reading

Aspaturian, Vernon V., ed., *Process and Power in Soviet Foreign Policy* (Boston: Little, Brown, 1971).

Bruce, James B., *The Politics of Soviet Policy Formation: Khrushchev's Innovative Policies in Education and Agriculture* (Monograph Series in World Affairs) Denver: University of Denver, 1976).

Brzezinski, Zbigniew K., and **Samuel P. Huntington,** *Political Power: USA/USSR* (New York: Viking, 1965).

Chang, Parris H., *Power and Policy in China,*

2nd enlarged ed. (University Park, Pa.: Pennsylvania State University Press, 1978).

Friedgut, Theodore H., *Political Participation in the USSR* (Princeton, N.J.: Princeton University Press, 1979).

Gross, Susan, *Pluralism in the Soviet Union* (New York: St. Martin's Press, 1983).

Gustafson, Thane, *Reform in Soviet Politics: Lessons of Recent Policies on Land and Water* (Cambridge: Cambridge University Press, 1981).

Hoffman, Erik P., and **Robbin Laird,** *The Politics of Economic Modernization in the Soviet Union* (Ithaca, N.Y.: Cornell University Press, 1982).

Hough, Jerry F., *The Soviet Prefects* (Cambridge: Harvard University Press, 1969).

Hough, Jerry F., and **Merle Fainsod,** *How the Soviet Union Is Governed* (Cambridge: Harvard University Press,1979).

Juviler, Peter H., and **Henry W. Morton,** eds., *Soviet Policy-Making: Studies of Communism in Transition* (New York: Praeger, 1967).

Lampton, David M., *The Politics of Medicine in China: The Policy Process, 1949–77* (Boulder, Colo.: Westview Press, 1977).

Morton, Henry W., and **Rudolf L. Tokes,** eds., *Soviet Politics and Society in the 1970's* (New York: Free Press, 1974).

Ploss, Sidney I., ed., *The Soviet Political Process* (Waltham, Mass.: Ginn, 1971).

———, *Conflict and Decision-Making in Soviet Russia* (Princeton, N.J.: Princeton University Press, 1965).

Rusinow, Dennison, *The Yugoslav Experiment, 1948–1974* (Berkeley: University of California Press, 1977).

Schapiro, Leonard, ed., *Political Opposition in One-Party States* (London: Macmillan, 1972).

Skilling, H. Gordon, and **Franklyn Griffiths,** eds., *Interest Groups in Soviet Politics* (Princeton, N.J.: Princeton University Press, 1971).

Solomon, Peter H., Jr., *Soviet Criminologists and Criminal Policy: Specialists in Policy-Making* (New York: Columbia University Press, 1978).

CHAPTER SEVEN

Political Performance in Communist Systems

One year after Karl Marx's death in 1883, Friedrich Engels, using Marx's research notes and materials, wrote:

> Democracy in government, brotherhood in society, equality in rights and privileges, and universal education, foreshadow the next higher plane of society to which experience, intelligence and knowledge are steadily tending. It will be a revival, in a higher form, of the liberty, equality and fraternity of the ancient gentes.[1]

But what progress, if any, have Communist states made toward this higher plane of society called communism? To what extent have they furthered democracy, brotherhood, equality, and universal education? What do their records tell us about the cause of human dignity? Although most political science textbooks, including the bulk of this one, deal with Communist political systems from the top down, it seems reasonable to ask what the system has meant to the rank-and-file citizen. Therefore, this final chapter focuses on performance to attempt at least a partial assessment of what Communist states have accomplished for their people thus far.

[1]Friedrich Engels, "The Origin of the Family, Private Property and the State," reprinted in Robert C. Tucker, ed., *The Marx-Engels Reader* (New York: Norton, 1972), p. 659.

When we evaluate Communist systems, we should be aware that we have far less statistical data than we need and would like. Ideally, we should have statistical indicators describing the amount and distribution of each of the values in all Communist societies. Although we do have useful, albeit incomplete, indicators for most of the values, data shortcomings will force us to leave many of the questions unanswered. Some judgments will be left for the reader to make and others will be made more satisfactorily sometime in the future.

We should also caution readers to be sensitive when evaluating and comparing systems at different levels of economic and political development. Whereas the Soviet Union is clearly an industrialized state and has had nearly 70 years to develop socialism, China is more backward economically and younger politically. Factors such as these influence what states have been able to accomplish and certainly affect their contemporary performance levels. Although we cannot qualify all of our judgments, readers should be aware of, and sensitive to, these facts.

As outlined in our introduction, we evaluate the political performance of Communist Party states in two different respects. First, we attempt to *appraise* the leaders' and systems'

143

general records in allocating the four values. Have their goals and actions resulted in democracy or dictatorship? In respect or suspicion? In welfare or poverty? In enlightenment or ignorance? Then, we try to *explain* why the values have been allocated in the ways that they have and why these allocations have resulted in particular outcomes.

POWER AND POLICY: DEMOCRACY OR DICTATORSHIP?

Democratic power relationships are viewed as important and necessary features of both socialism and communism by Marxist-Leninist leaders. Vladimir Ilyich Lenin once went so far as to say that socialism could not be successful and communism would not be achieved unless "full democracy" was implemented. But what have Communist Party states done to promote the form of socialist democracy that they so fervently espouse? What *goals* were set, what *actions* taken, and what *outcomes* experienced in the Soviet, Chinese, and Yugoslav cases?

A number of *goals* have motivated Soviet policymakers concerning the distribution of power. Some goals involve the encouragement of more mass and expert involvement in the decision process, goals that seem to promote movement toward both increased democracy and incrementalism. However, the primary goal—the maintenance of Communist Party control over a centralized decision-making process—seems to be much less democratic in nature. In a sense, then, the goals are conflicting. The primary goal has been fairly constant throughout the entire Soviet experience and aims to ensure the Communist Party of the Soviet Union's (CPSU's) leading role in the political system. Even after 60 years of Soviet socialism, the CPSU is unwilling to allow organized opposition to challenge its privileged role in the political arena.

At the same time, party leadership appears to be increasingly cognizant of some of the major costs of excessively centralized rule. One important cost involves the loss of

decision-making expertise that exists among different specialized groups and individuals in the society; the second concerns the apathy, alienation, and lack of political support that can develop among a noninvolved citizenry. As a result of this awareness, the party leaders have advanced two other goals concerning the distribution of power within the Soviet system. The first involves the expansion of the influence of ministerial and scientific centers and organs in the policy process. Aware that the central party leadership is not the repository of all expertise and knowledge in the modern era, party leaders have attempted to increase the involvement of these specialized scientific complexes in the policymaking process by delegating increasing power to these lower level institutions. By drawing new actors into the policy process, they hope to make the decision-making process more efficient and scientific.

Another important goal involves increasing the level of mass political participation. Although prohibiting political activity in opposition to party policy, the leaders recognize the benefits of an active, participant society and, therefore, encourage the involvement of the Soviet people in the building of communism. Encouraging citizen participation in a broad range of social and political tasks is viewed by the Soviet elite as a valuable strategy for increasing support and commitment to the system.[2]

The Soviet leaders have undertaken a variety of actions to achieve these basic goals. They have prohibited any challenges to the leading role of the CPSU; they have sought and encouraged the advice of specialized government and scientific complexes; and they have promoted mass involvement in the political system. For the most part, the party's actions have met with success. The CPSU has not been challenged. Its powerful, dominating role is as secure as ever. In addition, considerable evidence suggests that government and scientific experts have been given a wider role in policy-

[2]See Theodore H. Friedgut, *Political Participation in the USSR* (Princeton, N.J.: Princeton University Press, 1979).

TABLE 7.1 Political Participation in the Soviet Union, 1954–1976

Group	1954–1955 (in millions)	Percent Increase 1954–1963	1963–1964 (in millions)	Percent Increase 1963–1976	1975–1976 (in millions)
Adult population	120.8	16%	140.0	17%	163.5
Party members and candidates	6.9	51	10.4	51	15.7
Deputies to local soviets	1.5	27	2.0	13	2.2
Trade union members	40.2	60	68.2	57	107.0
KOMSOMOL members	18.8	17	22.0	59	35.0
Controllers	apparently 0	–	4.3	118	9.2
Activists in independent organizations	?	–	20.0	55	31.0
People's auxiliary police (*druzhinniki*)	0	–	5.5	27	7.0

SOURCE: Adapted from Jerry F. Hough, "The Brezhnev Era: The Man and the System," *Problems of Communism* 25 (2) (1976):10.

making and have had a significant impact upon policy.[3] Finally, the data presented in Table 7.1 illustrate that the state has expanded the level of political participation among the Soviet population. After spending three years as chief of the Moscow bureau for the *Washington Post*, Robert G. Kaiser observed that "there is probably no society in the Western world with as large a percentage of politically active citizens."[4] Yet, although many citizens are politically active, they are expected to participate within bounds prescribed by the CPSU. At the same time, we should not underestimate the meaning and significance of this activity. Like citizens throughout the world, most Soviet people support their government and are quite satisfied to participate in the activities available to them.[5]

The Chinese Communists have also been guided by the primary goal of maintaining the party's leading and unopposed political role. This, however, has not always been the case. During the Great Proletarian Cultural Revolution (GPCR) in the late 1960s, Mao Zedong set aside this goal and allowed the Chinese Communist Party (CCP) and many of its leading officials to be challenged by critical groups and individuals, such as the radical Red Guard. During this tumultuous period of Chinese development, Mao's goals of increased participation and equality came into conflict with the party's leading role. A number of specific actions, such as mass demonstrations, assaults on party officials who were taking the bourgeois line, and the dismissal of ranking party elites challenged the unchecked CCP leadership role. In addition, a series of actions leading to higher levels of power decentralization to the provincial and local levels, including the factories and work places, resulted in a major flattening of the traditional power hierarchy.[6]

China's record on the power value during the Maoist and the more recent reformist peri-

[3]See, for example, Peter H. Solomon, Jr., *Soviet Criminologists and Criminal Policy: Specialists in Policy-Making* (New York: Columbia University Press, 1978).

[4]Robert G. Kaiser, *Russia* (New York: Atheneum, 1976), p. 137.

[5]For a critical and provocative review of the power and democracy question in the USSR, see Roy A. Medvedev, *On Socialist Democracy* (New York: Knopf, 1975). Although Medvedev is an uncompromising Russian dissident, he remains a Marxist and believes the only possibility for satisfactory change lies within the existing system.

[6]During the GPCR, increased worker participation in management was accompanied by increased management participation in production. Managers were expected to assume part of the manual workload just as workers shared in the management of the enterprise. See, for example, Mitch Meisner, "Report from China: The Shenyang Transformer Factory—A Profile," *China Quarterly* 52 (1972): 717–737.

ods suggests elements of both democracy and dictatorship. Although party dominance remains, we should not overlook evidence of genuine participation. A leading expert put it in the following way:

> Organizational, social, and political constraints notwithstanding, significant nonritual participation does take place in China, under conditions well understood by all participants. Although there appears to be infrequent use of formal "democratic" instruments, and although mobilization instruments do not often serve as effective input channels, alternate forums allow for important, if limited, forms of genuine participation.[7]

Victor C. Falkenheim goes on to suggest that informal lobbying and personal networks constitute the basic techniques by which citizens pursue their goals.

The mass-line idea, one of Mao's important inventions, continues to influence citizen/party power relations in the post-Mao era. The mass line is a pattern of reciprocating communications between party members and the masses. Although this concept reserves primary decision-making power for the party and does not allow meaningful popular influence at the national level, it may provide the masses some minimal level of input and facilitate mass influence at lower levels of government. Because of the way the mass-line idea links masses with the party leadership, it aids the process of policy implementation at all administrative levels. Most recently, the reformist leaders under Deng Xiaoping have experimented with a host of urban, rural, government, and party reforms. A central objective in all the reforms has been to expand individual initiative in Chinese affairs. Although the role of the party is to be reduced—for example, it is to play a lesser role in personnel appointments (*nomenklatura*)—it certainly will not be eliminated. Great change is taking place in China today; however, the Communist Party remains in firm control.

Significant change is also taking place in Yugoslavia. Yugoslav leaders appear dedicated to their experiment in self-governing socialism, an innovative and serious effort to develop equalitarian democratic power relations at lower levels in their society. Basing the self-management system on the goal of decentralized, democratic administration of social, economic, and political affairs, the Yugoslavs have taken numerous actions to implement their experiment at the local level of government. Beginning in the 1950s with workers' councils in factories and then expanding them over the years to include democratic forms of administration in other organizations, the Yugoslav Constitution *requires* self-management in all social, economic, and political bodies. Every school, factory, and organization is required by law to manage its own affairs. Yet, levels of participation and influence are certainly less than the ideology calls for.[8] Additionally, ultimate policymaking power at the federal level is still reserved for the central organs of the party. After partially withdrawing from power in the 1960s—only to witness a dangerous rise in interregional political conflict—the League of Communists of Yugoslavia (LCY) reasserted the party's leading role and now views itself as the primary political power. "We Communists are in power in this country," proclaimed a leading official of the LCY: "As the most responsible, progressive and most conscious part of the working class, the League of Communists holds the power in its hands."[9]

Yugoslav leaders have been guided by two primary and conflicting goals concerning the distribution of power in their political system. Although earnestly pursuing the democratic ideals of self-governing socialism, they have been unwilling to relinquish the party's leading role, which would be required in a system of genuine democracy. Yugoslav leaders want

[7]Victor C. Falkenheim, "Political Participation in China," *Problems of Communism* 27 (3) (1978): 31–32.

[8]See Gary K. Bertsch and Josip Obradović, "Participation and Influence in Yugoslav Self-Management," *Industrial Relations* 18 (3) (1979): 322–329.

[9]*Ideological and Political Offensive of the League of Communists of Yugoslavia* (Belgrade: Secretariat for Information, 1972), p. 46.

In Yugoslavia's system of self-management, citizens are encouraged to participate in the affairs of all social, political, and economic organizations. Here is a meeting of a workers' council in a machinery factory near Belgrade.

both self-management *and* party rule and have undertaken actions to pursue these conflicting principles. Although it is conceivable that the post-Tito leadership will continue to pursue both goals simultaneously, many observers call attention to the inherent contradiction between the two and contend that genuine democracy can never be attained when one group of party elites is allowed a privileged and more powerful role in the political system.

The outcomes in Yugoslavia have reflected these competing and conflicting goals. Self-management has made considerable inroads into power relations within the society. Many of the authoritarian arrangements of the past have been replaced with more democratic processes involving large and varied groups of people. But the process of democratization is still incomplete and is likely to remain that way as long as the LCY maintains its dominating role.

In comparative terms, we can conclude that the national policy process in each of the Second World states is carefully orchestrated by the Communist Party. No organized opposition is permitted; there is little open and free public debate of political issues outside of the party organs; and there are no truly competitive elections where national leaders can be selected by the broader populace. Yet, although it

certainly would be misleading to label the political process democratic, it is in some ways unfair to call it dictatorial. Communist Party states are not dictatorships in the sense that one person or a small group of people dictates every policy outcome. At the regional and local levels, political choices are often the consequence of a wide variety of debates and discussions. Even at the national level of government, where the party leadership takes greatest interest and is most closely involved, the leaders probably aggregate and arbitrate competing interests just as much as they dictate. As Mao observed, it is the leadership's role to synthesize. In this process of arbitration and synthesis within the party and government machinery, the participation of diverse groups and political actors within the bureaucracy is often extensive and intense. Alternative policy actions are discussed and debated and, in some cases, the party leaders see their policy preferences defeated.

The term *dictatorship* is inaccurate, but even more so is the term *democracy*. It is true that there are some democratic features in the policy processes of Communist Party states, particularly at the local levels of government. Taking the lead in experimentation and innovation, the Yugoslav experience in self-management exhibits many forms of participatory democracy and is a genuine effort to devolve some policymaking powers and responsibilities to industrial organizations, to lower levels of government, and to the mass populace in general. Although in the past Communist Party states criticized the Yugoslav's experiment in self-management as revisionism and viewed it with reluctance and suspicion, different forms of self-administration and worker participation within their own centralized state and economic systems are creeping in. The Chinese were once the most critical of the Yugoslavs' experimentation, but now they too are experimenting with self-management.[10] Even the Soviets note that "the objective need to

[10]"Self-Management Enlivens Enterprises," *Beijing Review* 23 (12) (1980): 25-26.

consolidate and improve centralized management of production is coupled with a search for ways and means of improving the democratic forms of economic management."[11] In recent speeches, Gorbachev has spoken favorably of self-management and the further development of socialist democracy. In a December 1984 speech to an ideological conference and in his electoral address of February 1985, he made numerous positive reference to self-management (which, he noted, Lenin "never had counterposed to Soviet state power"), to the various interests of different social groups, to involving the work force more fully in the affairs of their collective, and to the need for greater "openness" (*glasnost*) in party and state life. To what extent these statements are empty rhetoric, only the future will tell. At the least, however, they call attention to the need for democratic developments in Soviet society.

Finally, at issue here is what exactly is meant by the term *democracy*. With the typical conception of rule by the people in mind, the Communist leaders contend that their high levels of citizen participation qualify them as socialist democracies. True, most all these states are characterized by high levels of participation in sociopolitical affairs, but most participation is still restricted and constrained by general party policy and does not encourage the free thought and choice that genuine democracy presupposes.

Why do Communist Party states have elitist political systems that are neither full dictatorships nor genuine democracies? What determinants have caused this? In the environmental realm there are a number of historical, cultural, and socioeconomic factors that have pointed the countries away from democracy. First, the historical traditions of most of the countries had a very weak democratic base. Most were states characterized by autocratic, imperial rule in which elitist, nonparticipant political cultures developed among the leaders and masses alike. The autocratic rule of tsarist

Russia, imperial China, and Yugoslavia, for example, promoted a culture and set of traditions that did not prepare the countries for democratic rule. Robert C. Tucker, Alfred Meyer, and Gabriel Almond have pointed out that the Communist systems derive their values, including their political values, as much from their cultural past as from the tenets of Marxism.[12] Hence, it was relatively easy and not particularly surprising that the new Communist regimes carried on in the undemocratic tradition.

Individual factors—that is, real live humans—and political realities have also affected this developmental experience. Lenin and Stalin were leaders willing to forego democratic ideals to achieve political objectives. During the early, formative years of communist development, their totalitarian rule left a deep indelible imprint on the nature of Communist politics. The new Communist states of Eastern Europe and Asia adopted an ideology and form of government that was developed under the Stalinist regime. In some cases the Soviet form of elitist, Communist Party rule was forced upon them; in other cases the new Communist leaders chose, at least temporarily as in the case of China and Yugoslavia, to copy the Soviet model. In all countries, a Soviet style of Communist Party rule was established. Some, like China and Yugoslavia, were able to break free of Soviet control and experiment with some reforms. Others, like most of the countries of Eastern Europe, find the Soviet pattern of elitist rule forced on them still today. Furthermore, it should be noted that the original, and many of the current leaders, of the East European states were trained in the Soviet system of rule. They, too, were unwilling or, because of Soviet influence, unable to adopt a system of more democratic rule.

[11]B. Topornin and E. Machulsky, *Socialism and Democracy* (Moscow: Progress Publishers, 1974), p. 102.

[12]See, for example, Robert C. Tucker, "Culture, Political Culture and Communist Society," *Political Science Quarterly 88* (2) (1973): 173–190; and Alfred Meyer, "Communist Revolutions and Cultural Change," *Studies in Comparative Communism 5* (4) (1972): 345–372; and Gabriel A. Almond, "Communism and Political Culture Theory," *Comparative Politics 15* (2) (1983): 127–138.

Furthermore, the people of these new Communist Party states were not fully capable of accepting the responsibilities of democracy. Residing in economically deprived and less-developed states and growing up under autocratic systems of government, the mass populace was ill equipped to undertake the type of participation a democratic government requires. Over the last few decades, however, great changes have taken place among these populations. Today, they are uniformly literate (with some exceptions among the Asian states) and have the education and training necessary to become able participants in the political process. Party leaders, however, continue to be reluctant about providing the mass populace with more meaningful and far-reaching political choices. True, they have encouraged higher levels of participation, but the participants' freedoms of choice and action continue to be restricted by the principles of centralized party rule. Some observers predict that, as new leaders with higher levels of education and possibly less ideological world outlooks assume the top party posts in these states, there may be greater willingness to make meaningful movements in the direction of genuine democracy. The younger, more highly educated Gorbachev regime has been making some positive statements about the need for democratic reforms. Whether it will produce them, however, remains to be seen.

Finally, there are also structural factors that help us explain power relations in the Communist Party states. First, the traditional system of one-party rule is a powerful factor that impedes the development of more democratic political rule. Because it is extremely unlikely that the Communist parties will relinquish their leading roles, power concentrations within the one-party system will continue. Yet it is possible that semi-institutionalized competition within the single parties will evolve as the less authoritarian Second World states seek more effective ways of weighing policy alternatives.

Examples of political structures that could contribute to a broader sharing of power and, as a result, more equalitarian power allocations in the political process, are legislative institutions, like the Supreme Soviet in the USSR, the National People's Congress (NPC) in China, and the national assemblies of the East European states. Conceivably, these legislative bodies could evolve over the years to assume more powerful policymaking roles like that of the Yugoslav National Assembly. Also, lower-level representative bodies (local soviets) and work organizations could also evolve in the direction that Yugoslavia has taken. Although there is little evidence of impending change in most of the Communist world, recent events in both China and the USSR may be noteworthy.

RESPECT: COMMUNITY OR CONFLICT?

Westerners often suspect a general lack of concern among Communist leaders for their people. We tend to think that leaders are primarily interested in production quotas, military competition with the West, or foreign affairs. Such thoughts are, at least in part, misconceptions; Communist leaders recognize the great importance of people in national development and have shown concern for developing the personal traits necessary to facilitate their overriding goals. But to what extent have they succeeded in promoting secure and supportive relationships among their people and between the political authorities and the broader populace?

Lenin realized that the class divisions and ethnocentrism that plagued and contributed to the collapse of tsarist Russia would have to be resolved if he and the Communists were to be successful in developing a unified Soviet commonwealth. Social and national cleavages were deeply cast in the old Russian state; radical goals and policies were required to overcome them. The initial goal that guided the postrevolutionary leaders was that of state survival, which required at least a minimal level of societal cohesion and political integration. Over the longer run, the Communist leaders have sought to establish respect, trust, and a spirit of comradeliness among the diverse Soviet peoples. These traits, the leaders hoped, would contribute to the goal of a unified Soviet state.

To encourage the development of these traits, the leaders emphasized the common struggles of the Soviet peoples, the bonds that unite them, and the importance of cooperation and friendship among the different ethnic and national groups. The policies adopted by the Soviet leaders may have reduced some of the rampant Great Russian chauvinism of the past and may have done something to facilitate friendship and end discriminatory relations against and among the non-Russian peoples. However, recent research suggests that interethnic differences persist and the Soviet leaders have been unable to create what they refer to as a "fundamentally new social and international community" of "Soviet people."[13] Anti-Semitism among large sectors of the Soviet people continues and strong ethnonational tensions appear lurking beneath the surface. Contrary to their rhetoric, the Soviets have not solved their nationality problem.

Goals resulting in even less impressive actions concern the respect the leaders and government provide their people and, conversely, the trust and respect the people accord their government. When examining the espoused goals of the leaders, it is quite clear that they have recognized the significance of encouraging the support and trust of the masses. As we will see shortly, however, the Soviet leaders show little inclination to trust and support their own citizens.

The most significant action taken by the Soviet authorities concerning the promotion of the interpersonal and group respect involves the reduction of gross inequalities in the income and status hierarchies of the society. However, although more equal income and status systems have been established under Soviet communism, we should not assume that Soviet society is a homogeneous mass of equal and loving people. There is still considerable diversity of social characteristics and a good deal of the interpersonal and intergroup suspicion and particularism that these differences tend to generate.

Another significant shortcoming concerns the system's general disrespect for human rights and personal freedoms. Although requiring respectful and trustful relations among the Soviet people and toward the Communist Party and Soviet Government, the leadership has been reluctant to extend these relations to their people. Even though the majority of the population appears to support the system of government and its leaders, the leaders continue to treat the mass populace with a strong dose of disrespect, mistrust, and suspicion. Freedom of speech, travel to the West, and so on, are basic human rights the Soviet people deserve, but rights the leaders remain reluctant to accord them.[14]

The Soviet constitution promulgated in 1977 contained no basic legal changes concerning the rights and freedoms of the Soviet citizen. It elaborates in detail the citizen's economic guarantees that form the centerpiece of the Soviet definition of human rights: the right to housing (still in short supply), education, work, leisure, medical care, and maintenance in old age. Less prominent and heavily qualified are the political rights, including freedom of speech, press, assembly, demonstration in the streets, religion, and privacy. The constitution dilutes these rights by declaring that they are granted only "in conformity with the interests of the working people and for the purposes of strengthening the socialist system." An explicit limitation aimed at dissidents notes, "The exercise of rights and freedoms shall be inseparable from the performance by citizens of their duties." These limitations have been exercised against some of the Soviet Union's most distinguished citizens. The au-

---

[13]See, for example, Zvi Gitelman, "Are Nations Merging in the U.S.S.R.?" *Problems of Communism* 32 (5) (1983): 35–47.

[14]In 1974, the Soviet Union was one of 35 signatories to the Helsinki Accord, an agreement that, among other things, was to ensure the free exchange of ideas and people. To this day, the Soviet leaders have been unwilling to honor this aspect of the agreement.

thorities' repression of the noted physicist and former national hero Andrei Sakharov is indicative of how far the leaders will go to quash points of view that conflict with the party line. After earlier exiling and isolating the dissident Sakharov to the city of Gorki—which is off-limits to Westerners—Soviet authorities have used a wide variety of tactics to harass and repress him further in recent years. Both he and his wife Yelena Bonner have been isolated from friends and family and have suffered all sorts of contemptuous treatment over the last few years.

The very presence of dissident movements, associated with nationality, religion, and other interests in the USSR, indicates that some individuals and groups perceive a lack of respect and other important values.[15] Considerable evidence, including the way the authorities treat these groups, suggests that their perceptions are well-founded. Although the various groups are far too numerous to mention here, a few examples are illustrative. The Jewish movement gained momentum after the Middle East Six-Day War in 1967 and has actively pursued the right of Jewish citizens to emigrate. Although Jewish emigration increased in the early 1970s, Soviet emigration policy became exceedingly restrictive in the late 1970s and early 1980s. Religious protest and dissent by Orthodox, Catholic, and Protestant groups have called attention to the lack of religious freedom and lack of a separation between church and state. Finally, citizens intent on monitoring Soviet conformance with the Helsinki accords on human rights have called attention to the gap between Soviet pledges and practice. These people have been severely treated by Soviet authorities. Although Soviet accomplishments should not go unrecognized, neither should the shortcomings that are so courageously raised by these and other groups. The early performance of the new Gorbachev regime appears mixed. Although considerable attention has been given in speeches to themes of social justice, consultation, accountability, and openness, the authorities have continued their attack on what they refer to as "alien" and "decadent" tendencies in the arts, on dissidents, and others who are loathe to conform to Soviet norms.

As a result of the deep social and regional cleavages that divided traditional China, the goal of societal integration also received a high priority in postrevolutionary China. To unify the society and polity, Mao and the Communist leaders set out to transform the Chinese populace by developing a new socialist person. Emphasizing the themes of respect, equality, and comradeship, the actions of the leadership in the area of political socialization played a major role in uniting the Chinese people.

Perhaps the most significant outcome of Mao's policy was the impressive level of equality evident in the Chinese system during the 1960s and 1970s. In a society with a long and strong tradition of elitist, hierarchical relations, Mao's actions altered in a period of less than 30 years a social characteristic that many observers thought impossible to change. But, along with this trend toward increased equality in production came reductions in economic efficiency and development. The emphasis on equality has been sharply altered in recent years. Egalitarianism was deemphasized soon after Mao's death in order to promote higher productivity and economic efficiency.[16] Recent reforms have emphasized initiative, competition, and "getting rich" as more important to China than equality. What the present trends will do to interpersonal and intergroup relations in Chinese society is an important issue requiring further research. At the very least, present policy is likely to produce results at considerable odds with Mao's utopian visions of egalitarianism.

The low level of corruption and criminal behavior in contemporary China, in comparison with the USSR, testifies to the great strides the Chinese have made in establishing re-

[15] See, for example, Peter Reddaway, "Dissent in the U.S.S.R.," *Problems of Communism* 32 (6) (1983): 1–15.

[16] See William L. Parish, "Egalitarianism in Chinese Society," *Problems of Communism* 30 (1) (1981): 37–53.

lations based on respect and trust.[17] Once the "Sin City" of the Orient, contemporary Shanghai is now a bustling metropolis of industrious workers and shows few of the negative features associated with present-day cities in both the East and West. However, during the Maoist period, the Chinese incurred significant costs in terms of human rights and civil liberties as the leaders attempted to mold a population based on equality and conformity.

A major question confronting the contemporary Chinese leaders involves the extent to which they will guarantee secure and supportive relationships among their people in the political realm. Articles in unauthorized magazines in the late 1970s and early 1980s demanded due process under the law and a less oppressive, more open political and intellectual atmosphere. Although a leading party slogan in 1979 was "Everyone is equal under the law," many dissidents questioned this and continued their demands for greater constitutionalism. Recent reports from China call attention to some progress towards a rule of law. In December 1984, the Communist Party newspaper the *People's Daily* noted that authorities should respect the legal system. It argued that while party authorities had grown accustomed to replacing the law with verbal orders and "practicing arbitrary rule," now China "should see to it that the law will not change along with a change of leaders, nor with the change of the opinions and attention of the leaders." Recent reforms and new legislation call attention to some progress in the direction of constitutionalism in contemporary China.

In trying to achieve a secure and supportive community from a diverse grouping of nationalities and ethnic groups inhabiting their traditionally explosive area of Europe, the Yugoslav policymakers pursued goals rather similar to the Soviet and Chinese leaders. While

pursuing the common goals of integration and unity, however, they adopted policy actions earlier that showed greater respect for human rights and local autonomy. Yugoslav socialization policies were less coercive, more respectful of the people, and more patient concerning the considerable time required to bring about the desired changes. Government actions in the area of federalism and self-management, which granted high levels of political and economic autonomy to the various national groups and local organizations, reflected a higher level of respect for the interests and concerns of the diverse Yugoslav peoples.

Although the Yugoslav policymakers may have started earlier and followed higher ideals in allocating respect to all groups and regions on the basis of universalistic norms and principles, the regional groups, such as Albanians, Serbs, and Croats, have often been unwilling to accord respect and trust to one another. When faced with difficult political choices that critically affect the national republics and provinces—such as whether to take the profits of the richer republics to subsidize the development of the poorer—the leaders have tried to decide in the collective or Yugoslav interest. Some regional leaders, however, are still unwilling to place Yugoslav interests before the interests of their own national or ethnic group. As a result, political decisions often degenerate into nationalistic squabbles pitting one nationality against another.

The relatively higher level of ethnonationalism and interregional conflict exhibited in Yugoslavia is also due to the more open political environment. The Soviet leaders generally disallow public debate of regional rivalries and are more likely to punish a citizen for disrespectful or uncomradely behavior, yet the more open atmosphere in Yugoslavia allows such behaviors to surface. Many observers consider this feature a positive characteristic of more open societies and believe that the more repressive Soviet approach forces conflicts below the surface. Once repressed issues reach the surface, however, they tend to be more crit-

[17]Crime and corruption are continuing problems in Soviet society. See Peter H. Juviler, *Revolutionary Law and Order: Politics and Social Change in the USSR* (New York: Free Press, 1976).

ical and explosive than those that bubble up before they reach the critical stage.

The more open political environment in Yugoslavia has had both costs and benefits. It has given greater attention to individual choice and freedoms. Yet many Yugoslav citizens live in a less secure and more uncertain environment than do their Soviet counterparts. Although full employment is almost guaranteed in the USSR, high unemployment in Yugoslavia has forced many Yugoslavs to find work abroad. Many of them note, however, that the freedom to travel abroad and seek employment far outweighs the benefits of guaranteed employment.

In an age of global conflict and turmoil, Communist Party states have attempted to portray pictures of domestic peace and comradely cooperation. Compared to the religious warfare in the Middle East, for example, most Communist societies have been remarkably peaceful and stable in the 1970s and 1980s, at least on the surface. To promote the ideals of community and comradeliness, Communist leaders have emphasized the common, collective interests of their people and attempted to minimize their differences. Although there have been some notable exceptions over the years, such as the Soviet treatment of Jews, and various national minorities, their performances in allocating equal respect and deference to most national and ethnic groups comprising their states have been impressive.

At the same time, there have been periodic uprisings and demonstrations of national discontent. These signs of discord have resulted from what some individuals and groups perceive as unjust allocations of the values affecting the national groups. The revival of ethnonationalism and other displays of interethnic conflict in Yugoslavia and the underground national movements in the Soviet Union are examples of such perceptions. These and other flaws in the performance of the governments continue to mar what is generally an impressive record of community building.

More serious than the intergroup conflict within the states, perhaps, is the international tension between and among them. The Soviet Union, through the Warsaw Treaty Organization (WTO) and the Council for Mutual Economic Assistance (CMEA or COMECON), seeks to play a major role in promoting ''secure and supportive'' relationships among the East European countries. Although WTO has brought a certain amount of military security, there is reason to doubt how supportive the military and economic relationships really are. Anti-Soviet demonstrations and national movements broke out in East Germany, Poland, and Hungary in the mid 1950s and continue to simmer. The Czechoslovak liberalization movement in 1968 was in part an anti-Soviet movement and was ended abruptly by Soviet and WTO military intervention. The ongoing Polish crisis calls attention to continuing problems within the so-called socialist commonwealth. Although the dominating Soviets profess equalitarian and comradely relations among socialist states, there continues to be a Soviet lack of respect for the full sovereignty and autonomy of the East European nations. The Soviet Union remains an imperialistic power in Eastern Europe. This fact suggests continued tension and turmoil for the region.

When searching for answers to the continuing problems of ethnocentrism and national tensions among the states, environmental factors, such as culture and geography, play major roles. Historical evidence of Great Russian chauvinism, Chinese warlordism, and nationalism within Europe and Asia indicates that intergroup distrust and hostilities are not of recent origin. In fact, when viewing the fratricidal past, the present levels of respect and cooperation are quite surprising.

The individual forces, such as the behavior of the political leadership and changes in the attitudes and behaviors of the masses, have had a good deal to do with the interpersonal and intergroup relations in the contemporary period. Leaders like Mao Zedong and Josip Broz Tito were guided by the ideals of socialist brotherhood and unity, and they undertook a wide variety of actions to transform their ideals into realities. Basing their developmental strategies on universalistic ethics and emphasizing the common interests of different groups within the larger collective, the leaders sought to promote more equalitarian and respectful relations within their states.

Although the attitudes of ethnocentrism are difficult to transform and although there are still pockets of particularism and distrust in many Communist Party states, the overall change in belief systems is quite remarkable. The majority of citizens within these states enjoy secure and supportive relationships with others and reflect at least some of the attributes of a genuine political community. Personal attitudes concerning interstate (e.g., Sino-Soviet and Soviet-Polish) relations, however, are not nearly so amicable and will continue to be a source of tension in the future.

Some structural factors have contributed to the growth of community, whereas others have generated feelings of intergroup hostility. The high level of political and economic decentralization under the Yugoslav system of federalism has protected national rights and autonomy and given the South Slavic nationalities a greater feeling of security within the Yugoslav union. The lower level of decentralization within the Soviet system is a source of insecurity among many of the non-Russian nationalities and ethnic groups. For example, one of the structural factors prohibiting a higher level of integration among many of the Soviet nationalities is the fear of forced assimilation of the Russian language and culture combined with a corresponding loss of their own national or ethnic heritage. Because the Russian nationality dominates Soviet economic and political life and the Russian language has become the common language of the Soviet people, the continued threat of Russian dominance tends to generate distrustful attitudes among many non-Russian peoples.

The fear of Soviet dominance among the smaller East European nations has had a similar effect on the attitudes of their peoples.

Hoping to find their own place in the international community of nations, the East European states desire inter-Communist relations based on the concepts of national sovereignty and noninterference. The Soviets' use of the so-called Brezhnev Doctrine of Limited Sovereignty, which was used to justify the intervention in Czechoslovakia in 1968 and Afghanistan in 1980,—and the threat of intervention in Poland in the early 1980s—allows the East European leaders little freedom in the pursuit of their ideals.

In attempting to unite the socialist commonwealth, the Soviet leaders have relied on the arts of both persuasion and coercion. Their strategies have met with general success, but there are definite costs to the more coercive approaches. The Soviets' experiences in Afghanistan and Poland are illustrative of this. Although you can force a nation to assume an "orthodox" role in the socialist commonwealth, tactics of this nature often breed rebellion and discontent. These are not characteristics corresponding to the ideals of brotherhood and unity and do not represent respect and equality either among humans within a common society or among nations of the Second World.

WELL-BEING UNDER SOCIALISM: WELFARE OR POVERTY?

The value of well-being represents the area of social policy to which the Communist Party states attach great importance and in which they take great pride. Past improvements in the standards of living have been recorded in some of the countries, yet the absence of expected progress relative to the West has been a source of discontent and embarrassment in many.

In his speech to the 24th CPSU Congress in 1971, General Secretary Leonid I. Brezhnev identified the country's principal goal as raising the standard of living. At the 25th Congress in 1976, he reemphasized the goal by pledging:

> a further increase in the Soviet people's well-being, the improvement of their living and work-

ing conditions, and significant progress in public health, education, and culture.

At the 26th and 27th Congresses, party leaders reemphasized that the CPSU is committed to an increase in the level of social and personal well-being.

When examining the actions and outcomes, we encounter a mixed picture. In many respects, it is apparent that much has been done in the area of social services. The Soviet Union is a welfare state. Housing is exceedingly cheap although often in short supply; medical care, health services, and education are free; employment is guaranteed. Yet, when comparing the average Soviet citizen with a West European counterpart, he or she is clearly deprived of many goods and services associated with a higher standard of living. First, housing is still scarce, forcing families sometimes to share apartments or to wait for years to be provided an apartment suited to their needs.[18] Second, consumer goods are still in critically short supply. Although the average family eats and drinks reasonably well, Soviet department stores show a short supply and limited variety of modern appliances, clothing, and other consumer goods. True, the Soviet leaders continue to speak of altering this situation, but the extent to which change is possible under the present conditions of economic stagnation and exorbitant defense spending is a matter of some contention. Most observers believe that improvements in the consumer sector will be slow and flawed as long as the USSR continues its present level of defense procurement. One of the questions confronting the Soviet policymakers is that of guns versus butter, and no one should be more aware of the importance and meaning of this choice than the Soviet people. Recently, the leaders have been uncharacteristically frank in calling attention to social and economic shortcomings. Whether or

not they can do something about it remains an open question.

Even though the Soviet consumer fares poorly in comparison to consumers in the West, the average citizen is relatively content. Comparing living standards with the past and recalling the hardships and great deprivation suffered during World War II, the more elderly consumer recognizes improvements and is generally optimistic about the future. The younger generation is less likely to recognize the improvements and is more skeptical about the sincerity of the leaders' promises. One accomplishment of the Soviet leaders has been to keep mass expectations in line with the state's capabilities to meet demands. One reason for the strict limitations on international travel is to prohibit comparisons with living standards in the West. As long as the Soviet population bases its expectations on what can be realistically attained in their country rather than on what they see others enjoying in the West, the leaders are given additional time to raise living conditions to compete with Western standards. If the disappointing record of the 1970s and early 1980s is an indication of the future and if predictions of a further economic downturn in the late 1980s come true, the leaders' promises will ring increasingly hollow.

Because of the lower level of economic development and the much greater number of people, the problem of providing all citizens with a reasonable level of well-being has been much more severe in China. Accordingly, the primary goal guiding the Chinese policymakers in the postrevolutionary period was the provision of a minimal level of economic security.

These provisions in a historically underdeveloped area require high rates of economic modernization and industrial production. Although the Great Leap Forward and the Cultural Revolution created major discontinuities in the overall economic progress, industrial production grew at an average of 13 percent during the years 1949–1974. However, economic performance in later periods was more

[18]See, for example, Henry W. Morton, "Who Gets What, When and How? Housing in the Soviet Union," *Soviet Studies* 32 (2) (1980): 235–259.

Although Soviet cities are the scene of constantly growing apartment complexes, demand still far exceeds supply. Shown here is a "circle house" with enclosed shopping and entertainment facilities in the Gagarin district of Moscow.

problematical; although the average rate of growth during the period 1949–1960 was 22 percent, the rate for 1960–1974 was only 6 percent.[19] Recognizing the importance of the task before them, the current leadership has sought

Industrialization in the urban centers has drawn millions of workers from the countryside to the sprawling apartment complexes surrounding the older cities. Here, on the outskirts of Yugoslavia's federal capital, is a section of "new" Belgrade where many workers live.

to put China on a different course that will raise the rates of economic modernization and industrial growth to higher levels. Economic growth is clearly the nation's highest priority.[20]

In order to encourage economic growth, the current Chinese leaders have undertaken dramatic reforms. In the agricultural sector, they have broadened the rights of peasants to farm on their own and engage in profitable activities. In the industrial sector, they have reduced governmental control and placed greater emphasis on competitive market forces. The overriding goal in both agriculture and industry has been to promote initiative, competition, and efficiency. By so doing, the leaders hope to promote modernization and social well-being in China.

The present-day contrasts between Chinese and Western standards of living and levels of consumption are much greater than in the Soviet Union and Eastern Europe. Still, the Chinese populace has witnessed considerable advancements over the last two decades. One significant development in contemporary

[19]U.S. Congress, Joint Economic Committee, *China: A Reassessment of the Economy,* (Washington, D.C.: U.S. Government Printing Office, 1975), p. 149.

[20]Stuart R. Schram, "Economics in Command?: Ideology and Politics Since the Third Plenum, 1978–1984," *China Quarterly* 99 (September 1984): 417–461.

China, which will have consequences for the value of well-being, concerns the apparent movement from equality to equity. Although Mao's former social policy emphasized an equal distribution of well-being, there is now more emphasis on equity—reward on the basis of contribution. This means that inequalities are likely to increase within the rural sectors, among provinces, and between the countryside and the cities.

Perhaps the most significant advancement in Communist China remains that in the area of health care. Between 1952 and 1972, the number of doctors increased from approximately 39,000 to an estimated 457,000 (3200 persons per doctor).[21] Using paramedics (called barefoot doctors) to spread medical care to even the most remote village, the Chinese health system made impressive strides. In the words of one American expert:

> The accomplishments of the "sick man of Asia" [traditional China] in the face of severely limited resources and overwhelming problems are, after 23 years, unmatched in the history of the world. The accomplishments are evidence of what can be done when a goal is set and the population mobilized to do it.[22]

Some are concerned that the medical advancements of the past may be sacrificed under the "new pragmatism" of the recent period of modernization. Fears are expressed that the moderates' drive for more Western-style modernization will have negative consequences for Chinese medical care. They believe that recent moves toward a more "professional" (i.e., Western) model of health care and away from the paramedics and barefoot doctors may have more costs than benefits.[23]

[21]E. Grey Dimond, "Medicine in the People's Republic of China: A Progress Report," *Journal of the American Medical Association* 222 (9) (1972): 1158.

[22]Victor W. Sidel, "Medicine and Public Health," in Michel C. Oksenberg, ed., *China's Developmental Experience* (New York: Academy of Political Science, 1973), p. 119. Also, see Anelissa Lucas, *Chinese Medical Modernization* (New York: Praeger, 1982).

[23]See, for example, Ruth and Victor W. Sidel, *The Health of China* (Boston: Beacon Press, 1982).

Although Yugoslavia is also a welfare state, in the sense that the public sector plays a primary role in providing social services for the people, the Yugoslav system has allowed for at least two decades greater individual opportunity with regard to increases in personal well-being. Evidence of this freedom of opportunity is everywhere: automobiles crowding the streets of even the most provincial cities; private homes being built in villages and towns; and summer homes in the mountains and along the Adriatic. The policymakers have taken specific actions to make this possible. For example, the level of allowed income inequality has been greater than in the Soviet Union, China, and other East European states. In addition, laws allow Yugoslav workers the opportunity to travel to, and work in, the capitalist countries of Western Europe. After a period of a few years, these workers are in a position to return home with a new auto and the cash required to build a comfortable private home on the city's outskirts.

The policymakers have also undertaken other actions affecting the allocation of well-being among the Yugoslav populace. One crucial decision involved the adoption of a competitive, market-oriented economy that promotes competition among firms and that also features some of the less desirable concommitants of Western economies, including embarrassing income inequalities, spiraling inflation, unemployment, and worker strikes. Although Chinese and Soviet society have traditionally exhibited a drab uniformity in consumer goods, housing, and social services, Yugoslavia is a picture of contrasts. Poverty and affluence exist side by side. A peasant's deteriorating cottage is bordered by a beautiful new house built with Deutschmarks sent home by an enterprising Yugoslav worker abroad. Mercedes share crowded streets with horse-drawn wagons and archaic trolleys. In a land of traditional contrasts, Communist social and economic policies have added a mark of their own.

Well-being is one of the values that is more amenable to quantitative evaluation and com-

Preventive medicine is doing much to heal the country once known as the "Sick Man of Asia." Here, young and old gather for daily exercises in front of an import–export firm in Beijing.

parison. A useful way of examining and comparing government actions, for example, is to see where they spend their money. Table 7.2 indicates how much money each government spends annually per person for the military, education, and health. Examining military

Factory workers' flats usually consist of one room inhabited by parents and child. Kitchens and bathrooms are generally shared with other families. Although this space seems inadequate by Western standards, it is a tremendous improvement over the prerevolutionary period.

spending first, the USSR spends far more per person (and overall) than any other Communist Party country. Although it spends somewhat less per person than the United States, it spends far more as a percentage of the gross national product (GNP). The two superpowers are clearly the big spenders in the defense sector. China has comparatively little to expend and does invest less per capita in the military sector than any of the East European states.

Turning to education expenditures, the USSR and East Germany are the clear leaders, although both spend substantially less than the United States. The education and health expenditures of the Laotians, Vietnamese, and North Koreans are extremely low and, as we will see later, explain the low quality of health care and schooling found in these countries. When combining health and education expenditures and comparing them with military expenditures, some interesting findings appear. Whereas the United States, for example, spends $632 per person a year on defense and $1010 on health and education, the Soviets spend $490 and $344 respectively. U.S. defense spending per capita may surpass the Soviet's, yet the United States does invest compara-

TABLE 7.2 Public Expenditures per Capita: Military, Education, Health

Country	Military (U.S. $)	Education (U.S. $)	Health (U.S. $)
Albania	71	na	26
Bulgaria	133	176	85
Cambodia	na[a]	na	na
China	28	17	6
Cuba	114	162	50
Czechoslovakia	180	182	176
East Germany	360	304	341
Hungary	103	201	127
Laos	na	na	1
Mongolia	108	60	12
North Korea	73	39	3
Poland	121	135	164
Romania	61	117	149
Soviet Union	490	231	113
Vietnam	17	6	1
Yugoslavia	113	124	138
USA	632	571	439

[a]Not available.

SOURCE: Adapted from Ruth Leger Sivard, *World Military and Social Expenditures, 1983* (Leesburg, Va.: World Priorities, 1983), pp. 38–41.

tively more in the education and health care sectors.

Actions in terms of government expenditures are of course related to policy outcomes. Table 7.3 provides a number of indicators of such outcomes, describing levels of health care, nutrition, and the physical quality of life in Communist Party states. Examining the number of people per physician in the first column, we find that the Soviet Union has the best ratio in the world (270 people for every physician). With the exception of the Albanians, the European Communist Party states also do very well on this indicator. The Asians do very poorly. The second column, describing the population per hospital bed, reflects the same trends. Viewing the next two columns, Cuba, Czechoslovakia, and East Germany have the best record on the infant-mortality and life-expectancy indicators among Communist Party states. The Soviets and other East

Europeans do quite well on these indicators, whereas the records of the Asians, with the exceptions of the Chinese and North Koreans, are extremely poor. Clearly, these indicators of health care correspond with the health expenditures described in Table 7.2.

When examining the three indicators of nutrition in Table 7.3, the Soviets and Europeans do quite well once again, whereas the Asians lag far behind. Cambodia (Kampuchea) and Laos are among the few states in the world with calorie-supply-per-capita levels below 2000. Cambodia (Kampuchea) suffered tragic losses in the 1970s through starvation and war. In 1975, the country had a population of approximately 8 million. By 1980 as many as 4 million had died. No nation on earth suffered more in the past decade than this once tranquil and fertile land.

The final column in Table 7.3 contains data purporting to indicate the physical quality of life. Claimed to be an unbiased nonideological and nonethnocentric index ''reflecting important elements that should be included in a humane existence,'' the indicator is based on infant mortality, life expectancy, and basic literacy data.[24] Rankings of countries worldwide range from a high of 98 for Iceland, Japan, Netherlands, and Sweden to lows of 15 for Guinea-Bissau and 21 for Afghanistan.

According to this indicator, Communist Party states reflect some important differences in the physical quality of life. The Asian states rank very low and appear to have physical quality of life standards similar to many states in the Third World. The USSR and East European states rank considerably higher and compare well with the industrial states of the First World.

Although the measure is useful in assessing the physical quality of life around the globe, it is not very helpful in discriminating among the more industrial countries of East

[24]For a discussion of the index, see Morris David Morris, *Measuring the Conditions of the World's Poor* (New York: Pergamon, 1979), pp. 20–40. Of course, there are many other factors that are important to and affect the ''quality of life.''

TABLE 7.3 Health, Nutrition, and Physical Quality of Life (PQLI)[a] Indicators

Country	Population per Physician	Population per Hospital Bed	Infant Mortality[b] Rate per 1000	Life Expec-tancy	Calorie Supply[c] per Capita	Protein Supply per Capita	Percent of Population with Safe Water	PQLI[d]
Albania	890	154	48	70	2,837	83	na	77
Bulgaria	410	90	20	73	3,638	102	na	91
Cambodia	na[e]	951	212	40	1,795	42	45	36
China	2,250	506	56	64	2,472	65	na	76
Cuba	640	221	19	73	2,717	71	62	93
Czechoslovakia	360	80	17	71	3,472	99	78	91
East Germany	490	94	12	72	3,746	102	82	4
Hungary	400	109	23	71	3,533	94	44	91
Laos	17,290	1,022	129	43	1,856	50	48	28
Mongolia	450	92	55	63	2,711	101	na	80
North Korea	na	832	34	64	2,972	84	na	78
Poland	520	133	21	72	3,545	105	55	93
Romania	680	113	29	71	3,396	97	na	91
Soviet Union	270	82	36	70	3,389	100	na	90
Vietnam	4,330	270	90	63	2,029	49	24	73
Yugoslavia	690	167	33	70	3,528	101	58	86
USA	550	171	13	74	3,652	107	99	96

[a]PQLI = physical quality of life index.

[b]Deaths under one year per 1000 live births.

[c]Per capita supply of food, in calories and grams of protein per day.

[d]The PQLI is based on three indicators: infant mortality, life expectancy, and basic literacy.

[e]Not available.

SOURCE: Adapted from Ruth Leger Sivard, *World Military and Social Expenditures, 1983* (Leesburg, Va.: World Priorities, 1983), pp. 38–41; and George Thomas Kurian, *The New Book of World Rankings* (New York: Facts on File, 1984), pp. 331–332.

and West and between the United States and the USSR. We are all aware of some important differences in the quality of life that the measure simply does not reflect.

Although all Communist leaders are committed to improving the quality of life of their people, the way in which they go about it and the priority given this goal in relation to others, such as national defense, is a matter of differing interpretations. There are some leaders and many citizens in these states who are in favor of reducing the level of defense spending and, perhaps, the level of industrial investment so that spending in the consumer and social services sectors can be expanded. Although these points of view have been registered by articulate and respected spokespersons, the concern

with national defense and industrial development apparently remains paramount in the minds of the majority of Soviet policymakers. Conceivably, arms agreements between the East and West and expanding trust and cooperation could lead to reduced defense spending and a corresponding increase in investments related to the well-being of the populace.

Communist policymakers are also confronted by other difficult questions of socialist economics. For example, how do you establish a welfare state, ending exploitation and reducing income and status hierarchies, while simultaneously stimulating higher levels of production and economic output? The performance record of most socialist states is mixed in these respects and all have had particular difficulties with the second objective. The record is quite impressive in the welfare area—that is, most all citizens eat well, are adequately clothed and housed, and enjoy reasonable health care—yet the productive output in the socialist states has suffered. Soviet agricultural production in the 1980s, for example, is not that much greater than it was at the turn of the century. The Chinese economy continues to fall farther behind the growth and development of the economies of the Western world. Unless major advances are made in the area of production, Communist leaders are going to find it increasingly difficult to attain the advanced level of social well-being they so earnestly desire.

The basic question confronting the policymakers is how to stimulate the productive output of the individual worker and the firm without relying excessively on the capitalist system of monetary rewards—which, the Communists argue, results in exploitation and injustice. Can Communist leaders find reward structures and general economic mechanisms that will ensure or surpass the productive output of the Western systems without accepting some of their less desirable features? Obviously, the tra-

ditional communist system of restricted monetary rewards combined with symbolic recognition, such as medals and other forms of commemoration, for outstanding work have not done the job. Not only does the output lag considerably behind the West, but so does the quality of the goods produced. This poor performance led to economic reforms, first in Yugoslavia, then in China; and now they are being seriously considered in the Soviet Union. Communist leaders continue to search for methods to promote productivity and efficiency. So far, they have found that there are no easy answers.

In attempting to account for the lingering difficulties of the Second World states in the welfare area, the environmental, individual, and structural explanatory factors are useful. One important environmental factor is the general level of economic underdevelopment found in most states before the advent of Communism. Only in Czechoslovakia and East Germany did the Communists encounter economic settings that resembled Marx's expectations of economic abundance. In every other state, with the partial exceptions of some of the

The bustle of traffic in downtown Budapest suggests the impact of consumerism on Hungarian society.

other East European states, the picture was one of primitive, agrarian economies, many of which had barely entered the industrial age. Even in the more developed states, the economies had been devastated by World War II and had to be rebuilt by the postwar leaders with little outside assistance. Although the Marshall Plan greatly aided the reconstruction of Western Europe, the Communist Party states chose to manage on their own.[25] The plight of some of the East European states was worsened as the Soviet Union undertook the wholesale movement of factories and productive equipment to the USSR in payment for wartime damages. Therefore, the postwar starting points for the Second World states were considerably below much of the First World. Yet, when pairing countries with similar economic starting points—for example, East Germany and Czechoslovakia with West Germany and Austria, or the USSR and other East European states with Japan, Italy, and the Iberian states—it appears that the western states have outperformed the eastern according to most indicators in the economic and welfare sectors.

Individual determinants have also affected the level of economic development and the state's capacities for providing the value of well-being. The leaders of all the countries were initially committed to increasing the economic output of their states through a strategy of forced savings and industrialization. Although Yugoslavia and China departed somewhat from this approach in the 1950s and 1960s, the general strategy was one in which the industrial sector was emphasized at the expense of the welfare and consumer realms. This developmental strategy did boost industrial potential, but the advancements came at great human costs. The construction of heavy industries often meant shortages in medical care or in consumer goods. These countries did not have the capacities to meet both industrial

Contemporary China is a blend of the new and the old.

and welfare needs and decided to emphasize the former. The leaders were willing to incur these costs over the short run to develop the industrial capacity to protect their states, and then, hopefully, they would begin to meet human needs over the long run. The workers did not always support the regime's economic policies and vented their misgivings through absenteeism, low output, and inefficiency. This human element's effect on the performance of the economy will be of considerable importance in the coming decades.

The economic system itself must be considered as a structural determinant affecting levels of well-being within the Communist-run states. The command-type socialist system adopted in most of the states allows the leaders considerable control in allocating such resources as income, housing, and health care among the population. The centralized socialist economy has also served, in some significant respects, to impede higher levels of well-

[25]The Soviet leaders denounced the Marshall Plan as a device to control Europe, refused to participate in the program, and denied participation to the East European states.

being. Tending to thwart some of the initiative and competition found under private ownership, and often allowing great waste and inefficiency, the economic systems have not permitted the societies to produce to their full capacities. If higher and more efficient levels of production could be achieved, the system would be in a position to enlarge allocations to the welfare sector and, as a result, improve the level of well-being among all its citizens. The unfulfilled promises and shortcomings of Communism became poignantly apparent in Poland in the 1970s and early 1980s. The Polish people grew increasingly dissatisfied with their economic situation.

At least partially aware of the shortcomings of the command-type system, policymakers and their advisors throughout the Second World are searching for new economic forms that may help rectify present problems by borrowing some of the more desirable features of capitalist systems. Yugoslavia and Hungary, and, more recently, China, have been in the forefront in economic experimentation. Although it is too early to evaluate all their effects, the more decentralized, competitive systems appear to alleviate some of the costs of the traditional, Soviet command-type model by stimulating higher levels of output and by making production more responsive to the laws of supply and demand.

ENLIGHTENMENT: ERUDITION OR IGNORANCE?

Policy choices concerning the nature and distribution of enlightenment—what one should know about oneself, one's work, and one's world—have been the focus of considerable controversy and debate in political systems throughout the world. Should the goal be the development of a broadly trained citizen in the humanistic, liberal tradition or the development of a more narrow, ideologically trained citizen? Should enlightenment be spread among the entire populace or concentrated in a smaller sector? These and other choices also confront policymakers in Communist Party

states as they attempt to mold populations likely to facilitate their overriding objective, the construction of communism.

Soviet policymakers have been guided by the goal of what they call the molding of a new man. Brezhnev defined this individual in his speech to the 24th CPSU Congress as someone with "a high level of culture, education, social consciousness, and inner maturity." The proper policies for ensuring the development of such a citizen have been the subject of numerous policy debates. In April 1958, for example, First Secretary Khrushchev criticized the Soviet educational system and demanded fundamental and far-reaching changes. In September of that year, Khrushchev published a memorandum on school reorganization that proposed, among other things, that continuous academic education be abolished and that all students be required to combine work with study. Finally, in December 1958, a set of educational reforms was adopted and—surprisingly—departed from Khrushchev's earlier proposals "not only in detail but in basic principles."[26] According to scholars who have studied the policy debate, Khrushchev was overruled as a result of the influence of a variety of individuals and groups who disagreed with his proposals. This example illustrates the high level of concern with education policy and also exhibits the importance of political debate and the influence that specialized interests can have on the making of policy.

Contemporary Soviet education attempts to provide both ideological and modern academic and cultural training. The Soviet people are uniformly literate (99 percent), have a solid basic education, and are challenging the West in many areas of scientific inquiry. However, with the strong emphasis on strict and narrow ideological training, the vast majority of the people are woefully lacking in accurate information and perspective about life and politics in other parts of the world.

[26]Joel J. Schwartz and William R. Keech, "Group Influence and the Policy Process in the Soviet Union," *American Political Science Review* 62 (3) (1968): 840–851.

The total revolution envisioned by Mao and his colleagues, abolishing the old and establishing the new, required the widespread allocation of what might be called a Maoist conception of enlightenment among the Chinese people. Mao thought all Chinese citizens should be selfless, imbued with a collective spirit, and willing to endure personal hardships in service to the public good. They should possess a keen class consciousness and be both a Red and an expert in their work place. Mao and the CCP leaders undertook a variety of actions to develop these new minds, new outlooks, and new behaviors. They adopted a strategy of political socialization that utilized indoctrination in the schools, mass media, and the arts. The printed and spoken word was to serve the revolution, and the goal of a politically conscious populace was a necessary ingredient leading to victory.

Although some of the outcomes of the Cultural Revolution remain unclear, the fanatical devotion to Mao's word has all but disappeared in contemporary China. The authoritarian reformers under Deng Xiaoping have deemphasized Mao's teachings and political conformity and emphasized pragmatism and productivity.

Enlightenment in contemporary China has come to mean something quite different than it did during the Maoist period. Today, there is more emphasis on a Western-style education. Training in the sciences, humanities, and other fields has taken an equal, or even more important, position alongside politics and ideology. With the new conception of enlightenment come new challenges for the Chinese. Because advanced education cannot be guaranteed to all, some sectors of the population will no doubt become more highly educated than others. Who makes these choices and on the basis of what criteria? Although some policy actions are still to be taken, the present emphasis seems to be on merit and achievement, a criteria that may promote development and modernization while contributing to increasing inequalities in the Chinese system. One thing, however, is clear. If the

As illustrated by these three students at the Technical University of Jiaotong, contemporary Chinese education now places a higher emphasis on science than on ideology.

present policies continue, the enlightened Chinese citizen at the end of the next decade will look far different from his or her counterpart at the end of the last.

Over the last few decades, the Yugoslav leaders have attempted to promote an educational system that would, as stated in their education laws:

> Contribute to the building up of an all-around personality, of an independent and a critical spirit possessing intellectual, high character, and moral and working qualities of the citizen of a socialist community.[27]

[27]Vera Tomich, *Education in Yugoslavia and the New Reform* (Washington, D.C.: U.S. Government Printing Office, 1963), p. 109.

To an extent greater than any other Communist Party state, the Yugoslavs have encouraged the development of an all-around personality, an endeavor that has required a much more open, less-ideological educational environment. The style and content of instruction is very similar to what we know in the West.

In attempting to develop the system of self-managing socialism, the Yugoslav leaders have been guided by the overriding goal of developing a citizen trained for self-management. The 1970 resolution on education states the goal explicitly in noting that young people must "become fit for direct decision-making on the conditions and results of their own work," and that they should have "a fully developed personality, educated and capable to perform its functions in the complex conditions of life and work."[28]

To implement these goals, the leaders have followed a strategy of political socialization and instituted an educational system intended to prepare the society for self-management.[29] Like other social organizations, schools are to be self-managed and provide students with firsthand experience in participatory democracy. Although the socialization experience is decidedly focused on youth, actions have been taken to prepare older sectors of the population for the responsibilities of self-management. Workers' universities and in-service training are provided to better equip them to help administer the affairs of their firm or other place of work.

Although there is much we do not know about the outcomes of the Yugoslav approach (as is true with the Soviet and Chinese approaches), most observers agree that the Yugoslav populace is generally committed to the principles of self-management even though it is sometimes reluctant to assume the responsibilities participation requires. By most Western standards of enlightenment, the Yugoslavs are the most enlightened of all the Second World societies. The less coercive actions of a more open educational system, a freer exchange of ideas and opinions, and a high rate of international travel have resulted in a surprisingly well-rounded, sophisticated populace in this historically backward area of the Balkans.

Comparatively speaking, what kind of citizen will contribute most to the supreme goal of all Second World leaders, the construction of communism? Might it be the ideological zealot of the Maoist period? Or is the more well-rounded, less dogmatic citizen more likely to possess the blend of political consciousness, knowledge, and patriotism conducive to developmental goals? Ultimately, the leaders of the Second World states must determine who is really enlightened and, furthermore, whether their conceptions of enlightenment will really contribute to a higher level of human dignity and societal well-being.

We should not conclude without recognizing some of the major advancements recorded in this value area. At the turn of the century, education was a value reserved for the privileged few in Russia, China, and many other Second World societies. Today, it is a right guaranteed to all citizens. Educational opportunity in Communist states is probably as open and as nearly equal as anywhere else in the world today. Second, we must recognize the great impact education has had on development in these states. The rapid transformation of backward, traditional countries into powerful states can in large part be attributed to advancements in the educational sector.

The data presented in Table 7.4 give us a clearer idea where Communist countries stand. Cuba has as good a teacher-to-population ratio as does the United States. The USSR's is only slightly poorer. Although the East European states compare favorably with the Western world, the Asians lag considerably behind. Cambodia (Kampuchea) and Laos

[28]*Resolution on the Development of Education on Self-Management Basis* (Belgrade: 1971), p. 9.

[29]For an excellent account of the Yugoslav strategy and an appraisal of its success, see Susan Lampland Woodward, "Socialization for Self-Management in Yugoslav Schools," in Gary K. Bertsch and Thomas W. Ganschow, eds., *Comparative Communism: The Soviet, Chinese, and Yugoslav Models* (San Francisco, Calif.: Freeman, 1976), pp. 307–319.

TABLE 7.4 Education and Communication Indicators

Country	School-age Population per Teacher	Percent of School-age Population in School	Percent of Women in Total University Enrollment	Literacy[a]	Phones per 1000	Radio Sets per 1000	TV Sets per 1000	News-papers[b]
Albania	36	61	44	72	5	74	4	54
Bulgaria	32	57	53	94	116	242	186	234
Cambodia	99	23	19	48	1	15	4	10
China	40	59	30	66	28	57	4	8
Cuba	23	68	46	95	33	295	129	91
Czechoslovakia	35	59	41	99	196	289	280	304
East Germany	35	62	47	99	176	383	342	517
Hungary	26	59	47	99	107	252	258	242
Laos	67	42	26	44	2	94	na	4
Mongolia	45	61	71	95	25	99	3	69
North Korea	73	64	na[c]	85	na	40	na	20
Poland	37	55	50	99	88	295	224	237
Romania	33	62	43	98	56	144	167	181
Soviet Union	26	59	50	99	80	490	303	336
Vietnam	54	62	32	87	1	121	26	10
Yugoslavia	33	60	40	87	71	207	192	103
USA	22	85	49	99	770	2,099	624	282

[a]Represents percent of adult population (over 15) able to read and write.

[b]Daily newspaper circulation per 1000 population.

[c]Not available.

SOURCE: Adapted from Ruth Leger Sivard, *World Military and Social Expenditures, 1983* (Leesburg, Va.: World Priorities, 1983), pp. 21–29; and George Thomas Kurian, *The New Book of World Rankings* (New York: Facts on File, 1984).

rank extremely low on all the indicators of educational performance. In Cambodia, for example, over 75 percent of their school-age children are *not* in school, few of their women are in universities, and only one-half of their people are literate. According to most all conceptions of enlightenment, the Cambodians and Laotians are in dire straits.

The last four columns in Table 7.4 summarize communication indicators and also call attention to the differences between the European and Asian Communist states. China and the other Asian states rank low on all indicators. The Soviet Union and most of the East European states rank extremely high, even higher than the United States, on newspaper circula-

tion. The governments have invested heavily in getting the party's word before their publics.

Although education and communication represent a relatively free and open search for truth and understanding in most Western countries, they remain strictly disciplined activities in Communist-run states. Television, the press, and educational curricula are all carefully controlled by party authorities. These same authorities take part in and condone systematic distortions of history. Whether these policies are conducive to long-term developmental goals is a problematic question that depends very much on one's personal attitudes concerning freedom and control, creativity, and conformity. For those adhering to Western value systems, there is considerable reason to be critical in this area of policy and performance.

In conclusion, we can ask: What environmental factors, such as ideology and culture, influence what Communist citizens know about the world and the process by which they come to know it? Most of these populations inherited cultures that were historically denied free access to information and ideas. The present policies of ideological training and party control are not practices, therefore, that represent a sharp break with the past. Rather, the states' control of the socialization process and educational policy are features of thought control to which most of these populations have long been accustomed.

When examining individual factors, however, we find that the present-day leaders are committed to promoting mass education and have been willing to pay the high cost that this task requires. Most Communist policymakers have been generous in their spending on education, as illustrated by their expenditures devoted to education (see Table 7.2). Communist Party countries tend to allocate a higher percentage of their GNP to education than most countries in either the First or Third World.

In the eyes of the leaders, the major human obstacles to their conceptions of enlightenment have been the reluctance of some sectors of the population to support fully the system's ideology and to display their support in acceptable forms of political activity. The undesirable attributes of apathy and alienation are still apparent among many sectors, including the young, and will have to be eradicated before enlightenment policy can be called an unqualified success.

Lastly, structural factors, such as state controlled educational systems and party domination of the mass media, explain a good deal of Communist policy and performance in this value area. Educational policy, although not immune from competing interests and debates over financing and so forth, is one area where long-term rational comprehensive planning is possible. On the basis of these plans, policymakers have undertaken major programs and provided massive funding to establish the socializing institutions capable of developing a new socialist citizen. From sports arenas to ballet theaters, from day care centers to workers' universities and scientific institutes, the Communist Party states' investment in promoting their concept of human development is one generally unparalleled in the contemporary world.

COMMUNIST POLITICS, VALUES, AND HUMAN DIGNITY

Is politics of any significance in explaining the allocation of values and their impact on human dignity in Communist systems today? Can any of the variations in the distributions of values or the plight of human dignity be attributed to political factors? Does the ideology, nature of political leadership, or policy-making system make a difference? When addressing these questions, we ought to recognize that considerable research has indicated that economic development may be the most powerful factor affecting people. As demonstrated in Table 7.2, richer countries have more to spend on their people than poorer countries. The United States has more to spend per capita on defense, health, and education than does the Soviet Union and East European countries. These states, in turn, have more to spend than do the less-developed countries of Asia. The level of economic development makes a great difference. But once we accept this fact, we confront some important question of interest to the student of politics. First, does the type of political and economic system affect the process and speed of economic development? Second, does the type of political system have any significant impact on either the amount of expenditures invested in different policy areas (e.g., defense versus health) or the distribution of policy outcomes (e.g., education and health care) among different sectors in the society? Concerning the first question, it appears that both capitalist and Communist, democratic and nondemocratic, systems can grow economically and industrialize. Abram Bergson's comparative study of economic growth in Communist and non-communist nations at similar levels of development showed rather similar growth rates.[30] Some Communist states grew quickly while others did not. The same was true for non-communist states. However, although Communist states can grow economically, we should note that they have done so by strictly controlling capital and suppressing consumption. They have chosen industrial and military development and suppressed demands for consumption and welfare. Economic growth under communism has often come at the cost of human welfare. This, of course, has implications for the state of human dignity in Communist states today.

Concerning the second question—that is the impact of the type of political system (e.g., Communist or non-Communist) on expenditure patterns—some research has shown the influence of the political system to be weak if not nonexistent. For example, after examining expenditures for national security and a variety of social and domestic programs in six Communist Party and six capitalist countries, Frederick C. Pryor concluded that political systems provide essentially the same types and levels of public expenditures and services for their people.[31] On the other hand, some have suggested that the type of political system does make a difference. Classifying political systems into three regime types (established democracies, innovative-mobilizational or Communist autocracies, and traditional autocracies), Alexander J. Groth argued that their policies are substantially different from one another.[32] In another analysis of 59 countries, including 11 Communist Party states, Groth also concluded that ideologies and political systems do make a difference:

> The findings reflect not merely higher social welfare benefits among socialist states—at generally lower direct cost to the worker—but also more consistent, more homogenous levels of benefits among these states, as compared with states at similar levels of development.[33]

Although some of the studies appear to be contradictory, most invesigations show that politics and political systems do affect people. Leaders and governments, for example, do much to determine public expenditures, the distribution of values within a society, and the human dignity of individual citizens. Table 7.2 suggests that the pattern of expenditures varies significantly between the USSR and the United States. The USSR invests considerably more per capita in its military relative to health and education than does the United States. Other comparisons suggest differences in expenditure patterns that seem to be related to political forces. Furthermore, ideology and political systems appear to be even more powerful in determining how values are distributed within systems. Expenditure data may suggest how much a government spends in a particular policy area, like health, but it does not reveal what sectors in a society enjoy the health care. Political factors can often explain such situations.

Data on the distribution of values tells us who gets what and how much. In the Second World states, most governments have eradicated extreme haves and have nots. Although the Chinese spend relatively little on health care, for example, all Chinese are guaranteed free access to medical care regardless of their social position. Most other Communist Party states do the same. By determining where monies are spent and who gets what and how

[30]Abram Bergson, ''Development under Two Systems,'' *World Politics* 23 (4) (1971): 579–617.

[31]Frederick C. Pryor, *Public Expenditures in Capitalist and Communist Nations* (Homewood, Ill.: Irwin, 1968).

[32]Alexander J. Groth, *Comparative Politics: A Distributive Approach* (New York: Macmillan, 1971).

[33]Alexander J. Groth, *Worker Welfare in the Marxist-Leninist States: A Comparative Perspective, c. 1975.* (Paper presented at the Meeting of the International Political Science Association, Moscow, USSR, 1979).

much, Communist Party governments have a powerful impact on the lives of their citizens.

By influencing government expenditures and the distribution of values within the society, political factors in Communist Party states can have a powerful impact on the human dignity of the millions of people living under communism. But what political factors are of the most importance in Communist systems?

On the basis of our study, three political factors seem of major importance in Communist systems. The first of these—Marxist-Leninist ideology and the national adaptations of this doctrine—serves as a major political force in all the Communist Party states. Although interpreted and used somewhat differently in the various systems, the ideologies of means have served as general frames of reference, or guides to action, and are used by the leaders as they confront the challenges of our age. The interpretation and application of the ideologies; the flexibility, dogmatism, or self-righteousness in their uses; and the emphasis on one set of ideological values versus another—all have a clear and powerful impact on the allocation of values and the course of human dignity.

The second important political feature of Communist systems influencing the distribution of values is the nature and structure of strong personal leadership. Individual leaders like Lenin, Mao, and Tito were powerful, revolutionary leaders who presided over political processes that changed the course of Soviet, Chinese, and Yugoslav history. In addition, the power elites with whom they worked, and by whom they were replaced, were dedicated social and political engineers devoted to the construction of communism and to using the means required to bring about progress toward this end. Sometimes, new elites have brought in new ideas. The pragmatic, authoritarian reformers in present-day China have brought in new ideas that are having a significant impact upon the allocation of values and the course of human dignity in China. Mikhail Gorbachev and the new members of the Soviet Politburo

can have the same impact in the USSR. Political leadership is a powerful force in all political systems and it is particularly so in Communist systems.

The third important factor involves the centralized structure of policymaking in the one-party state. Operating within a centralized, comparatively closed environment, Communist leaders have been relatively free to set goals, adopt policies, and, then, mobilize human and nonhuman resources to attain them. The centralized structure of politics within the one-party system, in other words, has proven to be a powerful determinant influencing the allocation of values and overall government performance.

These three factors—ideology, leadership, and a centralized policymaking process—are in some respects strengths of Communist systems. They allow a political process that can sometimes move with vigor and efficiency to address and resolve some of the pressing needs and problems of modern life. When examining the performance of Communist systems in some of these areas, such as education and health care, areas in which the Communists place high priority and can utilize the three political attributes to attain them, we find satisfactory, if not outstanding, performance records. But—and this is very important—although ideology, leadership, and centralized policymaking have great strengths, paradoxically, they also have great weaknesses. In their fervent efforts to tackle the pressing problems of modern life, Communist elites have often violated the interests and dignity of the primary objects for which they labored: the men and women of socialist life. In struggling to industrialize, wipe out illiteracy, and provide medical care, they have ignored some of the other needs and rights of their people. As a result, when we examine performance records in other value areas related to human dignity, such as the leaders' willingness to accord their people trust and respect or to allow them meaningful participation in the decision-making process, their records are found want-

Antiaircraft missiles on display in Moscow's Red Square at the anniversary celebration of the Great October Revolution. Although heavy spending in the military sector has moved the USSR into "superpower" status, it has meant considerable deprivation for the consumer.

ing. The picture, in other words, is mixed; there are significant accomplishments alongside tragic costs.

In evaluating the Soviet Union, some years ago, Zbigniew K. Brzezinski and Samuel P. Huntington noted:

> All the strong points of the Soviet system—in ideology, in leadership, in policymaking—would be impossible to duplicate in a society which protects the liberty of the individual.[34]

Therefore, the ideology, leaders, and centralized policy process that have encouraged significant advancements in some performance areas have by their very nature brought about significant costs in others. Although the denial of Western standards of liberties and democracy have allowed Communist systems to advance in ways non-Communist systems sometimes find difficult, this has often come at considerable sacrifice to the cause of human dignity.

THE FUTURE

As students of politics, we should recognize that we have no crystal ball when viewing the future. The options and trends are never as clear as we would like them to be. Often, different analysts see different things. But, although there is not complete consensus on the future, or the nature of change, in the Soviet Union, China, and other Communist Party states, there is agreement on the basic and significant fact that these societies are changing. Certainly, we encourage you to stay abreast of change in these countries and see for yourselves where they are heading. We cannot cover all of the developments and trends in this short conclusion, yet we would err by not drawing your attention to some recent, important developments that may provide some insight into the future.

[34]Zbigniew K. Brzezinski and Samuel P. Huntington, *Political Power: USA/USSR* (New York: Viking, 1963), p. 413.

When viewing the performance of Communist systems in terms of their stated objectives—and, in terms of the Communist ideals of democratic rule, trust and respect, equality and well-being, enlightenment and comradeship—we saw that they are not performing well. In the Soviet Union, there have been certain achievements but obvious and glaring failures. The new leaders recognize that they must do better to achieve the level of performance they desire and in order to compete with their peers in the West. This requires change and reform. Economically speaking, Secretary Gorbachev has recognized the need for a decisive breakthrough in the economy. In recent speeches, he has repeatedly emphasized that "there is no alternative to it." Gorbachev and other members of the Politburo are stressing the need to accelerate scientific and technical progress, and to improve training and skills at all levels. Gorbachev himself has championed new forms of work organization in both industry and agriculture.

The stated principle of the Soviet reforms is "greater independence, greater responsibility." Gorbachev has also argued that "more energy should be devoted to a search for the most suitable forms and methods of combining the economic interests of society, the work collective, and the individual." One senses that while economic objectives are the key motivations behind these reforms, sociopolitical concerns about expanding self-management and socialist democracy also enter in. However, although there is much discussion in the Soviet Union today on the need to "improve the economic mechanism," there is still considerable uncertainty on how it should be done. What seems to be different in the present period is the desire to take action, to move decisively with energy and resolution. The ability to do so and the resulting performance of the Gorbachev leadership in the economic sector will be an important key to the Soviet future.

Secretary Gorbachev also seems to recognize the need for change in the broader sociopolitical sphere. In the short time he has been in office, he has set about rejuvenating the political leadership. He has brought younger, better educated, more technocratically minded officials into the leadership system. He has continued Andropov's campaign on social discipline and campaigned against bribery and corruption. He has sought to strengthen discipline in the work place and to strengthen law and order more generally; and, significantly, he has continued earlier campaigns against "alien ideas," "decadent tendencies," and dissidents such as Sakharov and Medvedev. But at the same time, he has emphasized a number of reforms that have a distinctly democratic ring about them. Speaking of the further development of the Soviet political system, Gorbachev has emphasized the themes of socialist democracy and self-management; greater emphasis on openness, consultation, and accountability; recognition of the various interests of different social groups; social justice, and the like. Whether or not these are the real themes guiding the future development of the Soviet system, or empty propaganda having little relation to reality, only time will tell. But many observers comment that Gorbachev is a "take charge" leader, a man "who wants to get the Soviet Union moving again."

The Chinese system is today unmistakably the scene of remarkable, dramatic change, what Deng Xiaoping has called "the second revolution." The pragmatic modernizers, led by Deng, have undertaken far-reaching reforms that are moving China significantly away from the Maoist system. In the economic realm, they are decentralizing agriculture and returning to family farming. This has enormous implications for the lives and fortunes of 80 percent of China's population. The reforms emphasize "entrepreneurship" and broaden the rights of peasants to farm on their own. Among the new policies are loosening restrictions on trade and mobility, the right to acquire the means of production, and the hiring of labor. The reforms have resulted in significant increases in agricultural production.

The pragmatic modernizers are also bringing industrial reform to China. The overriding goal is to reduce centralized, hierarchical controls and to promote initiative, competition, efficiency, and accountability. Emphasizing the reduction of centralized planning and administrative control, the reforms are based on a vision of industrial development made more efficient by market (rather than central planning) forces. Enterprises are to become "relatively independent entities" encouraged to pursue their economic interest within prescribed, but considerably liberalized limits. In Chinese terms, the enterprises are "to be judged by consumers in the marketplace so that only the best survive." Joint ventures, foreign investment, and even wholly foreign owned enterprises are being encouraged through the new "open door" policy of foreign economic relations. Armand Hammer of Occidental Petroleum Company, the American industrialist who has done considerable business with the Soviet Union in the past, recently signed a $600-million contract with the Chinese to develop the world's largest open pit coal mine.

However, while economic indicators in China have been up in recent years—in 1984 farms and factories outdid the previous year's performance by 14.2%—the reform of China's huge, backward economy is not an easy task. In 1985 many concerns were being expressed about inflation, corruption, and other ills often associated with the capitalist economies of the West. But although these concerns seem to be slowing the reforms, they are not halting them, at least at the present. When looking at these trends in the economy, we should take care not to overstate them. It should be noted that the state will remain the crucial power in the economy. Although the market will play a role, it will do so within governmentally prescribed limits.

The reforms of the "second revolution" are also spilling over into the political realm. There seems to be more emphasis on law, and perhaps a bit more toleration of dissent. At the time of this writing, there are hundreds of protesters camped on the steps of the Peking city Communist Party headquarters. Evicted from the capital during the Cultural Revolution, they are demanding in 1985 their right to return. Al-

though a tame (and perhaps unsuccessful) protest by Western standards, it is a major departure from the Maoist period. There have also been significant changes in the Party and governmental systems. Provincial and local organs were reformed in 1983 and 1984; younger, more highly educated officials were recruited to facilitate the goal of modernization. The personnel appointment system was decentralized and the role of the party in making appointments (nomenklatura) was reduced. Again, however, one should not overestimate the reforms. While a loosening of party controls has come with economic reforms, dramatic political liberalization is not currently in the cards. A significant diffusion and sharing of political power has not yet come to China.

Reform came to Yugoslavia much earlier than China. But the reforms proved to be no panacea. Yugoslavia today is a country confronted by pressing challenges that threaten the very survival of the state. It is a country beset by extremely serious economic problems, by resurgent internationality difficulties, by critical intellectual dissent, and by the increasing ineffectiveness of the governing elite. Caught in the incremental process of muddling through, the Yugoslav government is an immobilized captive of the pluralistic, heterogeneous society within which it operates. As a result, it is bogged down in the competitive, factionalized politics that its political and economic reforms helped create. The next decade will be a critical period in the history of the Yugoslav experiment.

The challenges and uncertainties surrounding some of the other Communist systems are even greater. Poland, for example, remains a country in crisis. At the outset of the decade, the Communist leaders confronted Solidarity (the now-outlawed free trade union movement) and its popular leader Lech Walesa's challenge to traditional Communist Party rule. Poland was on the verge of major disorder. Although Polish Communist military leader Wojciech Jarulzelski has attempted to reestablish law and order in this fragile country, he has not been able to solve the deep and fundamental problems confronting Poland. The Polish economy is beset by continuing difficulties; the Jarulzelski regime has little respect and authority; the people are frustrated, disillusioned, and explosively sullen. Because of Soviet interests and influence in Poland, the Jarulzelski government has little room to maneuver. The Polish experience in the 1980s raises new questions about the future of communism in this troubled society.

Communism is also facing pressing challenges in Southeast Asia. Vietnam is in desperate economic straits. Hundreds of thousands of Vietnamese, shocked and disillusioned by what communism has brought to them, have fled the country, often risking and losing their lives. Laos, where approximately 40,000 Vietnamese troops are stationed, is being drawn increasingly into the Vietnamese orbit and is also in dire economic straits. Cambodia (Kampuchea) has been devastated by internal turmoil and its bloody feud with Vietnam. Ho Chi Minh's vision of a progressive communist federation in Southeast Asia has proven to be a tragic illusion.

While calling attention to problems and challenges, we are not predicting that these states will be consumed and vanquished by them. To the contrary, most states are likely to hobble along and muddle through. Although often being diverted by military competition and foreign policy intrigues, most states will continue to search for policies to meet the needs of their people and to improve the quality of life under socialism. At times, the emphasis will be on economic growth and material rewards and incentives; at other times, policies will promote equality and the collective good. Sometimes the process of policymaking will be rational and more comprehensive; at other times, short-term and incremental. But, in all cases, the approaches will never be cost-free. A more centralized Soviet approach may facilitate greater decision-making efficiency; a more decentralized approach may show greater respect for human rights and democracy. It seems an unfortunate but inevitable law of politics that all these strengths have accompanying weaknesses. A high level of centralization, with its emphasis on efficiency, generally means limitations on individual freedom and initiative; an expansion of more humanistic values and increasing personal choice, on the other hand, brings about difficulties in the centralized coordination of the system. How leaders decide to apportion these strengths and weaknesses explains the great diversity of politics one finds among Communist Party states in the Second World today.

Suggestions for Further Reading

Baum, Richard, ed., *China's Four Modernizations* (Boulder, Colo.: Westview Press, 1980).

Bergson, Abram, and Herbert S. Levine, *The Soviet Economy: Toward the Year 2000* (Winchester, Mass.: Allen & Unwin, 1983).

Bowers, John Z., ed., *Medicine and Society in China* (New York: Josiah Macy Foundation, 1974).

Brown, Archie, and Michael Kaser, eds., *Soviet Policy for the 1980s* (Bloomington: Indiana University Press, 1982.

Butterfield, Fox, *China: Alive in a Bitter Sea* (New York: Times Books, 1982).

Byrnes, Robert F., ed., *After Brezhnev: Sources of Soviet Conduct in the 1980s* (Bloomington: Indiana University Press, 1983).

Commisso, Ellen Turkish, *Workers' Control under Plan and Market: Implications of Yugoslav*

Self-Management (New Haven: Yale University Press, 1979).

Curry, Jane Leftwich, *Dissent in Eastern Europe* (New York: Praeger, 1983).

Chalidze, Valery, *To Defend These Rights: Human Rights and the Soviet Union* (New York: Random House, 1974).

DiMaio, Alfred John, Jr., *Soviet Urban Housing* (New York: Praeger, 1974).

Field, Mark G., ed., *Social Consequences of Modernization in Communist Societies* (Baltimore: Johns Hopkins University Press, 1976).

Frolic, B. Michael, *Mao's People* (Cambridge: Harvard University Press, 1980).

Hanson, Philip, *The Consumer in the Soviet Economy* (Evanston, Ill.: Northwestern University Press, 1968).

Herlemann, Horst G., ed., *Quality of Life in the Soviet Union* (Boulder, Colo.: Westview Press, 1985).

Johnson, D. Gale, and **Karen McConnell Brooks,** *Prospects for Soviet Agriculture in the 1980s* (Bloomington: Indiana University Press, 1983).

Kaser, Michael, *Health Care in the Soviet Union and Eastern Europe* (Boulder, Colo.: Westview Press, 1976).

Kelley, Donald R., *Soviet Politics in the Brezhnev Era* (New York: Praeger, 1976).

Lane, David, *The Socialist Industrial State* (Boulder, Colo.: Westview Press, 1976).

_____, *The End of Inequality? Stratification under State Socialism* (Baltimore: Penguin, 1971).

Lardys, Nicholas R., *Economic Growth and Distribution in China* (New York: Cambridge University Press, 1978).

Lasswell, Harold, Daniel Lerner, and **John D. Montgomery,** *Values and Development: Appraising the Asian Experience* (Cambridge: MIT Press, 1976).

Medvedev, Roy A., *On Socialist Democracy* (New York: Knopf, 1975).

Mieczkowski, Bogdan, *Personal and Social Consumption in Eastern Europe* (New York: Praeger, 1975).

Oksenberg, Michel C., ed., *China's Developmental Experience* (New York: Academy of Political Science, 1973).

Osborne, Robert J., *Soviet Social Policies: Welfare, Equality and Community* (Homewood, Ill.: Dorsey, 1970).

Pryor, Frederic L., *Public Expenditures in Communist and Capitalist Nations* (Homewood, Ill.: Irwin, 1968).

Schapiro, Leonard, and **Joseph Godson,** eds., *The Soviet Worker: Illusion and Reality* (New York: St. Martin's Press, 1981).

Spechler, Dina, *Permitted Dissent in the USSR: Novy Mir and the Soviet Regime* (New York: Praeger, 1982).

Triska, Jan F., and **Charles Gati,** eds., *Blue Collar Workers in Eastern Europe* (Winchester, Mass.: Allen & Unwin, 1981).

Wesson, Robert, *The Aging of Communism* (New York: Praeger, 1980).

PHOTO CREDITS

INDEX

Falkenheim, Victor C., 146
Family, role of in political socialization, 58
Fatherland Front (Bulgaria), 15
Federal Assembly (Yugoslavia), 115–117
Federal Chamber (Yugoslavia), 115–116
Federal Executive Council (Yugoslavia), 117–118, 119, 124
Fine arts, and ideology, 62
Fischer, Leon, 84
Five-year plans, Soviet Union, 121–123, 132
Formosa, see Taiwan (Formosa)
Four values, xii; enlightenment, xii, xiv–xv, 77–80; enlightenment and performance appraisal, 163–167; power, xii, xiii, 66–72; power and performance appraisal, 144–149; respect, xii, xiii–xiv, 72–74; respect and performance appraisal, 149–154; well-being, xii, xiv, 74–77; well-being and performance appraisal, 154–163
Friedrich, Carl, 126

Gang of Four, 91, 99
Georgiev, Kimon, 15
German Democratic Republic (GDR), see East Germany
Gheorghiu-Dej, Gheorghe, 15
Gierek, Edward, 75, 132n
Global Monitoring System (GMS), xvii
GNP, 33; of East Germany, 24; per capita, 35–36; of Soviet Union, 24, 26. See also Economic growth
Gomulka, Wladyslaw, 15, 75, 132n
Gorbachev, Mikhail, 32, 93–94; and economic reform, 32, 33, 138, 171; and human rights, 151; on self-management, 148
GOSPLAN (Ministry of Planning, Soviet Union), 119
Gottwald, Klement, 14
Government: of China, 113–115, 119; in Eastern Europe, 118; relationship to Community Party, 84, 105, 121–124, 134–135; role and influence of, 108–109, 118, 124; of Soviet Union, 109–113, 118–120; of Yugoslavia, 115–118, 119. See also Communist Party; Policymaking
Gray, Jack, 81
Great Leap Forward, 27
Great Proletarian Cultural Revolution (GPCR), 27–28, 34–35, 145
Griffiths, Franklyn, 127
Gripp, Richard C., ix–x
Gromyko, Andrei, 97, 119
Gross National Product, see GNP
Groth, Alexander, 168

Hammer, Armand, 172
Hammer, Darrell P., 85–86, 99–100, 112, 121
Handbook of the Party Official, The, 113
Health care, 36, 40, 158–160; in China, 157; in Soviet Union, 160; in Yugoslavia, 160
Ho Chi Minh, 17, 18
Hooliganism, in Soviet Union, 137
Hough, Jerry F., 102, 112–113, 127
Hoxha, Enver, 14
Hua Guofeng, 95–96, 99, 115

Human dignity, and politics, xii, 167–170
Human rights, 74; in Soviet Union, 150–151
Hungary, 15–16, 21
Huntington, Samuel P., 135, 170
Hu Yaobang, 96, 120

Ideal citizen, 165; in China, 64–65; in Soviet Union, 63–64; in Yugoslavia, 65–66
Ideology, 54, 78–79; and education, 59–62; and human dignity, 169–170; vs. knowledge, 64–65; Maoist, and medical profession, 34; and mass media, 62; and policy interplay, 131
Incrementalism, 130, 140–141
Industrialization, 34, 35. See also Economic growth
Information, access to, 166–167
Internationalism, 46

Jarulzelski, Wojciech, 172–173
Jiang Qing, 91

Kaiser, Robert G., 145
Kampuchea, see Cambodia (Kampuchea)
Keech, William R., 127
KGB (Committee for State Security), 63
Khmer Rouge, 17
Khrushchev, Nikita, 43, 79, 87, 92; and educational reform, 163; on Stalin, 69
Komsomol, see Communist Youth League (Komsomol)
Korea, division of, 12. See also North Korea
Kuomintang (KMT), 10

Lane, David, 113
Laos, 17, 165–166. See also Southeast Asia
LCY (League of Communists of Yugoslavia), 84–85, 116, 121, 130, 146–147; Executive Committee, 124; regional organizations, 88–89; rotation and succession of leaders, 103
Leadership, political, 20, 91–96, 103–104, 169–170. See also individual leaders
League of Communists of Yugoslavia, see LCY (League of Communists of Yugoslavia)
Le Duan, 17
Lenin, Vladimir Ilyich, 5–6, 7, 8, 83–84, 92, 144, 149
Lenski, Gerhard, 41
Li Dazhao, 10
Ligachov, Yegor, 94
Literature, and ideology, 62
Little Red Book, 34, 59, 78
Liu Shaoqi, 99
Li Xiannian, 115
Long March, 11

Mao Zedong, 10–12, 26–27, 34–35, 95, 98–99, 131, 132, 139, 145–146, 151. See also China, People's Republic of, Maoist period
Market socialism, 28
Marx, Karl, 3–5, 24, 29, 30, 36, 46
Mass-line concept, 146